D1292896

Imagining Ichabod

MY JOURNEY INTO 18TH-CENTURY AMERICA
THROUGH HISTORY, FOOD, AND A GEORGIAN HOUSE

PAULA BENNETT

Photographs by SANDY AGRAFIOTIS

BAUER AND DEAN PUBLISHERS
NEW YORK

To my supportive mother, Toby, who often said,
"I know there is a book in you;" and to my loving father, David,
who had hoped to one day write his own.

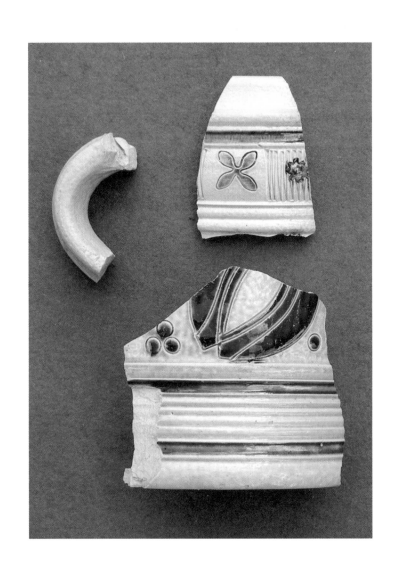

Chronology OF OUR PROPERTY AT OLD FIELDS

unknown	William Spencer the elder, after whom the William Spencer Garrison was named, takes up residence at Old Fields during the later half of the seventeenth century. The construction date of the house William occupied is unknown.
ca 1690	The William Spencer Garrison is established.
1696	The childless William Spencer dies and his nephew Humphrey Spencer inherits the land and buildings at Old Fields. The date Humphrey moved to the property is unknown.
1699	First liquor license is granted to Humphrey Spencer, suggesting an active tavern on the property starting in 1699.
1701	Mary Cutts marries Humphrey Spencer.
1712	Humphrey Spencer dies and his widow, Mary, is granted a liquor license.
1740	William Spencer sells his great-uncle's property to Ichabod Goodwin.
ca 1740–1750	The Goodwins likely build a new house.
1742	The first Ichabod Goodwin (the Captain) moves to Old Fields with his wife, Elizabeth, and their three children: Hannah, Mary, and Dominicus.
1769	The last year a liquor license is granted to anyone residing at Old Fields.
1774	Elizabeth Goodwin, wife of the Captain, dies.
1777	The first Ichabod Goodwin, the Captain, dies at Old Fields.
1794	The Goodwin house burns down. Soon after, the Goodwins rebuild in the style of the older structure. This is the house standing on the property today.
ca 1797	Wall stenciling done in the master's bedchamber.
ca 1800	After the house is rebuilt, the fireplace in the dining room is modernized.
1814	The third Ichabod Goodwin dies at age forty-four.
1825	Mary "Molly" Goodwin, wife of the General, dies.
1829	The second Ichabod Goodwin, the General, dies at Old Fields.
1843	Andrew Goodwin, who was head of the household at the time of his father's death, dies.
ca 1865–1880	The bay window is added to the southern elevation in the study. A two-story structure (presumably a railroad house) is placed off the southeast corner of the rebuilt house, and a hallway connecting this two-story addition to the original main house is added. Both are visible in a photo of the house dated ca 1880.
1869	Andrew's son, the fourth Ichabod Goodwin, dies.
1905	Sophia "Lizzie" Hayes Goodwin, wife of the fourth Ichabod, dies.
1930	The fourth Ichabod's son, William Allen Hayes Goodwin, dies.
1958	William's daughter Elizabeth Hayes, the last Goodwin to live at Old Fields, leaves.
ca 1958–2004	Various owners reside at Old Fields, the first after Elizabeth Hayes moved out, was a distant relative of the Goodwins.
2004–2016	The Bennett's tenure at Old Fields.

Detail of a 1755 map of British and French settlements in North America. Berwick is in the northern (unmarked) section of the Massachusets Bay Colony, separated by New Hampshire.

Contents

*At left, three fragments of German Westerwald stoneware
dating from the early to mid-1700s.*

Spencer & Goodwin FAMILY TREES

WILLIAM SPENCER THE ELDER (ca 1631–1696)

Nephew **HUMPHREY SPENCER** (1674–1712)

in 1701 married
MARY CUTTS (1675–ca 1734)

Children

WILLIAM (ca 1706–unknown)
Sarah (1709–unknown)
Samuel (1711–unknown)

"The Captain"
THE FIRST ICHABOD GOODWIN (1700–1777)

in 1729 married
ELIZABETH SCAMMON (1710–1774)

Children who lived past infancy

Hannah (1730–1775)
Mary (1736–1774)
Dominicus (1741–1807)
ICHABOD (1743–1829)
Samuel (1745–unknown)
Elizabeth (1748–unknown)
Sally (1754–1825)

"The General"
THE SECOND ICHABOD GOODWIN (1743–1829)

in 1768 married
MARY "MOLLY" WALLINGFORD (1750–1825)

Children who lived past infancy

The third Ichabod (1770–1814)
Thomas (1772–1822)
Betsey (1774–1790)
Anna (1776–1818)
Abigail (1777–1851)
Hannah (1778–1820)
Mary (1779–1831)
ANDREW (1784–1843)
Sarah "Sally" (1786–1870)*
Olive (1789–1791)
Dominicus (1791–1814)
James (1793–1884)

*The General and Mary's daughter, whose recollection of the house fire was written down by her great-nephew William Allen Hayes Goodwin.

ANDREW GOODWIN (1784–1843)

married
ELIZABETH WALLINGFORD (1794–1874)

Children who lived past infancy

ICHABOD (1819–1869)

John (1825–1911)
Andrew (1838–unknown)

John Goodwin (left)
and his older brother,
the fourth Ichabod.

PHOTOGRAPHER UNKNOWN

THE FOURTH ICHABOD GOODWIN (1819–1869)

in 1850 married
SOPHIA "LIZZIE" HAYES GOODWIN (1824–1905)[†]

Child

WILLIAM (1853–1930)

WILLIAM ALLEN HAYES GOODWIN (1853–1930)[§]

in 1883 married
MINNIE WEEKS (1856–1916)

Many children, including

ELIZABETH HAYES (1895–1992)[‡]

[†]Lizzie recorded her brother's memories of the Marquis de Lafayette's visit in 1824.
[§]In 1890 William read excerpts from the 1778 military diary of his great-grandfather, a lieutenant colonel at the time
of writing the diary, to the Maine Historical Society.
[‡]Elizabeth was the last Goodwin to live at Old Fields and the recipient of the letter written by her father, William,
in which he recorded his great-aunt Sally's memories of the house fire.

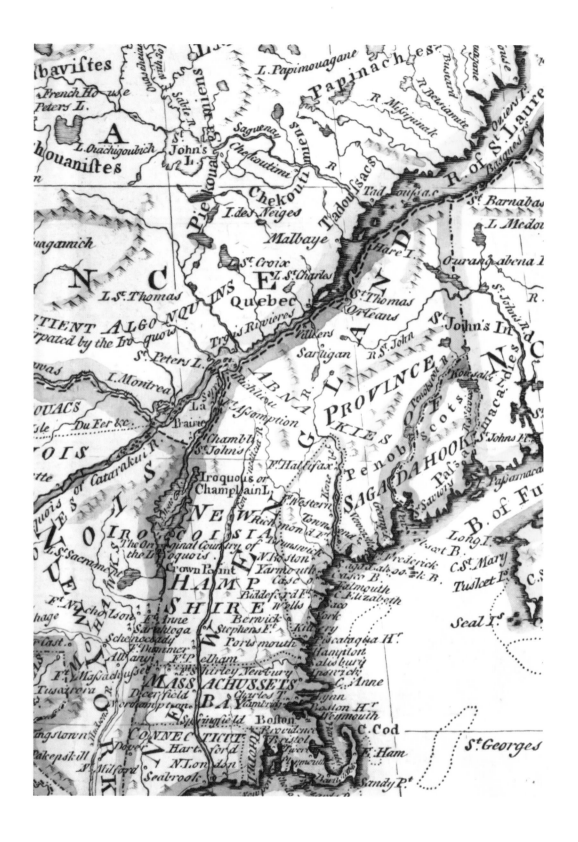

Imagining Ichabod

Historic New England, or 200 Years and 450 Miles from My Hometown of Baltimore

I have always been drawn to the beauty of handmade objects, the taste of properly grown food, and a life lived on a more human scale. I have always wanted to live a life somewhat removed from the "modern" world of today—a life more rooted in the past, or at least my idea of the past. Even as a child, I had a recurring fantasy of happily living off the land in some remote cabin in the woods. This daydream was powerfully reinforced when I first saw *Gone With the Wind* and heard Scarlett O'Hara's father urgently declare, "Why, land is the only thing in the world worth workin' for, worth fightin' for, worth dyin' for, because it's the only thing that lasts." The belief in the importance of land, both for its permanence and for its ability to sustain us, would influence many choices I made as an adult.

My husband, Harvey, and I share the same aversion to the all-too-common quarter-acre lot. In 1974, long before we moved into our historic house in southern Maine, complete with its four and a half acres, we bought our first home on the outskirts of Montgomery County, Maryland. Chosen mainly for its two acres (which to us, being city dwellers, seemed huge), the property had fruit trees, and wild watercress growing in the rivulet winding through the backyard. The house even came with an already-planted vegetable garden bearing ripe tomatoes, squash, and green beans.

Our next move took us to Baltimore County and the chance to live closer to the family's philatelic auction house—*philatelic* being a fancy word referring to stamps. Hoping for a more self-sufficient existence, we purchased seven unimproved wooded acres and removed as few trees as necessary for a four-thousand-square-foot vegetable garden and the energy-efficient home we had designed—a passive-solar house with mostly south-facing windows, ceramic-tile floors for heat retention, virtually no interior walls, and sliding shoji screens for privacy; in other words, a *very* 1980s house.

Aside from some solar gain, we heated this house almost entirely with wood, much of it harvested from our own acreage. Throughout the months of July, August, and September, our daughter, Jessica, and I would often be found picking wild grapes or blackberries. The reward for our aching arms and scratched fingers was homemade grape sorbet or black-berry cobbler. I also made jams and most of our own bread, and sewed clothes for both Jessica and myself. Although I was not yet trying to re-create an eighteenth-century world, I was certainly reviving elements of a past time.

Years later when I joined the family business and had to abandon my semi-home-steader lifestyle, or *pioneering* as one friend jokingly called it, I thankfully never had to fully embrace the fast-paced, high-tech world of the latter part of the twentieth century. Working with stamps infused our day-to-day routine with an old-time aesthetic. Handling these delicate pieces of paper demands a slow-paced, nonmechanized process, far removed from the pressures of most of today's business models. The philatelist (in this case, Harvey) must take his time, carefully holding each small stamp with a pair of tongs or tweezers, painstak-ingly examining the front and back for tiny flaws, subtle repairs, and printing intricacies. This hands-on task can give one a sense of peace and calm. There really is no way to speed up or mechanize the process.

The business expanded within a year after I joined, and we began to include historic documents in our sales—including texts by Abraham Lincoln, John Adams, and Isaac Newton. Working with these documents written on frail paper, often hundreds of years old, transports one back in time. The aroma and feel of the paper and the beauty of the handwrit-ing all contribute to the sensation of being in an earlier era, before mechanized typesetting.

SOON AFTER WE MET, Harvey and I recognized that we shared a love for American history that was equal to our passion for music and cooking. We learned that we had read many of the same biographies in our youth, not only those of George Washington and Ben Franklin but also of lesser-known colonial figures such as Jewish financier Chaim Solomon and a young girl named Molly Pitcher, who brought water to the Americans fighting at the Battle of Monmouth in New Jersey.

My fascination with history, specifically the early history of the United States, began when a visit to Colonial Williamsburg in 1956 opened a door onto the world of the eight-eenth century. For my eight-year-old self, walking through the beautifully furnished rooms and hearing stories told by the elegantly costumed women was a transforming experience.

Watching the bakers in the Raleigh Tavern, walking the brick paths, and riding in a horse-drawn carriage were life-changing. After that trip, I was captivated by our colonial past, and over the years the attraction continued to grow.

As a young married couple, Harvey and I decided to take a weekend drive to Colonial Williamsburg. It was on that trip in 1972, sixteen years after my first visit, that we both developed a strong affinity for eighteenth-century architecture, decorative objects, foods, and beverages. That trip to Colonial Williamsburg was the first of many throughout the next forty-plus years (and counting) of our marriage. On future visits we were captivated by the cooking demonstrations, inspired by the sight of a roast of beef set before a blazing fire, juices dripping. We enjoyed the smell of wood fires burning as we walked along Duke of Gloucester Street, lined with classic examples of restored and re-created eighteenth-century homes and shops. We were especially drawn to the beauty and balance of the period's designs and the quality of the craftsmanship. As Richard Todd, author of *The Thing Itself*, wrote, "A sense of proportion seems there and then to have been universal" in the design and architecture of eighteenth- and early-nineteenth-century America, where even "everyday objects had a quality that today seems to require genius to achieve."[1]

While living just outside Baltimore, we often visited the eighteenth-century brick homes of Fells Point and toured the early-nineteenth-century Fort McHenry and the iconic Phoenix Shot Tower. It wasn't until we moved to New England, however, that we felt truly immersed in our country's history. Our adopted hometown of South Berwick, Maine, sits in a region rich with history. Originally known as Kittery, this area was settled by the early 1630s and incorporated by 1647. Across the New Hampshire border is Dover, founded in 1628, and only twenty minutes' drive away is Portsmouth, founded five years earlier, in 1623.[2] Marblehead, Massachusetts, first settled in 1629, is within close driving distance, as is the equally charming Ipswich, founded in 1630. Every one of these New England towns boasts wonderful intact examples of Early American architecture, both *first period* (1620s–ca 1725) and *second period* (1726–1780).[3]

Harvey and I often take spur-of-the moment drives to visit these places. To walk around these historic towns settled just after the arrival of the first Pilgrims in 1620 is to walk through history. Many of the homes—once owned by signers of the Declaration of Independence, governors, and wealthy ship owners—have been turned into historic house museums. Then, there is our own home: the General Ichabod Goodwin House, thought to have been built at the end of the eighteenth century.

I AM THE TYPE OF PERSON who believes decisions should be acted upon without delay. Harvey, on the other hand, likes to take his time and ponder, seeing eight sides of any issue. In making our decision to move north, however, Harvey was as driven as I was and the process went very quickly, even for us. It would not have been worth mentioning if we had done everything more slowly, say over the course of a year or so; instead, we went into hyperdrive. In March of 2004 we started looking for a historic house in Maine, more than four hundred miles from my hometown. We found our house in June, settled in September, and moved in on the last day of October—all in less than five months. And so it was that Harvey and I found ourselves, at ages fifty-eight and fifty-six, respectively, living in historic New England in an eighteenth-century house.

The move meant leaving Maryland, where I had lived my entire life, where I met my husband, and where we built our auction business and our passive-solar house. We left behind our friends, family, and business offices—all that was familiar to us—and yet, since that Halloween Day, we have not once regretted our decision.

When Harvey and I moved into our new home, we found a photo that had been left behind by someone who had lived here during an earlier era. We readily took over as the photo's custodians, cherishing this memento from our house's past. The image shows a man and a woman seated in a horse-drawn carriage, seemingly ready to ride into town. I would have enjoyed such a ride myself, unhurriedly clip-clopping along at four miles per hour, able to absorb the landscape as it slowly unfolded before the open carriage. It seems quite clear to me that the splendor of the American countryside was much easier to appreciate before six-lane highways and sixty-five-mile-per-hour speed limits.

I like central heating as much as the next person and I try not to glorify the past. Antibiotics, anesthesia, and indoor plumbing—all are conveniences for which I am extremely grateful. Still, there is a part of me that wants to reject at least some aspects of the society we live in, with its factory farms and inexpensive manufactured goods from China. I believe that much has been lost in our never-ending need for the next high-tech toy. Our current lifestyle, one in which tweeting and texting have become all-consuming activities, lacks something fundamental.

This is the story of how Harvey and I came to live with our country's past—its history, architecture, food, and drink. We began to cultivate a slower, less technology-based existence, cherry-picking from the eighteenth century and incorporating those "pickings" into our twenty-first-century lifestyle. It all started with a visit to a bookstore.

Undated photograph of
Elizabeth Hayes Goodwin
and her older brother
Wallingford in front of the
north-facing carriage house,
built in the 19th century.

The Stars Align and an Epiphany Leads to Maine

It was 2003 and a typical July day in New York City. Needing a respite from the steamy streets, I wandered into the dim, cool interior of Rizzoli Bookstore, then on Fifty-Seventh Street. I headed for the back room where I knew I would find the massive table stacked with lavishly illustrated books on interior design. When I stopped in front of the table, my eye was quickly drawn to a red, white, and blue cover. I picked up the book—*American Farmhouses* by Leah Rosch—and began leafing through it until an image of a beautifully paneled keeping room in an eighteenth-century Connecticut farmhouse stopped me from turning the page.[4] That was it. I was mesmerized. I kept gazing at the photo, trying to identify the feeling the room evoked in me. Unexpectedly, I felt connected to that old room as if I was being absorbed into our nation's history. I suddenly wanted to immerse myself in our colonial-era past and our years as a fledgling republic. I realized right then, while standing in Rizzoli, that at some point in the future I would need to move from our modern home in Maryland to a historic house in New England, a house with a wonderful old keeping room just like the one in the book.

There have been only a few times in my life when a completely new path has suddenly opened up to me. I call these my *epiphanies*, and one took place that day in 2003, almost a year before we found ourselves buying an eighteenth-century house in South Berwick, Maine (about ten miles north of Portsmouth, New Hampshire). Not part of that day's epiphany was the knowledge of when exactly I would make that move, or where I might find this historic house; and, of course, my husband would need to know of this pending disruption to our lives. I tucked the idea of living in an eighteenth-century house into the back of my mind, purchased the book, and went out into the stifling heat.

The west-facing façade of the
General Ichabod Goodwin
House, ca 1795, hints at the
8½-foot ceilings of the ground
floor. Thankfully, this view
does not show much of the
mid-1980s addition to the far
right. It is easy to step back in
time and imagine the house
just after the earlier additions
of the bay window and the
two-story "railroad" house,
made between 1865 and 1880.

BUSINESS TAKES US TO MAINE Although the nature of our business (philatelic auction-eering) had taken us to almost every state in the nation—as well as various countries in Europe and Asia—it wasn't until 2004 that we had our first opportunity to visit Maine. It was March and a client requested that we visit him in Damariscotta to view his stamp collection. Always needing material for our next auction, we quickly made arrangements for the eight-hour drive from Maryland to southern Maine, planning to spend the night in the nearby resort town of Kennebunkport. Harvey would finally get a chance to see the rocky coast of Maine, an image he had romanticized since his childhood.

A New Englander, my father had introduced my brother and me to the roadside restaurant Howard Johnson's, or HoJo's, as some fondly call it, with its deservedly famous fried clam strips. With that childhood tradition in mind, Harvey and I made sure to indulge in a fried lunch at one of the local clam shacks en route to our meeting. Happy after our seafood repast, we went to view what our client had to offer. The collection turned out to be too small to consider, but the trip was certainly worthwhile.

We allowed ourselves one extra day for exploring Kennebunkport and the charming adjacent town of Kennebunk. That was enough. In just those few days, Harvey and I fell in love with Maine, or at least with this picturesque area close to the top of the Eastern Seaboard. We were taken by Kennebunkport's stunning beaches, the amazingly clean air, the ever-changing tidal rivers, and, best of all, the abundance of wonderfully preserved examples of Early American architecture. Maine was the ideal place to pursue my dream. I had always proclaimed that one day I would live where the air is clean, and since my epiphany I had known that my future home would also be steeped in American history.

Fortunately, my husband and I almost always find ourselves on the same page, with the caveat that occasionally a mutually agreed-upon decision is preceded by one of my very long and somewhat argumentative monologues. This time, however, my husband needed no convincing. As soon as we returned from the trip, I began hunting through online real estate sites for our future historic home. On the second day of my search, I came across a listing for the General Ichabod Goodwin House in South Berwick. The images were fabulous. This eighteenth-century house had retained many of the period details I had found so compelling in Leah Rosch's book. Not only did the house come with a historic-sounding name, it had numerous working fireplaces, intact gun posts, wide-plank painted pine floors, windows with many of the original "wavy" glass panes, and a front door framed by classical Ionic columns with an early Georgian pediment above. The Goodwin

House had somehow managed to escape the destructive renovation mania imposed on so many period dwellings. I eventually learned that the same family had occupied the home for over two hundred years, and I imagined each succeeding generation of Goodwins embracing the original character of the house, content to live as their ancestors had, rarely feeling the need to modernize. Of course, there were modern elements, such as the plumbing in the ca 1870 addition where the bathroom and kitchen were located.

Now, before falling asleep each night, I found myself visualizing the double front doors with the early Georgian pediment above and thinking that the Goodwin home might just be the historic house I was hoping to find.

A FORTUITOUS PHONE CALL In June Harvey and I held one of our philatelic auctions in New York City. The morning after the sale's conclusion as we were getting ready to head back home to Baltimore, I received a phone call from my younger brother, Neil. The two of us chatted about the auction results, and as I was about to hang up, my usually reticent sibling suggested, "Instead of going straight home, why don't you and Harvey drive to Maine and look for a house?"

My brother is not the type of person to give advice, so I took his suggestion seriously. Harvey and I rarely take off more than a day or two, and certainly not after an auction when so many details needed to be addressed, yet after a brief discussion, we surprised ourselves by agreeing to actually follow my brother's offhand suggestion. Within the hour, we were driving away from the hotel, and rather than making the familiar right turn onto Park Avenue to Fifty-Seventh Street and heading west toward the Lincoln Tunnel and points south, we turned left onto Park and headed north, back to Kennebunkport.

Just over five hours later, we arrived in the center of town, parked the car, and went straight to the real estate office we remembered on Main Street. We asked Heather, the only agent still on duty at that hour, to arrange a few viewings for the next day. We told her we were looking for older houses in the area (and in our price range), and specifically asked to see the Goodwin House.

The following morning, with Heather as my guide, I went in search of our historic house while my stressed-out husband remained in our hotel room, buried in a myriad of post-auction logistics like checking credit references and commiserating with the under-bidders. After she had shown me two houses that did not come close to my vision, Heather fnally took me to see the Goodwin House. On that initial visit, I entered through the

nineteenth-century addition. I walked quickly as I made my way to the main section of the house, barely glancing at the 1980s kitchen. I noted with some appreciation the nineteenth-century hallway that connected the addition to the original late-eighteenth-century structure. After passing through, I stopped to admire the mixed-period dining area with its bay window and faux-grained painted wooden doorway. Yet it wasn't until I entered the first of the eighteenth-century twin parlours that the house started to reveal some of the promise I had seen in the photos online.

As I walked into the Goodwins' *best parlour*— as the room would have been referred to in the 1700s—I observed with much delight the many eighteenth-century architectural features: the lovely old glass, the heavy moldings, the raised paneling above the fireplace, and the built-in shelves to the right of the hearth. This house confirmed Richard Todd's statement on the superb proportions of Georgian architecture. As I gazed out the expansive, west-facing windows, I was captivated by the timelessness of the view they offered. I later discovered that this same view had likewise been appreciated by Sarah Orne Jewett (1849–1909), the nineteenth-century American novelist and a friend of two Goodwin women who had lived in our home. In her novel *The Tory Lover* Jewett describes the vistas as seen from the house across the road—the home of the famed shipbuilder and merchant Jonathan Hamilton:

> *You could look up the wide fields to the long row of elms by General Goodwin's, and see what might pass by on the Portsmouth road. You could also command the long green lane that led downhill toward the great house; also the shipyard, and, beyond that, a long stretch of the river itself.* [5]

After taking pleasure in the beauty of this room, I stepped through the charming Georgian entryway, with its period winding staircase, and into the second of the twin parlours.[6] Here was an equally handsome room. Though lacking the massive moldings and raised paneling of the first parlour, it had excellent proportions and a handsome fireplace surround of eighteenth-century delft tiles depicting biblical scenes (see below). These old rooms were just beautiful, yet it was not until I entered the keeping room that I knew I was home. There was a charming old hutch against one wall and a back staircase that was something I had only read about in books. And then I saw the hearth. One glimpse of that eight-foot-wide, five-foot-high walk-in fireplace and I could immediately visualize Harvey roasting our Thanksgiving turkey. There was no question, this house was my epiphany made manifest.

The next day, my husband tore himself away from the demands of the business and went with me to view the Goodwin house for himself. Harvey shared the same visceral reaction. This house felt like home. We could easily see ourselves walking from the parlour to the front hall every evening and climbing the winding staircase as we headed for our bed.

A few weeks later, we purchased the General Ichabod Goodwin House and scheduled the settlement date for September 10, 2004.

THE HOUSE AND ITS FIRST INHABITANTS Now that the house was truly ours, the hunt for its history became my single focus outside of our business. What could I discover about the Goodwin House? Why does our home look like it was built around 1740 when we were told it was built fifty years later? And who were the first Goodwins to live here?

Kent MacNown, owner of the Goodwin home in the 1980s and early 1990s, had given us a spiral-bound notebook entitled *Oldfields, The General Goodwin House: An Assemblage of Oldfields' History, Pictures, Happenings & Memorabilia*. It contained clippings and stories he had assembled, including original documents from the Goodwin family. From this compilation, we learned that the Goodwins' early-Georgian-style home had been rebuilt after a fire at the end of the eighteenth century; the new house being built to look "precisely like the old one," thus explaining the stylistic anachronisms. Kent also wrote that an Ichabod Goodwin moved with his wife and children to our property in 1742. I later learned that this property had originally been owned by the Spencers, who in 1740 sold the land and all of its buildings to the Goodwins; yet William Spencer did not relinquish the property for two years, adding a stipulation to the deed that he could remain in his residence until 1742.[7]

This collection of stories provided enough information to start my own inquiries. Intitially unaware of the Spencer connection, I began researching the Goodwins who had built our house, searching the Internet for any details I could find about that first Goodwin and his immediate family.

I discovered that the Ichabod mentioned in the notebook was made a captain of his local militia in 1758 and that his second-oldest son to survive childhood, also named Ichabod, was promoted to the rank of major general in 1787. It is this son after whom the house was named. Citations relating to these first two Ichabods—or as we came to call them, the Captain and the General—mainly describe their participation in various wars.

Regardless of the lack of personal information, I was enchanted with the idea that the first two Goodwins to live on our property were both Ichabods. I then learned that two other Ichabods had subsequently been born in our home and that members of the Goodwin family had lived in the house continuously until 1958, when Elizabeth Hayes Goodwin moved out at the age of sixty-three (in fact, it was Elizabeth and her brother, who were photographed in the horse-drawn carriage). Eventually, as I continued my Internet searches I was able to establish a rough genealogy of the Goodwins who lived here between 1742 and 1958 and learned how their lives were intertwined with local and national history. I also discovered that our property and the surrounding area were both referred to as Old Fields, named after the old Indian fields that were here before the settlers took over the land. Harvey and I readily adopted this name for our new home.

A RATHER CURIOUS COINCIDENCE   Just a few weeks after we had purchased the Goodwin house, my online hunt revealed a wonderful piece of Goodwin ephemera. I located a cover—in postal-historian terminology a cover is simply an envelope, in this case, an envelope measuring three and a half by six and a half inches.[8] The cover was for sale on the website of a postal history dealer in Vermont. At the bottom left of the cover was handwritten "one Single letter" and it was signed "Ichabod Goodwin Maj. Genl." I immediately contacted the seller and purchased the cover along with its attached letter. When the item arrived in the mail a few days later, I excitedly opened the package to find our first

Goodwin document, one that could connect me to their history. I brought the envelope to my husband. Naturally, as a professional philatelist and postal historian, his eyes immediately went to the upper left corner, where the "straightline" postmark date—September 10, 1810—was stamped ("straightline" because the town and date are arranged in a straight line rather than the more common circular configuration). Harvey and I looked at each other, both of us with eyes opened wide in amazement. We would be settling on our house exactly 194 years, *to the day*, after the major general had mailed this letter.

On the tenth of September, 2004, Harvey and I signed the closing documents and put the General's letter in the study from whence it came.

Furnishing Our Home to Evoke the Eighteenth Century

During that first winter, Harvey and I embarked on a mission to furnish each of the eight rooms in the original part of the house to look as they might have in 1795. Coming from a contemporary home with a Japanese farmhouse influence and no walls, we would essentially be starting from scratch. We moved in with only a few pieces of furniture—an old sofa, a Japanese-inspired dining table with its three chairs and bench, and a reproduction four-poster bed I had purchased just before moving.

In re-creating our home as it might have looked at the end of the eighteenth century and not wishing to leave everything to my imagination, I embarked on an intensive study program. To begin, I turned to books on eighteenth-century houses and sought out galleries featuring American and British paintings with subject matter that might offer some insight into domestic interiors. Harvey and I also made frequent day trips to tour the eighteenth-century properties of Historic New England and the National Society of the Colonial Dames of America.[9] Later, we took longer drives to study the decorative arts wings at New York City's Metropolitan Museum of Art and the Museum of Fine Arts in Boston. Even on a business trip to London, we spent a day at the fascinating Dennis Severs' House.

Each house museum, painting, and book on Georgian interiors was a window providing insight into the eighteenth-century use of fabric, arrangement of furniture, and placement of accessories, but nothing was as instructive to our mission as the two invaluable documents we found among the Goodwin family papers.

While on one of my Internet searches, I learned that Elizabeth Hayes Goodwin, the last Goodwin to dwell at Old Fields, had donated a collection of family papers to Dartmouth College. I contacted the library, made an appointment, and Harvey and I were off on the two-hour drive to the charming town of Hanover, New Hampshire. Having the chance to handle those delicate Goodwin family documents was an unexpected gift—though, of course, the actual "handling" was done by Harvey, who was used to working with such fragile paper. As Harvey unfolded and refolded the various documents, we discovered many fascinating details about our first Ichabod's ancestors and descendants. There was a letter praising the bravery of a Goodwin who lived in England in the 1600s and a wonderful trove of letters written in the middle of the nineteenth century by Sophia Hayes Goodwin, wife of the fourth Ichabod Goodwin to live at Old Fields. Sophia's letters were delightful to read, containing lots of chatty tidbits, but we were somewhat disappointed that the collection did not include any personal letters written by either of the first two Ichabods.

As we continued sorting through the documents, I was thrilled to discover several heirloom recipes, including one for preserving beef, dated 1799; but then we came across the real treasure—the home inventories of the Captain, dated 1777, and of the General, dated 1829. Now we knew the specific furnishings and objects with which they had lived, including "armed chairs" and a card table, mirrors, silver, and pewter. Aided by the inventories and my newly acquired understanding of Early American architecture and interiors, we began to furnish our home.

The critical first step was to choose appropriate paint colors. We immediately fell in love with the historical colors of the London-based Farrow & Ball. To our eyes, the greens, the creams, and the earthy reds were perfect. Moreover, the period finish the company offers—the one called Dead Flat—is most reminiscent of the surfaces of the finer homes of the eighteenth century and seemed an ideal choice. For the keeping room, whose walls were a dark red when we moved in, we decided on a deep cream, as it would make the room brighter, even on the cloudiest days; we went with a lighter cream for the dining room. The green for the larger of the twin parlours is based not only on similar greens in historic house museums such as the Silas Deane House in Wethersfield, Connecticut, but also on the shade of green in the ca 1890–1900 wall covering still in the two-story front hall of the old house. I could easily see one of the Goodwin women in the early twentieth century purchasing the fashionable, tapestry-style wallpaper to go with the existing wall color of the best parlour.

Once the walls were done, we focused on the windows and floors. Noting that the scale of the patterns on most fabrics woven today is not compatible with the proportions of our rooms and windows, we were happy to discover in England fabric and rugs made on reproduction equipment, scaled to complement our Georgian interiors.

To replicate the look of eighteenth-century carpets, we chose wool rugs made in twenty-seven-inch strips, crafted by Stourvale Mills in England. The carpet patterns the mill uses are designed from documentary evidence, using authentic colorways from the 1790s through the beginning of the twentieth century. Then, through a local decorator, we ordered our upholstery and curtain fabrics from the Gainsborough Silk Weaving Company in Sudbury, England. The mill still weaves textiles on twenty-one-inch looms, just as the English mills did in the seventeenth and eighteenth centuries, and their patterns are based on cataloged archives from as early as the sixteenth century.

One thing I found interesting about the use of fabric in eighteenth-century interiors was how the same textile pattern was typically used for everything in the room, from the upholstery to the curtains. I chose to follow historic precedent in the dining room and used the same toile pattern for both the curtains and the upholstered seats of the chairs. Similarly, in the bedroom I used the same fabric for the bed hangings and the window curtains. I chose a simple tie-back curtain for the windows in the bedroom and opted for an elaborate classic swag for the curtains in the parlour downstairs to underscore the more formal nature of that public room.

We were now ready to focus on furniture and accessories and began to haunt antique stores and auctions. We were selective, constantly asking each other whether this chair or that table would help implement our desire to conjure up the past, or whether this or that object was in keeping with the aesthetic of the times. Alternatively, we wanted to avoid any items that might appear as if they were purchased as a collection for display purposes only (pewter gill measures, for example).[10]

After a short time, I came to realize that furniture and decorative objects of later eras were simply not suitable for our Georgian rooms. Just as I felt the patterns on fabrics made on new equipment seemed too large, I found the painted designs on most nineteenth-century porcelain too bold and the carvings on machine-made furniture after around 1830 too precise, too perfect. With that in mind, we narrowed the search, looking primarily for items of a 1700 to 1800 vintage that would emphasize the Georgian era's desire for balance and symmetry, enhancing the beauty of our house's proportions.

THE KEEPING ROOM The first room we wanted to concentrate on was the keeping room. Given its central importance as a cookery, dining room, laundry, and family room all in one, I am confident that the Goodwins would have set up the keeping room before any other.

The original keeping-room hutch now stores our special pieces, including reproduction and 18th-century glass stemware, redware, and pewter dishes. At the bottom of the photo is a sugar cone we stumbled upon in an antique store in Jamestown. The metal sugar nipper (to the right) is used to "nip off" the amont of sugar needed for a recipe or a hot drink.

When I picture the first Ichabod in 1745, with his wife, Elizabeth Scammon, their five children, and their servants—or the second Ichabod and his wife, Molly Wallingford, in 1789 with their ten children—it is easy to imagine how crowded this room would have been throughout the day, its numerous occupants bustling about, cooking, washing, ironing, husking corn, and carding wool. Of course, our keeping room would never be quite so active as it was for the Goodwins. And Harvey and I had a single focus when it came to furnishing this room: we wanted to restore the room to just one of its essential functions—a cookery. As the keeping room had been used as a family room for a good part of the twentieth century (with the hearth partially hidden by beadboard), we were anxious to begin using the space as it had originally been intended. This was of prime importance given our shared passion for the culinary arts.

Initially, we added items that New Englanders would have used every day—redware pottery bowls and jugs, pewter plates and mugs. We then moved on to the finer pieces that might have been reserved for special occasions—a tea and coffee set of Chinese export porcelain, silver tankards and sauce boats, bone flatware, and creamware. We soon began to use the home's original hutch for storing many of our dishes, pots, pans, and the majority of our serving pieces.

We were then ready to move on to the larger items. I could not envision the keeping room cluttered with furniture, especially when I consider the number of people who would have shared the space. There would have been a few chairs for the adults in the family, and most likely a table for preparing the meals and perhaps even a separate table for dining. This latter table might have been folded up and placed against a wall when not in use, thus allowing for more floor space. With these thoughts in mind, it was time to start looking.

Ever devoted to its history, dear old New England abounds in small antique shops lining its coast and dotted throughout its interior. For Harvey and me, it became a cherished pastime to drive along the scenic back roads of Massachusetts, New Hampshire, and Maine, searching for that special piece, one that would have looked familiar to the first Goodwins. Early in our search it was our good fortune to come upon a wonderful seventeenth-century English gateleg table. Wonderful, because the oak had darkened beautifully over its four-hundred-plus-year existence, and good fortune because, being English and not American, we could afford it. We had learned very quickly of the scarcity, and thus the high price, of American antique furniture from the seventeenth and eighteenth centuries. As a result, our home is furnished mostly with English furniture.

I suppose it's not surprising that we have been criticized by fellow historic house owners for our purchases. In their purity, they insist that Old Fields should be furnished only with American-made pieces. It is not that we disagree. We would love to have had a house filled with Early American examples; unfortunately, though, our budget scarcely allowed for this costly nod to letter-of-the-law authenticity.

To help justify the purchase of pieces made in England instead of here in the colonies, I thought back to our visits to earlier sites like Plimoth Plantation, where some of the small thatched-roof homes were furnished with large cabinetry—case goods that, we were told, were brought over from England by the more well-to-do Pilgrims. In the earliest days of the colonies, skilled cabinetmakers were scarce; moreover, trade regulations between the American colonies and England required that the colonists send all of their highest-quality lumber to England. This wood from old-growth forests was used by British cabinetmakers to construct tables, chairs, and other case goods, some of which were then exported back to the colonies. As a result, a considerable number of furnishings in Early American homes were, in fact, English made.

As we had no difficulty envisioning Daniel Goodwin, the Captain's grandfather, who arrived by the mid-1600s from England,[11] bringing this folding gateleg table with him, Harvey and I felt comfortable with our first major acquisition. With our rationale intact, we continued shopping. We gradually added an eighteenth-century tavern table—the original kitchen island—and a superb group of ironware utensils that included a grill, a griddle, and a wafer iron. Harvey and I also found trivets—very handy for cooking with pans over a bed of coals. Bit by bit we filled the gaps in our inventory, every addition enhancing our ability to immerse ourselves in early-1700s cookery.

THE ELUSIVE FIRE BUCKET   There is still one important item we have yet to acquire, an item found in every colonial New England household and one that certainly would have hung in the Goodwins' keeping room—the obligatory fire bucket. These colonial homes were made of wood, and heating and cooking were all done with fire. Any random spark from the hearth, or excess grease on the flue, could easily and rapidly lead to disaster. So, soon after relocating to South Berwick, we felt the need to find a fire bucket to hang from our mantel, and we added this object to our furnishing wish list.

Each August since our move to Maine, Harvey and I had attended the major antique show in Concord, New Hampshire. This was where, in 2007, we spotted the perfect fire bucket. From experience, we knew to arrive early on the first day to avoid the crowds and shop our favorite vendors before the hungry hordes depleted their stock. So we arrived thirty minutes before the show began, and once the doors opened we began our hunt. Walking down the first aisle, I noticed an excellent example of a fire bucket—a nice deep green with its leather intact. I checked the price tag, noted what seemed like a reasonable price, and pointed it out to Harvey, who responded, "That is nice. Let's think about it as we finish walking down the aisle." After about five minutes of browsing, I told Harvey he should go back to purchase the bucket while I looked at some pewter kitchenware. Soon— too soon—he returned. The bucket was being purchased by someone else just as he had arrived back at the stand.

In the many years since spotting that fire bucket at the Concord show, we have not yet found a suitable substitute. So from time to time, when I think about how nice that deep-green leather bucket would have looked hanging from a nail on the side of the hearth, I have to remind Harvey that he who hesitates is lost.

HEARTH COOKING FIT FOR A KING, OR AT LEAST FOR A WHOLE LAMB   Soon we added two seventeenth-century solid oak dining chairs and one early-eighteenth-century slat-back side chair with a rush seat (Harvey and I like to point out that the latter is one of our few authentic American antiques). We decided to place the gateleg table and the chairs along the back wall of the keeping room, by the hearth. This location has proved to be the perfect setting for our more rustic dinners, especially during Maine's long winters, as whichever side of your body is nearest the fire benefits from the radiating warmth. Unfortunately, relying on a fire for comfort means that one side of you is always cold, or "frozen," as an eighteenth-century memoirist more accurately noted. [12]

Harvey and I were not total novices when it came to cooking in an open fireplace. We had been roasting meat and poultry on a spit since 1983. The inspiration for open-hearth cooking came in 1982, before we began designing our Baltimore house. While on vacation in San Francisco during the spring of that year, we made a pilgrimage to Berkeley just to have lunch at Chez Panisse Café. There, owner Alice Waters, one of the original proponents of eating local, had her chefs cooking on a wooden-handled grill—replicas of which were available for purchase at the restaurant. We immediately ordered one of our own and had it shipped to Baltimore. As soon as we were back home we asked our blacksmith to make a roasting spit in the exposed central chimney we had already designed. We purchased

a Chez Panisse cookbook, and after a somewhat steep learning curve that first year, we were able to put the grill and spit to great use.

In Baltimore, our first foray into hearth cooking was a grilled butterflied leg of lamb for a few relatives one year for Passover. I recall how Harvey proudly took the lamb off the grill and placed it on the wood carving board. As I began to slice the meat that had looked perfect on the outside, we were startled to find the lamb absolutely raw on the interior— much to the chagrin of our hungry guests. To avoid such disasters in the future, we spent the next few months cooking over the hearth's fire, just for ourselves, to learn to regulate the time and temperature when cooking over an open flame. Soon we were cooking our Thanksgiving turkeys and Christmas geese on the spit. A few times we even attempted homemade pizza in the brick oven. During most of our years in the Baltimore house, however, we were too busy with the auction business to really explore our new passion.

It wasn't until we moved to Maine and were ensconced in our eighteenth-century environment that we truly became motivated to explore the ancient technique of spit-roasting and preparing foods in a brick oven. Our attraction to historic cookery began with the techniques and recipes used long ago, as we tried to adhere to the ingredients that would have been available in colonial New England. Until Maine, I hadn't approached cooking with a concern for historic authenticity, though I had always had an interest in cooking traditional dishes. Perhaps this interest grew out of my exposure to the many old-time Jewish recipes prepared by my grandmother who had emigrated from Lithuania at the end of the nineteenth century. Then again, I also enjoyed treating my father to some of the old-fashioned specialties of his native New England. So aside from my grandmother's *tsimmes* (sweet potato and carrot casserole) and *helzel* (goose-neck skin with bread stuffing), I often made Early American dishes like Indian pudding, split-pea soup, and baked beans; and while I wasn't specifically using historic recipes, I later realized that my cooking choices often resembled those of the late seventeenth and eighteenth centuries—lots of butter, a liberal use of spices, herbs, Madeira, and definitely no 2 percent milk, only whole milk, and, of course, heavy cream for the desserts. I have also always been a big believer in cooking from scratch, whether I am making breads, meat stocks, stuffings, or soups. So while I may not have been actively seeking historic authenticity, I was already cooking in the spirit of those earlier times.

How exciting, then, to finally move to New England and have the chance to develop what had been a pastime. Not only would I begin to research recipes contemporary to our new home's original occupants, but we now had this fabulous, spacious walk-in hearth in which to make them. At Old Fields we had a hearth large enough to cook a whole lamb. If only we could fit enough people at the dining room table. We did eventually invite twelve guests over to enjoy the half of a lamb we had purchased, though due to time constraints we cooked one quarter of it—more than sufficient to leave everyone full by evening's end.

We soon came to use the hearth for much of our cold-weather cooking.[13] We loved the fact that this fireplace still had the original crane[14] (a clever piece of equipment that I have yet to see being used in American restaurants employing wood-fired cookery, probably due to the space needed to properly operate the device). Now, in addition to spit-roasting, we were able to make soups, stews, and New England's much-loved boiled dinners, all by hanging a cast-iron kettle from our crane—Ichabod's crane, as Harvey, the avid punster, likes to call it.

To enhance the feeling of an eighteenth-century lifestyle, we began to use our central heating system sparingly, setting the thermostat at around fifty degrees; any lower and we were afraid that the pipes of our hot-water baseboard system would freeze. Harvey and I like this kind of energy efficiency on a bone-chilling day in winter. This gesture has its practical upside as reflected in our lower oil bills and, of equal importance, the warmth provided by the remaining coals of the hearth fire is more acutely felt. We also choose candlelight over electricity while eating our meals in both the keeping room and the dining room—although the rooms were wired for electricity sometime before we arrived, we have only a few outlets for lamps that Harvey uses when he cooks after the sun goes down. To my mind, feasting by candlelight on a game pie that was baked in the brick oven, or enjoying a soup or stew that has simmered all day over the fire, takes one back to the tastes and scents of hundreds of years ago. This sensation of a bygone time is especially poignant in the keeping room, where every detail, from the darkened old oak of our table to the blazing fire in our enormous hearth, evokes an eighteenth-century tavern (we later discovered just how accurate that sensation was).

We had always used a dimmer switch to lower the recessed lights in our Baltimore home and then lit candles to supplement the muted light, but now we were inspired to a new level in our eighteenth-century home. We soon began to dine exclusively by candlelight, even for the many dinners in the twentieth-century addition. We noticed that any room, regardless of the architecture, becomes softer and conveys an earlier sensibility when electric light is eliminated. Also, a dim room, lit only by candles, helps one focus on the meal as the outside world fades into the background, instilling a sense of calm and creating an atmosphere that both Harvey and I have come to prefer. It is always with some sadness that we greet the beginning of daylight saving time each year.

AN UNANTICIPATED ENTRY INTO A PREELECTRICAL AGE Our first winter in the Goodwin home brought unexpected insight into just how central this amazing eight-foot-wide hearth must have been to the Goodwins' world.

We lost our power for six days during an unusually potent snowstorm in early March, less than five months after moving to Old Fields. It was the time of year when the snow is especially wet and heavy and can easily down just about every power line around. Of course, well pumps do not function without electricity, so there was no running water for the kitchen and no functioning bathrooms. And with outside temperatures falling to about twenty-five degrees, that one fire in our hearth had to be constantly fed. I can attest to the great effort it must have taken to keep warm as we spent a goodly part of each of those six days chopping and hauling wood to keep our home fire burning. We could now see for ourselves why the majority of indoor activities took place in the keeping room, with other areas set aside for special occasions only.

Bundled up in as many layers as we could wear and still be able to maneuver, we spent much of the rest of each day preparing breakfast, lunch, and dinner. In the mornings, we had to first get the fire going, then boil the water (we used fresh snow), grind the coffee beans (it takes a lot longer in a hand grinder than you might think), and toast the bread on a long fork held in front of the fire. It felt like as soon as we had finished eating, it was time to start the preparations for our next meal.

In the evenings, we read by candlelight, *candles* plural, as our twenty-first-century eyes required at least three candles to decipher the printed page. We recalled being told on one of our many house tours that Thomas Jefferson, for one of his fancier parties, decided on the "extravagance" of nine candles. Certainly, a single candle would have sufficed for his normal evening activities. I imagine that our profligate use of candles would have been frowned upon as a spendthrift indulgence. When friends came to visit, they joined us by the fire and we would spend hours chatting over cups of hot chocolate. It truly felt the way we imagined the good old days to have been, or, to be realistic, the *mostly* good old days, depending on who you were.

During those six long days, we also began to appreciate our massive central chimney. While it would take American-born British inventor Count Rumford until the end of the eighteenth century to design a truly efficient fireplace such as the ones we have in our dining room and bedroom, those well-blackened bricks lining our hearth absorbed enough heat from that constantly fed fire to provide at least some minimal warmth to the surrounding rooms; surprisingly, the hearth fire warmed even our second-floor bedroom.[15] I can also now vouch for the effectiveness of down comforters, especially in conjunction with thermal underwear and two winter bathrobes. Yes, I actually wore one robe on top of the other. Something tells me those hearty Yankees did not feel the need to pile on quite so many layers of clothing. I believe that a nightshirt or nightgown and cap were all that those intrepid New Englanders required.

If you're wondering how we dealt with the lack of a functioning well pump, the truth is, it wasn't easy. Luckily we had a friend who on the third day loaned us a small generator that could at least operate the pump to keep the toilets flushing. Even while we were somewhat grateful for the insight into the labor-intensive lifestyle of those first Ichabods, after six days with no radio or television, no computer, and no bath (I used bottled water for morning ablutions), we decided discretion was the better part of valour and purchased our own generator, one that we have happily employed a number of times since our involuntary experiment in living as if it were the 1700s.

A PARLOUR ONCE AGAIN BECOMES A DINING ROOM   As soon as we had a functioning keeping room, it was time to turn our attention to decorating the slightly smaller, less formal parlour. There is something truly wonderful about this room. Perhaps it is the lovely fireplace with its antique delft tiles, and the sweeping views from the west-facing windows. Or maybe it is the generous, classic proportions of the room itself that makes the space so gracious and welcoming, encouraging us to sit and linger over dinner as the darkening evening renders the pressures of the outside world a distant memory. No matter the reason, it seems that virtually every visitor is struck by the beauty of this room as soon as he or she steps across the threshold.

I had learned from our numerous tours of historic house museums that toward the end of the eighteenth century, wealthy house owners in this country began to transform their informal Georgian parlours into formal dining rooms. With expanding wealth, those Americans who could afford it were able to emulate the more refined lifestyle of their Enlightenment-era English counterparts. Now they had the luxury of dedicating a room to the art of eating. Not only did they have the means to purchase a table and chairs designed

On clear days, the mid-afternoon sunlight streams through the nine-over-six windows and makes our dining room a perfect spot for a formal midday dinner.

specifically for dining, but they could also afford to acquire all the associated accoutrements—porcelain dishes, silver serving pieces, linens, and more. With that in mind, Harvey and I believed that the smaller of the twin parlours was indeed once a dining room and, in keeping with our mission, we were ready to return the room to its presumed late-eighteenth-century incarnation.

After painting the walls a light cream color to suggest the paler shades popular during the Federal period (1790–1830), we began to furnish the space. Harvey and I chose mainly late-eighteenth-century pieces, with one major exception—our contemporary Nakashima-inspired dining table of cherrywood with its accompanying bench and three chairs. These pieces were made by our talented cabinetmaker friend Robert Ortiz, and surprisingly they feel appropriate in the room. Our use of period linens and flatware modifies the table's more modern appearance; that and the handmade nature of the table and chairs help them blend into the Federal environment. To complete the room's decor, we added a mid-to-late-eighteenth-century lowboy and a marble-topped side table from the same period. Still, I felt the room needed something more.

One of my favorite aspects of eighteenth-century design is the focus on serving pieces that enhance the dining experience, turning the acts of serving and partaking of food into an art form. In this period you will find an abundance of specifically designed tableware—cobalt glass–lined saltcellars for individual use at the table, soup tureens designed to keep the contents warm, and many other specialty items for more genteel dining.[16] This was a far remove from a century or so earlier, when the knife was the main implement for getting food from plate to mouth (and often there was no plate; one simply used a slab of stale bread known as a *trencher*).

Always keeping an eye open for these graceful pieces, I noted a creamware epergne prominently placed on a table on the first floor landing of the Dennis Severs' House while visiting London. I fell in love with this exquisite, decorative centerpiece from the 1700s that's used for displaying fruits, nuts, and other sweetmeats served at a meal's end. I could easily picture just such an ornamental piece, perhaps in silver, gleaming on our marble-topped side table. After that visit, I started to look for one, but for years we had no luck on any of our antiquing road trips. At last, on Mother's Day in 2008, Harvey and I found a nineteenth-century silver-plated epergne quite similar in design to the one at the Severs' House. We found it at the Dining Room, a charming shop devoted to antique tableware, in Sheffield, Massachusetts (sadly, the shop was just about to go out of business). We purchased the epergne—the perfect Mother's Day gift—and I have never ceased to appreciate its beauty. I still take great delight in arranging displays for the dessert course, feeling almost like an artist as I try to create a tableau with aromatic oranges, golden pears, nuts, and plump, dark raisins still on the vine.

While dining in this former parlour, it is easy to feel a genuine connection to the General and his family. Our meals always bring forth thoughts of the past, and we can picture the Goodwins sitting around their dining table, similarly positioned by the fireplace (although our table is an Ortiz, not a Chippendale). Harvey and I imagine we are enjoying the same flavors as they did while we eat our hearth-cooked meat or sip the last of the Madeira in our glasses. This Portuguese aperitif, or dessert wine, was very popular in the eighteenth century and is the perfect conclusion to our meals here at Old Fields. As it was George Washington's favorite drink, surely he and his guests would have likewise lingered over their Madeira, reluctant to end the evening. Therefore, we raise our glasses to our first president and his fellow devotees who brought this lovely "old wine" to our shores.[17]

THE BEST PARLOUR Now that we had finished our ideal Georgian environment for dining, it was time to turn our efforts to the grander of the two parlours. Appropriately named, the best parlour was just that, the finest room in the house. It is in this room that the Goodwins and similarly prosperous families would have hung their most elaborate window treatments, placed their finest furnishings, and displayed their most expensive objects.[18] In this fashion, they were able to demonstrate their standing in the community and show off the wealth they had earned—or so we heard over and over again, while on house museum tours or at lectures, from the eighteenth-century Peyton Randolph House in Colonial Williamsburg to the seventeenth-century Chadbourne estate here in South Berwick. Harvey and I are not big on lavish displays. We both feel that a room with too many accessories or pieces of furniture can seem cluttered; yet, wanting the parlour to reflect its original function, we placed a few of our favorite treasures in this room—Harvey's beloved Liverpool jug, a tall piece of pottery with a bold engraving of a three-masted ship, and my own cherished China export tea set and silver tankards.

By the fall of 2006, we still needed furniture for the room. In November, while revisiting one of our favorite antique stores in nearby Wells, we fell in love with a pair of Chippendale-style chairs. The chairs weren't quite matching and both had a few minor repairs, so they were much less expensive than we had expected. We purchased the pair

and brought them home that day. In anticipation of acquiring just the right tea table, we placed the chairs in the best parlour and used a reproduction table we had purchased for another room as a temporary placeholder.

It wasn't until 2008 that we found a suitable table on one of our antiquing weekends. That summer Harvey and I ended up back in Sheffield in the beautiful Housatonic River Valley, still home to a stretch of antique shops although the Dining Room had since closed. By midafternoon Harvey and I found ourselves browsing in a store with a number of unusually attractive items. While we were chatting with the owner, the subject shifted to our business. It turned out that the owner was a client of ours and had just purchased some items from our most recent auction. It truly is a small world. After a lively discussion of stamps and how his father got him started in the hobby, he proceeded to show us a finely carved walnut English tea table, ca 1780. Because of the General's inventory, we know that he and Molly had such a table in their possession, and given how lovely this example was, there was no question that we would be taking it home with us.

Upon returning from Sheffield, Harvey and I were finally able to place those two chairs, purchased almost two years earlier, around our newly acquired tea table, centered in front of the fireplace. That evening we set out a pair of our favorite small wineglasses, opened up a 1989 Madeira, and took great pleasure in our new setting, though some special piece was still needed to complete the room.

THE MUSIC BOOK AND TWO TELEGRAMS There is a phenomenon often iterated in the philatelic world known as the *tyranny of the empty space*. For a stamp collector, the empty space in the album, with its identifying Scott Catalogue number (Scott Publishing Co. established this numbering system for collectors), represents a glaring void and a challenge. The need to fill that space is the collector's principal motivator (a true challenge given that so many of those Scott numbers represent stamps that are rare, elusive, and expensive). And so it was for Harvey and me, though instead of a blank spot on a stamp collector's album page we had the challenge of a blank wall or an empty corner in a room—a challenge that required our best efforts. Thus, with each trip to a museum we kept our eyes alert for inspiration, for pieces that would be appropriate for the unfilled spaces in the parlour.

Such was our state of mind on a visit to Colonial Williamsburg during Christmas week in 2008. While there we attended a delightful harpsichord concert in the parlour of the George Wythe House, and I immediately began to picture such a harpsichord in the corner of our own parlour. Upon returning to South Berwick, research was in order. Soon I located a website for an entire shop devoted to antique harpsichords, spinets, and pianos about 120 miles from Old Fields. Within a few days we were off to Rehoboth, Massachusetts, where the Harpsichord Clearing House offers dozens of antique pianos, each as wonderful as the other. After considering our options for more than an hour, Harvey and I decided on a 1795 Broadwood square piano, as the piano's earliest form was known. Amazingly, all but one of the strings were original.

Within a week, the Broadwood was delivered to Old Fields and placed along the south-west wall of the parlour. Before anyone could play it, we needed to find someone experienced in tuning antique pianos, so we reached out to the University of New Hampshire for a referral. We contacted the tuner they recommended, and he was at our door within a few days. It took him just over an hour to achieve the required pitches. As soon as he finished, he sat down on the chair and performed a lovely piece by Haydn, instantly transporting us back to the late 1700s. Of course, never having taken a single piano lesson, there was no way I could produce anything like the music we had just heard. Harvey, on the other hand, can play a simple Mozart tune, and we always insist that musically inclined visitors play our Broadwood so we can enjoy its wonderful sound.

This square piano also serves as a showcase for one of our favorite Goodwin finds—a music book. This prized possession almost slipped through our fingers a few years back. In February 2010, a local auction house was handling the papers of New Hampshire–born Tobias Lear, personal secretary to George Washington from 1784 through his presidency and until Washington's death in 1799.[19] The highlight of the auction was a 1781 map from the Battle of Yorktown. Clearly, the auction house had been unable to determine the map's true value, as they estimated the lot between $5,000 and $50,000. We tuned into the auction online and followed the live bidding until the map finally hammered down at $1 million (plus the 15 percent buyer's premium). While curious to know the outcome, we had not bid on that lot as our eyes were focused on another, decidedly more affordable one.

While previewing the collection, Harvey and I had noticed with great interest the lot containing "books from the library of Ichabod Goodwin, formerly Governor of New Hampshire." This former governor was a great-nephew of the General (and having stayed here at Old Fields while attending Berwick Academy, he was indeed the fifth Ichabod to live in the ancestral home). The lot's description included a music book dated 1819 and signed by an "Ichabod Goodwin," likely the governor, whose collection it was. Our plan

At left, two undated photographs of New Hampshire governor Ichabod Goodwin (1794–1882), great-nephew of the General. Below, the 1741 deed signed by our first Ichabod Goodwin and his wife, Elizabeth Scammon, selling a property they had owned in Kittery.

was to bid on the lot with the music book as well as two additional lots—one containing the governor's coin silver spoons; and the other including two telegrams sent to Governor Goodwin: the first reported the shooting of Abraham Lincoln and the second announced his death. We asked to be on the phone while each of these lots was called, assuming there would be little interest. Alas, we were quite mistaken.

For the first two lots Harvey and I were clearly in competition with another phone bidder. Each time we said "Bid," our unseen competitor responded by topping our price, until we were just about ready to stop. For the first lot, with the music book, the other bidder finally dropped out, and the library, complete with Governor Goodwin's music book was ours (for *only* 50 percent over the high end of the estimate; not exactly as bad as the Yorktown map, but we did spend a bit more than planned). The second lot proceeded along similar lines, with the other bidder again dropping out just before we reached our limit. Both times I felt the adrenaline rush so many of our own clients must feel when participating at auction via telephone. I now knew for myself the feeling of triumph when you call out your final bid and no response follows; there is a visceral reaction when you realize, with the ensuing silence, no one is going to top your price and the piece is yours.

Harvey and I were not so lucky with the lot featuring the two telegrams. Our competition kept topping our price, and we lost to their winning bid. But our disappointment quickly faded when one of our clients gave Harvey a call several days later. He actually knew the high bidder on that lot, and, aware of our interest in all things Goodwin, our client contacted us about another item in the lot he was sure we would want—a property deed signed before the Justice of the Peace, John Hill, by our first Ichabod Goodwin and his wife, Elizabeth, on November 10, 1741. That wonderful client of ours helped us obtain this most meaningful document, and for a very modest sum.

We continue to enjoy these items from the Tobias Lear Collection—the Goodwin music book, now perched on our Broadwood piano; the governor's shipping log and an album of photographs from the lot of "books"; the coin silver spoons, engraved *I Goodwin* in cursive, which we use for the dessert course; and, of course, the Captain and Elizabeth's deed.

Beginning to Imagine

Now that we had the best parlour properly furnished, Harvey and I began to entertain. As I wait for our guests to arrive, I try to picture the visitors who came to Old Fields over two hundred years earlier. Our house is on the east side of the original road to York and through the open doorway Molly or the General would have been able to see their guest arriving on horseback. Here they would have waited as the rider hitched his horse to the granite post that still stands at the top of our circular driveway. Or maybe their guest would

have come from the wharves, walking up the hill-side toward the Goodwins' front door.

Frequent visitors would likely have included their neighbors, the successful merchant Jonathan Hamilton and his wife, Mary, whose home, now known as Hamilton House, still stands (and can be visited) just across the way from Old Fields. The General would have beckoned Jonathan and Mary to enter, and if it was a cold winter day, quickly escorted them into the best parlour from the unheated entryway, motioning them toward the warm fire and the pair of armchairs listed in the General's inventory. I imagine that many evenings were spent in front of the Goodwins' parlour fire discussing current events, or perhaps determinedly avoiding controversial topics and instead talking about that timeless fallback—the weather—as they sipped their Madeira and enjoyed the ginger cakes that Molly might have proudly offered on her new set of Staffordshire ware.[20] Between sometime around 1785, when Jonathan Hamilton moved into the house across the street from Old Fields, and his death in 1802, the discussion on many evenings surely would have turned to British interference with the shipping of American goods to Europe prior to Jefferson's embargo of 1807.[21] In December of 1794, they probably shared their concerns about the recently signed treaty with Britain, drafted by John Jay and viewed by many to be insufficient to protect the shipping interests such as those upon which Hamilton's fortunes depended. [22] As the details of the treaty emerged, it become clear that Jay's document accomplished very little, serving merely to forestall a second war, although the treaty did allow a very young United States time to gain a more secure footing on the world stage before the War of 1812. Meanwhile, businessmen like Jonathan Hamilton suffered economic hardships as the British continued to illegally seize American cargo on the open sea.

Another serious concern for American shippers, one that directly affected Hamilton and his fellow townsmen, was the threat of pirates. William Furness, a seaman who lived near Quamphegan Landing, where today's Old Berwick Historical Society museum now stands, was appointed by Hamilton to captain his ship, the *Olive Branch.* In October of 1793, Furness and his crew of 112 sailors were captured by pirates off the coast of Africa en route to Portugal.[23] The men and women of Berwick would have read poor William's letter in the March 15 issue of *The New-Hampshire Gazette*, almost five months after their capture:

> *The labour is very hard, and they give us nothing but bread and water; and so little of that, that it is hardly sufficient to sustain life; and unless our humane Congress gives us some small allowance to alleviate our sufferings, we must continue in the most abject slavery....We were stripped of every thing when taken but life, and it is almost enough to take that.... destitute of every thing but horror.*[24]

Jonathan Hamilton's repeated requests for the federal government to pay the ransom, an amount that equaled $2,000 per man, would go unanswered for almost three years. In 1796 the American government finally paid off the pirates, and Captain Furness and his crew were liberated. William Furness returned home to Berwick, only to be captured again one year later, this time in the Caribbean.

Life today on the high seas may seem tranquil in comparison; yet, just a few years ago, Harvey and I found ourselves discussing a quite similar story about piracy when a Captain Phillips was taken hostage by a group of Somali pirates. As the biblical saying attributed to King Solomon states so accurately, "There is nothing new under the sun."

As I slide open the latches of the front double doors, I often imagine the Goodwins similarly swinging open these same doors as their neighbors climbed the wide, granite steps up to the house. Standing in the doorway, I am struck once more by our providentially well-preserved western panorama. Perched on top of a promontory overlooking today's Salmon Falls River, each year our property provides a New England–winter postcard vista of charming snow-covered fields and hills. Almost as if by design, there is a perfect red barn nestled within the gently sloping field before the river's edge. The picturesque rounded hills of Rollinsford, New Hampshire, rise just beyond, on the west bank of the Salmon Falls. And surely, just as I do now, the General and his wife must have paused to appreciate the sloping fields across the road and taken a moment to enjoy the fresh breezes that so often rise off the river below.

CONVERSATIONS OVER A GLASS OF MADEIRA During our first years here, Harvey and I used the parlour sparingly, as a refuge from the stresses of our then-hectic, twenty-first-century lifestyle and the round-the-clock demands of our auction house. On evenings when we needed to escape, we would enter the parlour at about five o'clock. I would take down the small glasses from the cabinet, and Harvey would pour each of us a glass of wine. The setting always worked its spell, and the stresses of the day were soon a distant memory.

Now in our semi-retirement, Harvey and I enjoy many more late afternoons in this lovely space devoid of the hum of electricity. Here, we pay tribute to the men and women of the eighteenth century who solved the problem of those bleak, preelectricity days of a northern winter through the strategic placement of mirrors and objects made of silver, brass, and glass. We can attest to the fact that these simple items effectively amplify a single candle's luminosity so that even one candle can light up a room almost as effectively as today's sixty-watt bulb, and certainly more beautifully.

The parlour is also the perfect spot for the occasional guest who has just enough time for a cup of tea and a bite of sweet. At other times, the tea table makes a lovely place to start a special meal or to enjoy a dinner's conclusion, providing just enough space for a simple dessert. Over the years, I have come to notice that one cannot really slump while sitting in a

Chippendale chair. You must sit upright, poised and alert, while sipping your glass of wine and conversing about weather or international issues.

While Harvey and I enjoy discussing politics with guests, when it is just the two of us, our conversations often turn to the day-to-day challenges we encounter in our business. I still remember well the time our computer crashed in the middle of a live auction we were holding in New York City. We had to cancel the sale and reschedule for the following week. This meant an additional ten hours of driving, plus unpacking and repacking all the lots, computers, and auction-related paraphernalia. As soon as we got home that evening, we retreated into our sanctuary. Trying to maintain a sense of calm, we carefully went through the logistics of notifying thousands of our clients, placating the unhappy consignor, arranging for temporary staff, coordinating schedules with the auction agents who needed to be present, and contacting the hotel to ensure that an auction room would be available within the next week or so. Happily, the soothing environment, accompanied by a glass (or two) of our Madeira, lowered our blood pressure, and we were able to clearly think through the entire process. Those kinds of difficulties aside, Harvey and I love sitting at our tea table in front of the fire, always grateful for an opportunity to appreciate the beauty of the room.

THE STUDY   The parlour done, we moved on to the fourth (and final) room on the main floor. Harvey and I believe that this smaller room was most likely partitioned off from the keeping room. The hearth in the keeping room, as it exists now, is woefully off center, abutting the southwest corner. Knowing the Georgian love of symmetry, why would the builder create a structure so inconsistent with the characteristics of the style?

One day, to test our theory, we measured the length of the eastern walls of both rooms. Adding these two measurements together as if the spaces were one unit, we found that the hearth is situated at the exact midpoint, just as Georgian architecture dictates. Harvey and I are now quite convinced that the smaller room, now our study, was walled off at some point after the house was rebuilt, possibly to create a place for the General, the master of the house, to work in solitude, away from the bustling activities of the keeping room.

Then one summer, our fifth at Old Fields, I came across an illustration of a tea table in Brock Jobe's book *New England Furniture*.[25] According to the caption, the table had originally been in the General Ichabod Goodwin House. Thrilled to find a photo of an actual piece of furniture that once resided in our home, I contacted the author to try to discover the table's location. When Mr. Jobe told me that, as far as he knew, the piece was in the hands of Historic New England, I was relieved to have some news, but also a little disappointed as I had held out hope that the table might be for sale.

I did a bit of sleuthing and learned that Elizabeth Hayes Goodwin had in fact donated the tea table to the heritage organization. I then emailed Historic New England to ask them about the table's whereabouts, and one of their staff informed me that the tea table, along with another piece of Goodwin furniture, was being stored at one of their properties—the Hamilton House. Since moving to South Berwick, Harvey and I have made frequent visits to the site, becoming friendly with Peggy Wishart, the property manager.

As the Goodwin tea table was not on display, we arranged with Peggy to view it in storage; unfortunately, we chose a sweltering afternoon in July. She took us up to the attic where, naturally, it was hotter still. In our excitement, Harvey and I were oblivious to the heat, for we found not only the tea table but also a large late-eighteenth- or early-nineteenth century secretary, and a pair of andirons that were not dissimilar from a pair we had acquired for the dining room fireplace. Peggy confirmed that the andirons and the handsome secretary had been donated by Elizabeth at the same time as the tea table. The style of the secretary places it between 1790 and 1820, or in other words, when the General and his family were living here and most likely after the house

The late-18th-century George III mahogany secretary we purchased for our study is similar in size to the Goodwin piece found in the attic of the Hamilton House.

45

was rebuilt. Harvey and I could imagine no room other than a study where such a considerably sized piece of furniture would have been placed. Surely, we reasoned, this supported our theory that the southeastern part of the keeping room had been partitioned off to create a study. There, seated at this secretary, the General would have taken care of his extensive commercial and political correspondence, and at this same desk he most likely wrote that letter in 1810 whose envelope bears the September 10 straightline postmark.

With a nod to the later modernization of the study—the addition of a Victorian bay window (ca 1871)—we added electric light when we moved in and now enjoy the room as a quiet place for reading without the need for candles. Following in General Ichabod's footsteps, we use the room for our own letter writing, although I cannot say that our correspondance displays the same careful penmanship as that of our General.

A FOUR UP, FOUR DOWN CREATED FROM A THREE UP, THREE DOWN   A typical floor plan in a Georgian-era house is symmetrical, the number of rooms on the ground floor mirrored on the second floor. Our house is currently a four up, four down, i.e., four rooms on each floor, but based on the smaller size of the study on the ground floor and the small room on the second floor adjacent to the master bedroom, Harvey and I strongly feel that the house was originally a three up, three down, with these two smaller rooms being partitioned off at a later time.

I use the small space on the second floor as a dressing room. It is simply furnished with a chest of drawers and a dressing table. I also included a rocking chair as a nod to the room's probable origins as a nursery. I like thinking of the early Goodwin women who might have rocked in this room while breast-feeding.

When I began to research the use of the four rooms on the second floor of the main house, I rejected the idea that the room adjoining the main bedchamber could have been a nursery as there was no fireplace and thus no way to provide warmth for the vulnerable infant. Then, during a tour of the Rundlet-May House in Portsmouth, the guide pointed out a room layout similar to that of our second floor and told us that the small room closest to the master bedroom was the nursery. That room also had no fireplace. I raised my hand and pointed out that without a fireplace the room would lack the warmth needed to protect a newborn during the cold winter months. The guide quickly disabused me of my modern understanding that a young child should not be placed in an unheated room. Colonial families evidently did not see newborns as more vulnerable than anyone else.

As the little ones reached an age when they no longer needed to be close to their mother, they would have graduated to one of the other two upstairs rooms, which likely held five of the six beds listed in General Goodwin's 1829 inventory (the sixth would have been in the master's bedchamber). Given that the General and his wife had eleven children (though not all survived childhood), the beds must have been shared by at least two, and probably three children at a time. These extra bodies, no doubt, provided welcome warmth during the winter months. In addition to their function as bedrooms, these upstairs rooms might also have been used for food storage. The attic, in addition to being used as a store-room, may have provided sleeping space for servants.[26]

THE MASTER'S BEDCHAMBER At last, it was time to create an eighteenth-century bedchamber. We had temporarily set up our bedroom in the northwest corner of the house, above the dining room. This was where we placed the reproduction antique poster bed we had purchased right before moving to Maine, which we were now ready to replace with a period-appropriate piece. From our various house museum tours, we learned that the master's bedroom in a Georgian home was invariably located over the best parlour, so we moved our bedroom into the southwest corner. The decorating process began with our commissioning a handsome documentary carpet of green, gray, black, and ivory from the same British company that had made the parlour carpet.[27] After placing the order, we discovered, while reading a book on the homes of the Founding Fathers, that the first chief justice of the Supreme Court, John Jay (the same John Jay who negotiated with England and drafted the treaty of 1774 in an attempt to avoid war), owned a carpet with an identical pattern and colorway—a happy coincidence.[28]

According to the inventory of General Ichabod, at least one bedroom had bed hangings, referred to as *curtains* in the inventory. I had always found the idea of a draped poster bed enticing, so I was looking forward to re-creating one in our room. During our hunt, we never did come across an eighteenth-century example; they must be rare indeed. We finally settled on an early-nineteenth-century four-poster bed that we found at Leonard's, an antique store in Providence, Rhode Island. While browsing their vast showroom we also acquired a late-eighteenth-century dresser. Our bedroom was slowly coming together, but we still needed fabric for the hangings.

We ordered the bed hangings from the same mill in England where we had purchased the fabric for the parlour. We chose a lovely pale yellow wool woven on their twenty-one-

inch reproduction loom, but before we could hang the fabric, a problem arose when we began to assemble the bed. Our ceiling was too low for the finials that topped the posts!

Our second floor pays for the generous ceiling height of the first floor, higher than found in many Georgian homes and quite a bit higher than typical first period houses. Of course, to allow for the grander rooms below, the height of the second floor was shortened by those same six inches. As a result, our finials had to be removed. This solution, proposed by the moving men, has a local historic precedent, as we later discovered during a tour of the Sayward-Wheeler House in York Harbor, Maine. There, the owners had to cut off a central finial of their prized tall clock and shorten the two flanking finials to fit the clock under their own low ceiling. I would never want to disfigure an irreplaceable antique—just as Harvey does not like the idea of altering items of philately—so, while I regret the removal of the finials on our nineteenth-century bed, I feel that our actions were not criminal as the bed is not a museum piece (our solution may even be justified by the similar actions of the Saywards or the Wheelers). The finials are stored for safekeeping until the day they can be reunited with their posts.

There was one other complication, though it was minor in comparison. Because the legs of our bed are quite a bit taller than those of most contemporary beds—low and sleek seems to be today's preferred profile—our mattress sits higher off the ground. As I am what Harvey calls *vertically challenged* at four feet ten inches, I had to immediately acquire library steps so I could climb into bed. Luckily, while we were at Leonard's we also found a reproduction set of library steps, so now I do not need to take a running leap each night to get into our rather high bed. Using that little set of wooden stairs was something I had always romanticized; so for me, climbing into bed is an especially pleasant ritual. Each night, as I enter our bedroom, I look forward to the inviting prospect of falling asleep under my "roof" of wool and silk, and I thank the quick thinking of the moving men that day.

MODERN ADDITIONS AFTER THE CIVIL WAR In early 2008, Harvey and I were talking to an architectural historian about the decidedly non-Georgian bay window in the study. To explain the late-nineteenth-century addition, the historian pointed out that throughout American history, soldiers from small towns would find themselves in cosmopolitan cities like Washington, D.C., or New York. They would be exposed to new architectural trends that often influenced upgrades they made to their homes after they returned from war. We know that during the Civil War a grandson of the General, the fourth Ichabod Goodwin (the third to head Old Fields), was sent to Washington, D.C., to help enlist men for the Union Army. At the time of his deployment, in 1863, the bay window was already a common architectural feature in Washington, adding valuable light and space to a room. Upon Ichabod's return, we can easily picture him regaling his wife, Sophia, with tales of the grand homes he had seen. We later learned that it was, in fact, Sophia who had the bay window added sometime after the war ended in 1865.[29] Our fourth Ichabod's descriptions must have been quite captivating.

It also seems that the "modern" two-story section of the house was added at around the same time. Connected to the original home by a Victorian hallway, this addition now houses our twenty-first-century kitchen on the first floor and, on the second, our master bathroom and a walk-in closet. According to the spiral-bound notebook assembled by the previous owner, it seems that this addition was a preexisting structure that was actually dragged from its original location and placed upon the foundation of a former building on our property (perhaps the house that belonged to the Spencers). Furthermore, as the story goes,

the first-floor room was a railroad station complete with ticket window, a feature that remains in our kitchen to this day, with the two rooms upstairs most likely used as bedrooms for the stationmaster and his family.

This structure might have been added to make room for those "modern" coal stoves that our fourth Ichabod would also likely have seen while in Washington. Since these stoves allowed one to cook without bending over an exposed flame, it is understandable that house-wives like Sophia, and her servants, would have certainly found the new stoves desirable.

According to MacNown's compilation, this was a "ticket window." An architectural historian believes it was used as a pass-through for food prepared in a ca 1870 kitchen.

THE WONDERS OF PLUMBING: AN INDOOR BATHROOM I have visited many historic houses in which a spare bedroom or two have been converted into bathrooms by the simple addition of plumbing, and so it was with the Goodwins' house. Our neighbor, an octogenarian who had considered buying the property from Elizabeth Hayes Goodwin in 1958, said that at the time he viewed the house there was a huge tin tub right in the center of the upstairs room that is now my walk-in closet. By the time we moved to Old Fields, the larger of the two upstairs rooms in our two-story addition (perhaps originally the station-master's bedroom) had already been turned into a bathroom. This bathroom exemplified the 1980s—the decade in which it was converted—with its gigantic Jacuzzi, all-white tile, and big mirror surrounded by glaring lightbulbs. My plan was to completely remodel this room to appear as if it were ca 1880, while keeping intact the plumbing.

First, I needed to demolish the white-tiled floor, eliminate the mirror and Jacuzzi tub, and get rid of the Formica-topped vanity that sat in the spot where I planned to install a gas fireplace. This was my first priority, for there is nothing more soothing to me than turning

on a warming gas flame with the simple push of a button on the remote while running water for the bath. No need to carry heavy logs from the shed, no flame to start from scratch, and no wood chips scattered around the floor and needing to be swept up (again, we cherry-picked from the past). Within a few minutes, my bathroom would get toasty warm, the perfect temperature for stepping into the

My antique claw-foot tub positioned just right so I can enjoy the light from the west-facing windows.

antique claw-foot tub we had imported from Europe. I could not wait. The one drawback of this cast-iron beauty, at least for those installing it, is that it is very, very heavy. While the renovations went forward, the antique tub languished in the garage until at last every other detail was in place and the construction crew could no longer stall. With a collective groan and loud complaints, the four men lifted the five-foot-five-inch tub, carried it out of the garage, into the house, and up the stairs to its final resting place. I truly felt bad for the crew with their herculean task, but I think even they recognized that the beauty of the antique claw-foot tub was worth the effort.

To finish my sanctuary, I had the workers install old pine flooring and cover the walls with a blue-and-yellow-striped wallpaper by Thibaut. I chose the paper as I felt it had a strong nineteenth-century sensibility, yet I could not believe what I found out a few months later when Harvey and I drove into nearby Portsmouth for lunch and a guided tour of the wonderful Moffatt-Ladd House. On the tour, we admired the furnishings of the first floor, remarking on the lovely documentary patterned rugs by Stourvale Mills—the very mill from which Harvey and I had ordered all our reproduction carpets—and the fine tea table in the parlour. But it was not until the tour guide took us to the third-floor storage area that we made a surprising discovery. The room was cluttered with numerous antiques, many housed in glass display cases. After a few minutes, the guide called our attention to a small piece of wallpaper inside a glass display box. This scrap of blue-and-yellow-striped paper, she noted, had come from the General Ichabod Goodwin House. Who knew that my choice of wallcovering for our bathroom would turn out to be so accurate!

INTELLIGENT DESIGN During those first few years at Old Fields, as our vision for an eighteenth-century home was being realized, we grew to appreciate the intelligent design of that era all the more. As we began to eschew electric lighting in our attempt to relive earlier times, we were ever more grateful for the classic Georgian nine-over-six windows. Their fifteen panes fill the room with light even during the impossibly short days of a Maine winter. We also came to understand why the main meal of the day was eaten at around two o'clock in the afternoon. From our firsthand experience we found it much easier to cook a fireplace meal while there is still sufficient daylight to see what you are doing, especially in the northeast-facing end of the house where it gets dark earlier. And here in Maine, it gets quite dark by three o'clock between November and February (hence the need for Harvey to use lamps when cooking during the winter).

By the end of 2008, we had pretty much completed the task of setting up our home. We came to admire its imperfect loveliness—slanted floors, anyone?—with its furnishings and accessories made almost entirely by human hands over two hundred years ago, truly a 180-degree turn from our passive-solar home in Baltimore.

PAINTING A PICTURE OF THE PAST   Here I am, in the eighteenth-century section of our home, trying to imagine the lives of the Spencer and Goodwin families who occupied this land from sometime toward the end of the seventeenth century into the nineteenth. Harvey and I eventually learned that a William Spencer was the first member of these two families to build on our land; but, in the earlier stages of my research, we knew little to no details about him or his nephew Humphrey, or his grand-nephew William, who sold the property to the Goodwins in 1740. And while we have always known more about the Goodwins, very little that we have learned involves the day-to-day minutiae of their lives. We have yet to find any letters dealing with their private concerns, or those of the Spencers before them. What did they eat and drink? What did they discuss in the evenings? I wanted to know more about both families and how our country's early history affected their daily lives.

Given that none of the Spencers to live here and neither of the first two Ichabod Goodwins was a John Paul Jones or a John Sullivan—two famous locals who were officers during the Revolutionary War—let alone a John Adams or a George Washington, their lives are essentially undocumented. With the limited information I had, my mind was free to roam, to fill in those gaps by creating a narrative of the families who lived here, but I also felt the need for my imaginings to be based on historic realities, so I continued my research. I needed to develop a more detailed understanding of the families who lived in Berwick from the end of the seventeenth century through the beginning of the nineteenth.

South Berwick, as part of the first permanent European settlement in Maine, is rich in history and abounds in resources such as the Old Berwick Historical Society (OBHS), with its vast collection of documents relating to the town's beginnings. It was in the OBHS archives that I found a neighbor's farming log written in 1791. Equally rich in information was the Internet, where even my earliest sporadic searches paid off with the discovery of sites teeming with details on early Maine, such as the website of the Maine Historical Society, in whose archives I discovered excerpts from General Ichabod's military diary that had been read aloud to the society by a Goodwin descendant in 1890. In the same archive I found the amazingly detailed book *Massachusetts Soldiers and Sailors of the Revolutionary War*, which contains a list of each deployment of our second Ichabod. In early entries he is listed as a lieutenant, then later a major general.

In addition to the General's military diary, I read history books on the military activities of early Americans. My understanding of the times was furthered by biographies, personal journals, and historical fiction. I even gleaned important details by carefully inspecting paintings contemporary to that time: a world of information can be found in scenes of cooking, drinking, enjoying music, playing cards, and even flirting.

The printed word and painted canvas definitely proved informative, but still more valuable were the conversations I had with local historians. I was soon able to embellish the family stories I had heard, thus grounding my imaginings in verifiable details about domestic life in New England in the seventeenth and eighteenth centuries. And of course, just by living day after day in the Goodwin home, I could envision the daily routines of its earliest inhabitants and how their lives were connected to the events taking place around them.

One afternoon, soon after completing the keeping room, I was seated at the gateleg table, sorting through dried beans—tomorrow's baked beans—lest there be small stones or debris. In my mind's eye I could see the General opening the door of his study in front of me and treading across the wide-plank floors of the keeping room. On a long winter evening, perhaps our second Ichabod would have gathered his children in this very room to regale them with colorful family stories such as the tale of the Wabanaki (a confederacy of five northeastern Indian tribes) and his grandmother, Mehitable (or Hetty, as she was often called).

MEHITABLE'S SAD TALE During our country's westward expansion, there were many conflicts between the settlers and the Native Americans (immortalized in Hollywood's numerous permutations of the "cowboys and Indians" story). Over a hundred years earlier in the Northeast, New England colonists had been at war with the native inhabitants upon whose land they had intruded.

At first, the colonists and those native to the land coexisted; their relations were peaceable. The English learned from the Indians how to adapt to the new climate and its flora and fauna, and the Indians enjoyed the conveniences of cooking implements, clothing, and guns for hunting. As the British population grew, however, the settlers overhunted the herds so crucial for the survival of the Indians and took over the farmlands and forests (ownership of land was a concept totally unfamiliar to the North American natives). The English dammed and polluted their streams, greatly affecting the populations of two important dietary staples, salmon and shad. Treaties were broken and promises left unfulfilled; worse, the colonists introduced diseases such as smallpox, to which the Indians had no immunity, resulting in drastic reductions in their populations. Alarm and distrust eventually led to conflict, and those in Berwick were directly impacted, including the Captain's own mother, Mehitable Plaisted Goodwin, whose story was immortalized by Cotton Mather in his *Magnalia Christi Americana,* published in 1702.

Mather was a famous seventeenth-century theologian who, while brilliant, unfortunately felt compelled to reinforce the rash judgments of his contemporaries, his own writings severely tarnishing his reputation by enforcing the belief that witches existed at the time of the notorious Salem witch trials. Nevertheless, it is this Cotton Mather who tells us of how Mehitable was captured in a devastating attack on Berwick in 1690, during King William's War. Twenty homes were burned and eighty to one hundred inhabitants were either captured or killed, including Mehitable and her husband, Thomas. Thomas was subsequently separated from Mehitable, who was taken north not knowing if her husband was alive. In the words of the famous preacher recounting Mehitable's forced march to Canada.

> *Mehitabel* [sic] *Goodwin, being a captive among the Indians, had with her a child about five months old; which, through hunger and hardship, she being unable to nourish it, often made most grievous ejaculations. Her Indian master told her, that if the child were not quiet he would soon dispose of it; which caused her to use all possible means that his Netop-ship might not be offended; and sometimes carry it from the fire out of his hearing, where she sat up to the waste* [sic] *in snow and frost for several hours until it was lull'd asleep.*[30]

Mather's story goes on to describe how Mehitable's baby was murdered, and how the unhappy mother continued on the long, arduous journey to Canada, where she was effectively enslaved by a French family in Quebec for another four years. Eventually the English, French, and Native Americans came to an agreement to ransom any prisoners still alive. In October 1695, a Mr. Cary was appointed to travel to Quebec aboard the *Tryal.* He returned to Boston with many who had been captured from Berwick, Dover, and York, including Mehitable.[31] Upon returning home, she found her husband alive and living in Berwick. Five years later, she gave birth to Ichabod, our Captain and the first Goodwin to live at Old Fields. Her gravestone still stands in the Vine Street Cemetery, just around the corner.

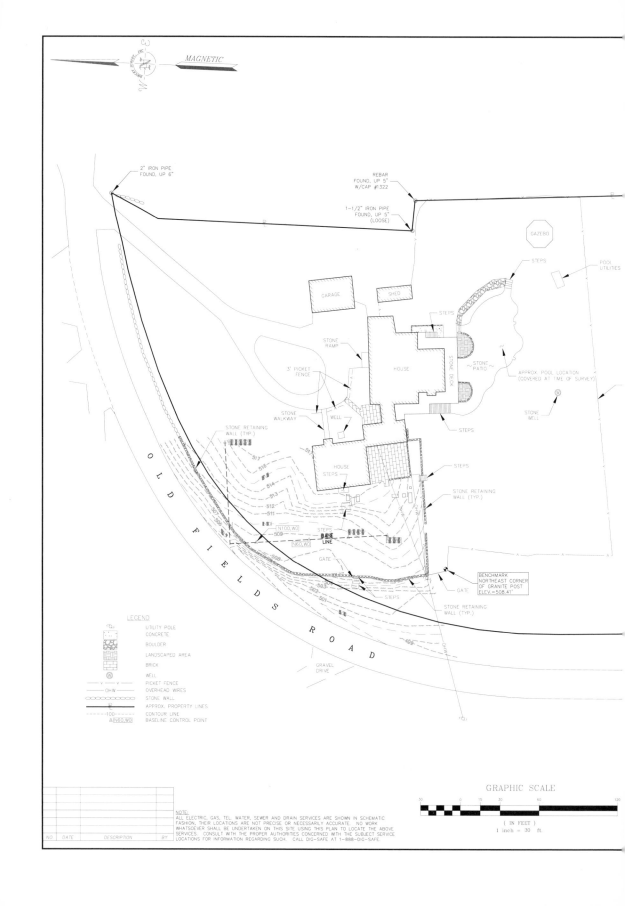

MAGNETIC

2" IRON PIPE
FOUND, UP 6"

REBAR
FOUND, UP 5"
W/CAP #1322

1-1/2" IRON PIPE
FOUND, UP 5"
(LOOSE)

GAZEBO

STEPS

POOL
UTILITIES

GARAGE

SHED

STEPS

STONE
RAMP

HOUSE

STONE
DECK

STONE
PATIO

3' PICKET
FENCE

APPROX. POOL LOCATION
(COVERED AT TIME OF SURVEY)

STONE
WALKWAY

WELL

STEPS

STONE
WELL

STONE RETAINING
WALL (TYP.)

HOUSE
STEPS

STEPS

STONE RETAINING
WALL (TYP.)

N100,W0

STEPS

BASE
LINE

N60,W0

GATE

BENCHMARK
NORTHEAST CORNER
OF GRANITE POST
ELEV.=508.41'

STEPS

GATE

STONE RETAINING
WALL (TYP.)

O L D   F I E L D S   R O A D

GRAVEL
DRIVE

LEGEND

UTILITY POLE
CONCRETE
BOULDER
LANDSCAPED AREA
BRICK
WELL
PICKET FENCE
OHW   OVERHEAD WIRES
STONE WALL
APPROX. PROPERTY LINES
--100--   CONTOUR LINE
N60,W0   BASELINE CONTROL POINT

GRAPHIC SCALE

(IN FEET)
1 inch = 30 ft.

NOTE:
ALL ELECTRIC, GAS, TEL. WATER, SEWER AND DRAIN SERVICES ARE SHOWN IN SCHEMATIC
FASHION, THEIR LOCATIONS ARE NOT PRECISE OR NECESSARILY ACCURATE. NO WORK
WHATSOEVER SHALL BE UNDERTAKEN ON THIS SITE USING THIS PLAN TO LOCATE THE ABOVE
SERVICES. CONSULT WITH THE PROPER AUTHORITIES CONCERNED WITH THE SUBJECT SERVICE
LOCATIONS FOR INFORMATION REGARDING SUCH. CALL DIG-SAFE AT 1-888-DIG-SAFE.

NO.	DATE	DESCRIPTION	BY

NCE: 1 OLD FIELDS ROAD
      SOUTH BERWICK, ME

URVEY PERFORMED BY J.M.L. & L.P.S. DURING 11/12 USING A GEODIMETER
  TOTAL STATION WITH A TDS RANGER DATA COLLECTOR AND A SOKKIA B21
VEL. TRAVERSE ADJUSTMENT BASED ON LEAST SQUARE ANALYSIS.

TAL DATUM BASED ON MAGNETIC ORIENTATION.

L DATUM BASED ON ASSUMED ELEVATION.

NOT A BOUNDARY SURVEY AND SHALL NOT BE USED AS SUCH. PROPERTY
HOWN HEREON ARE APPROXIMATE.

Location Map (n.t.s.)

1-1/4" IRON PIPE
FOUND, UP 10"

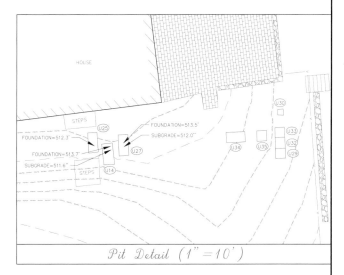

HOUSE

STEPS

U25

FOUNDATION=513.5'

SUBGRADE=512.0"

FOUNDATION=512.3'

U27

FOUNDATION=513.7'

SUBGRADE=511.6"

STEPS

U14

U30

U33

U34   U35   U32

U29

Pit Detail (1" = 10')

EXTENTS OF OLD
ROAD BED

SITE SKETCH
OF
1 OLD FIELDS ROAD
SOUTH BERWICK, ME

DRAWN BY:	M.W.F.	DATE:	DEC. 26, 2012
CHECKED BY:	M.W.F.	DRAWING NO:	3436A
JOB NO.:	3436	SHEET	1 OF 1

DOUCET
SURVEY INC.
Serving Your Professional Surveying & Mapping Needs
102 Kent Place, Newmarket, NH 03857
(603) 659-6560   http://www.doucetsurvey.com

The site map of 1 Old Fields Road, showing the house on the left, with some of the test pits dug in the western yard during the 2012 season (rectangular, numbered boxes). The excavation is headed by Dr. Neill De Paoli and sponsored by OBHS. At bottom right, note the 17th- or 18th-century roadbed of Old Fields Road.

4 *An Archaeological Dig*

"I'll get it," I shouted to Harvey. Although it was 2014 and the second summer in which we were attempting to be semi-retired, Harvey and I were each in our separate offices, on the phone with our auction-software programs at the ready.

Our home offices are one of the bonuses that came with the Goodwin house. At some point, most likely in the early nineteenth century, the Goodwins built a carriage house just slightly southeast of the keeping room. In the mid-1980s, the owner modernized the carriage house. He added an upstairs apartment where the hayloft had been, and on the first floor he incorporated an office fully wired not only for electricity but for computers as well—perfect for the networking system needed for communicating with our Baltimore employees. This first-floor room became my home office, and Harvey set up shop in another area of the carriage house that had been converted into a family recreation room.

We were both in our offices when we heard the raspy sound of the antique doorbell. I was confident I would find our "resident" archaeologist standing there; his now-customary ring of the doorbell still brings a sense of anticipation, letting us know that our auction work will have to wait as we follow him to the latest discovery.

IT BEGAN WITH A BROKEN PIECE OF REDWARE   How we came to know Dr. Neill De Paoli was the fortuitous result of a sagging northeast corner that had a broken piece of redware hidden within its walls (our fragment is pictured next to an unbroken plate on the preceding page).

By the start of 2010, our Internet searches had yielded valuable information on the Goodwins, yet many mysteries remained regarding the details of our house. One of the first things about the house I recall reading in that spiral-bound notebook was the story of the original Goodwin home being destroyed by fire—recorded in an undated letter written to Elizabeth Hayes Goodwin by her father, William Allen Hayes Goodwin, the son of the fourth Ichabod in the family to live past infancy and the third to head the household. Here is an excerpt from the letter in which William recalls his great-aunt's recollection of the fire that destroyed the original Goodwin home:

> *The house was burned about 1795, General Goodwin coming home from court late to dinner, a hurried fire caught the chimney and the house. Some of the furniture was saved. I have heard from my great-aunt Sally … who at the time was about 9 years old that they brought up milk pans from the dairy but threw the mirrors out of the window. General Goodwin immediately built the present house precisely like the old one.*

The exterior of our current house is typical of eighteenth-century Georgian architecture in America—a five-bay façade, centered by a pediment-topped entrance flanked by pilasters,

and with double-hung sash windows. Yet, despite our house being rebuilt after the fire at the end of the eighteenth century—according to the letter—many of the architectural details suggest it was built before 1750. Typical of houses built earlier in the century, our house has a single center chimney, not the two end chimneys common in American domestic architecture by the end of the eighteenth century. The later arrangement allowed for the commonly found central hall that runs the depth of the house, dividing the rooms symmetrically. Our house, of course, has no such central hall.

Also, at the end of the eighteenth century, interior trim would have reflected the Adamesque decoration already prevalent in England by the 1760s. Given the lack of such detailing in our home—we have no elaborate plasterwork or fireplace surrounds—it is hard to believe that the house was built after 1790. In addition, architectural historians have dated the semi-lunar pediment above our front door to 1750 or earlier, a few even suggesting that the style is more typical of the period around 1730.

Because of the many outdated architectural features (outdated by 1795), Harvey and I were inclined to believe William's statement in his letter that our house was built "precisely" like the one that had burned down, but we had questions. Did the Goodwins simply prefer the more old-fashioned style? Or was the small-town builder unaware of architectural changes at the close of the eighteenth century? And did the whole house burn down, or was the new home built around surviving remnants?

So, after living here for over five years and unable to discover anything through our research, we had begun to think we might need to enlist the aid of an architectural historian or archaeologist to help sort out the history of our house, specifically an expert familiar with Early American construction. Perhaps such a professional could help us unearth—no pun intended—the missing pieces.

The opportunity came that summer when we had our house's exterior painted. One day while his team was painting, our contractor pointed out that the northeast area of the house needed a bit of help. Seeing ourselves as stewards of this historic home, we immediately agreed that the somewhat costly but essential structural work should begin as soon as possible. In the process of the restoration, the keeping room's back staircase was exposed, and there a rather large fragment of redware was discovered tucked into the wall. This broken fragment most likely had been reconstituted as insulation. I later learned that in New England's cold climate, families commonly stuffed just about anything between their interior and exterior walls, hoping to decrease the amount of penetrating cold.[32]

We knew that dating the fragment wouldn't confirm the year our house was built, but we thought it might offer a clue. So that August, Harvey and I wrapped the piece of redware in a soft cloth and carried it across the street to the Hamilton House in the hope that one of the tour guides could shed some light on the subject. As luck would have it, the guide that day was Dr. De Paoli, who quickly identified the fragment as part of a very large milk pan. Not surprisingly, given our shared interests, the initial inquiry about the redware fragment quickly led to an animated discussion about our house, its history, and the mysteries that remained. As we left him to his work, we promised to stay in touch.

Many visits with Dr. De Paoli followed throughout the fall of 2010. At one point, he came over to examine the interior of our house, every inch, from the attic to the basement, from the nails to the window mullions, from the wood to the hardware. Dr. De Paoli looked at beams and window sashes, floorboards and raised paneling. He first inspected the attic— its paneling, flooring, and door framing—and then looked at the basement cabinetry and fireplace foundation. Alas, from that inspection, he found nothing that could be definitively dated prior to 1795.

THE WILLIAM SPENCER GARRISON   During an early exchange with Dr. De Paoli, I mentioned a map I had found in one of the first books I read while researching Old Fields—a little paperback entitled *The First Permanent Settlement in Maine*, written by Everett Stackpole (1850–1927), an esteemed local historian.[33] The map in Stackpole's book indicates the transfer of several tracts of the Spencer property to Daniel Goodwin (the Captain's grandfather) and Thomas Goodwin (the Captain's father). The map also identifies the site of the William Spencer Garrison at the western boundary of the property. I had known about a garrison being located here as it was mentioned in William Goodwin's letter to his daughter, but it was exciting to find documentary evidence confirming its existence.[34] When I described the map to Dr. De Paoli, he was captivated. Not only is he a professional archaeologist, he also has an extensive knowledge of early Maine history, with one of his primary interests being the study of how the settlements in Maine survived (or failed to survive) the tumultuous years of the French and Indian Wars (1688–1763).

The William Spencer Garrison, most likely built between 1675 and 1690, listed in a 1711 inventory of Maine forts in Berwick, was just one of the many fortified structures located throughout colonial Massachusetts, including the District of Maine, and New Hampshire, built for the protection of residents from Native American war parties—often a combination of native tribes and the French.[35] Many garrisons were simply a complex of buildings already located on a property. Some were surrounded by a tall wooden fence, or palisade, that provided a common border for defense. At least one building would usually be constructed of especially heavy logs with cut-in gun ports. Those fleeing the attacks would seek refuge at the William Spencer Garrison, some lodged in the main house while others would go to the dairy, barn, or other outbuildings.

According to Stackpole's map, the garrison was located on the east side of Old Fields Road, along the western boundary of our land at the juncture of the three main thoroughfares—Old Fields Road, Old South Road, and Vine Street—and where Vaughan Lane, the narrow road that leads to the Newichawannock River (or the Salmon Falls River, as it is now called), ends, along the edge of Jonathan Hamilton's estate. The archaeologist had been intrigued by the possibility that our property was the site of the William Spencer Garrison. By late fall of 2010, he was at our breezeway door, trowel in hand, anxious to begin his first test pit. The hope was to find some remnant of the garrison, an irrefutable "smoking gun," such as large amounts of gunshot or a fragment of a wooden palisade.

By the following June, Dr. De Paoli had set up an official excavation site on our property sponsored by the OBHS. Then, the summer after, in 2012, he organized a field school, and every summer since, for three to five weeks each June and July, students from across the United States have come to take part in the excavation. After the field school ends for the season, the digging proceeds with a few devoted volunteers through early November or until the ground is about to freeze. Over the years, Harvey and I have witnessed the progression of a growing series of pits paralleling the western elevation of the house. Upon viewing our now mangled west-facing yard, one might assume we had been invaded by a species of giant moles, yet Harvey and I are thrilled.

While Dr. De Paoli's original motivation for starting an excavation at Old Fields was to locate the exact site of the William Spencer Garrison, no smoking gun has been found to date. The only remotely military reference in the various documents we have researched is a mention of "Armes" and "powder and ball" in the elder Spencer's inventory. Harvey and I are far from disappointed, though, as countless details depicting the daily lives of the Spencers and the Goodwins have been brought to light by the dig, as well as some significant details about our home and the other structures on our property.

ARCHAEOLOGY PROVIDES A WINDOW ONTO THE PAST   I still remember the excitement generated by the archaeological findings in the summer of 2012. It was the first summer of the field school, and Dr. De Paoli, whom we knew well enough to call Neill by this point, came to the breezeway door that connects the 1870 addition to the carriage house where our offices are located, to tell us that he and his students had just uncovered the first fire remnants in the new pit started just to the right of the granite steps leading up to our front door (see photo on next page). Our resident archaeologist appeared exceptionally excited, and the three of us eagerly ran to the site. There, in the newly dug pit, about two feet down, we saw the irrefutable evidence of a fairly intense conflagration, one that had

been hot enough to burn brick and plaster and melt window glass. We stood on the edge of the pit, looking down at the charred and melted remains. We knew that those scorched chunks of plaster and brick, and pieces of broken glass were most likely from the walls, windows, and chimney stack that had once been part of the original Goodwin House.

That summer, Neill and his students would eventually isolate the remains of two different types of windows— both a casement (see right, window from the Richard Jackson House, Portsmouth, NH, 1644) *and* a sash window. These new findings meant that two sepa-
rate structures, built decades apart, likely burned together on that same site—one with casement windows, presumably an early house built by the Spencers, as casement windows were primarily found in colonial America during the seventeenth century; and the other structure with sash windows, presumably the original eighteenth-century Goodwin house built after 1740, as sash windows were not common until the beginning of the eighteenth century. This discovery suggests that the Goodwins either had built a "modern" extension to a pre-existing structure, or that they had an entirely new house built soon after purchasing the Spencer property. Given the contents of the letter written by William Allen Hayes Goodwin, I have always believed the latter, while the professional archaeologist withholds judgment until definitive proof is found. Either way, the findings indicate that an older Spencer structure was still standing at the time of the fire.

Then Neill made another important discovery while doing research at the York County Courthouse in Alfred, Maine. Their extensive archives contain their Registry of Deeds, a compilation of all commercial transactions in the county, starting in 1636, and therefore proving invaluable to our research. It is there that he came across the elder William Spencer's inventory, dated to the time of the elder Spencer's death in 1696. The inventory lists a "two-story building with two rooms on each floor." As our current house, the one built "precisely like the old one," is a four-up, four-down floor plan—or arguably it might have originally been a three up, three down, but not the two rooms per floor of the Spencer home—the Captain undoubtedly built a new structure on the property. But when it was built and how the Goodwins used the Spencer house remain undetermined. While we had filled in another large piece of the puzzle, Harvey and I still had many questions.

Neill continued to sift through the records at the York County courthouse. He soon learned that in 1696 the childless William had bequeathed his land and house to his nephew Humphrey Spencer. Neill also discovered a number of documents detailing the transfer of the Spencer property to the Goodwins in 1740, including the stipulation about the two-year interim. Did the Goodwins move into the Spencers' preexisting house in 1742? Or, is it possible they had a new house built during the two-year interim between purchasing the property and moving to Old Fields? Based solely on the stylistic dating of our house's architectural features—the one presumed to have been built "precisely" like the original—if the Goodwins did move into the Spencer house, then it is very likely that they built their new "modern" home soon after. Also, by the time the Captain purchased Old Fields, he was already a gentleman of means and likely would have wanted more than four rooms for himself, his servants, his wife, and their three children (with one more on the way).

Although the details of William Goodwin's letter seem accurate, the lack of specificity as to the extent of the damage is frustrating; plus when William states that the General "built the present house precisely like the old one" it sounds like our house was a complete rebuild. But as Harvey and I learned more about American architecture at the end of the eighteenth century, we noticed distinct inconsistencies with certain structural elements, leading us to question whether it could be possible that some parts of the original house had survived the fire and were incorporated into the rebuild.

The puzzle is ever expanding.

A RENEWED RESPECT FOR TRASH "You guys got a minute?" Neill inquired as soon as I opened the door, the ring of the antique bell still resounding. This oft-repeated question is his way of letting us know that he or an assistant has found an object worthy of an interruption to our workday.

For four summers, Neill had been digging tirelessly in our yard with his team of volunteers and field students. They had unearthed hundreds and hundreds of shards and intact objects in an attempt to discover what structures existed on our property between 1690 and today. In the summer of 2014 they had begun work on a pit directly in front of the northwest wing of the home. Standing in our open doorway, Neill informed me that they had just uncovered two more fascinating artifacts. One was the handle and bowl of a "battered metal seal-top spoon dating from about 1650 to 1675. The wear on the base of the spoon's bowl indicates the user was left-handed." The spoon was, to my mind, remarkably unspoiled, and it was easy to imagine William Spencer, Humphrey's uncle, dipping his seal-top spoon into a bowl of pea soup using his left hand.

The second artifact was a charming seventeenth-century brass or pewter Tudor rose button that may have "once adorned a man's doublet."[36] Neill mentioned that the Tudor rose button was a sign of "loyalty to the royalist cause of the Stuart monarchy." Notably, a similar piece was found by archaeologists digging on the nearby site of the well-appointed seventeenth-century home of Humphrey Chadbourne, the brother-in-law of Thomas Spencer, the elder William Spencer's father—albeit the Chadbourne piece was a much larger example used to adorn the harness of a horse.[37]

While these two objects were remarkable, some of the most intriguing finds to date were from an area explored the summer before. In 2013, Neill's team of archaeologists uncovered a stone-walled cellar probably connected to part of the older Spencer house. They found items dating from as early as the late seventeenth century and also items dating from the time we know the Goodwins were living on the property, so we know the Goodwins had used the cellar hole as a trash pit—a spot to discard daily rubbish as well as broken items no longer useful. A small-town resident in the eighteenth century certainly would not have received weekly visits from a waste management service as we do today.

The informative trash pit has told us much about the actual diet of the Goodwin household. A large array of bones and shells has been recovered, so we know that the early inhabitants of Old Fields ate a good deal of beef, lamb, and mutton, along with lesser amounts of clams, oysters, and fish, possibly both saltwater and fresh. And of course, pork, based on a large upper jawbone that was uncovered. When it was first discovered, the jawbone was assumed to be that of a wolf—a scary thought!

Besides being a place for everyday refuse, a trash pit served another purpose in the eighteenth century. When a younger generation took over the family homestead, they would use these pits for disposing of unwanted items that, in their eyes, probably seemed "old-fashioned." And it is for this reason, our resident archaeologist explained, that our trash

Top left, copper rosette. Top right, 18th-century pewter button with glass enamel decoration.

pit has a number of fragments from the late 1600s, presumably from when Humphrey Spencer moved to the property, and other fragments possibly dating as late as the 1770s, when the General took over the running of Old Fields from his father, the Captain; out with the heavy old pottery and in with the newer, more delicate ceramics listed in the General's 1829 inventory. One day, Harvey, Neill, and I, were standing around the perimeter of the trash-filled cellar hole. "Check this out," Neill instructed as he showed us a small object that looked like a fastening for a jacket. "This copper rosette," he explained, "would have been used to embellish high-end coats, dresses, and shoes. Such an ornamental fastener made of metal and wrapped in silk served to distinguish its wearer as a member of the gentility. It sure was one eye-catching way to convey his or her status." I could envision the Captain, now aged, wearing his beloved old coat, fastened with this copper rosette. That garment worn by the Captain until, literally, his dying days, might have been the first thing his daughter-in-law consigned to the trash pit after the funeral service late in 1777.

This trash pit has offered up other adornments such as shoe buckles, earrings, and an enameled shirt button. Based on these findings, one can reasonably speculate that the Goodwins dressed in a manner indicating a fair degree of wealth. By having a chance to handle actual objects from their lives, no matter how small the remnant, I can picture their dress and I can imagine their meals. I can "see" their eighteenth-century world. As my imagination gives shape to the Goodwins, I add this lovely copper rosette to our growing collection of artifacts found below the surface of our property.

THE TAVERN   As early as the first summer of the dig, in 2011, Neill and the volunteers began digging up a large number of fragments of ceramic wine jugs, tankards, mugs, and clay pipes dating from the eighteenth century. These fragments, combined with the records of annual licenses for serving alcohol found earlier in the York County Registry of Deeds, support the theory that there had been a tavern right here in our front yard starting in 1699, likely run out of the home of the Spencers and later taken over by Captain Ichabod Goodwin. For both Harvey and me, this was a fascinating possibility.

The licenses were granted by the town of Berwick, first to Humphrey Spencer in 1699, and every year thereafter until his death in 1712, when the license was granted to his widow, Mary, and finally to our first Ichabod Goodwin in 1742. The Captain had the license reissued almost every subsequent year until 1769, the last year for which we have a record of a liquor license. So aside from 1750 and 1753, when no liquor license is recorded, we know that a tavern operated at Old Fields without interruption between 1699 and 1769.

It seems logical that the Spencer house would have been maintained as the tavern, while the Goodwin family occupied the new house, or at least that is my educated guess. Although there is still no evidence to support my interpretation, Neill is not totally dismissive of the idea. During our many animated discussions about the property, we go back and forth, hypothesizing the chronology of the various structures. I always like to point out that we have also found nothing to prove that the Goodwins moved into the Spencer house or that they had built their early Georgian home when the style was no longer in vogue.

To date, the excavation has yet to reveal exactly where the Spencer house stood. Was the foundation on which the two-story railroad house now sits that of the Spencer home, as some locals have suggested? And why didn't the General rebuild this older structure after the fire? The latter question is perhaps easier to answer: as the last year Captain Goodwin was identified as tavern keeper was 1769, a few years before he died, they would have had no need to rebuild the Spencer home for use as a tavern. Also, what purpose did that older house serve between 1770 and the year of the fire, around 1795? We may never know....

Still, there are many things we do know. Neill's research revealed a large number of permit fees paid by Humphrey Spencer. These more expensive licensing fees allowed him to sell beverages with a higher alcohol content. We also know from Humphrey Spencer's inventory that the Spencers had a dairy and a distilling apparatus. No doubt this distillery was used to supplement the rum that Humphrey likely imported from abroad. And the Spencers may well have used butter and cheese produced in their own dairy in tavern meals.

With each passing year, the dig continued to provide evidence of tavern life. One of the most delightful archaeological finds was a small iron pincer called a *smoker's companion*. Used to grab a burning ember from the fire to light one's pipe, this utensil appears to be from the seventeenth century, based on its similarity to documented examples.

The fact that this fragile implement has survived intact, and in its current remarkable state of preservation, made this discovery especially noteworthy. Also, while not evidence of the tavern's existence, per se, this smoker's companion helped me imagine tavern life.

The Captain, clay pipe in hand, would probably have been seated by the fire, enjoying the attention of his patrons. They likely discussed current affairs, like the problems with the landing at Quamphegan (the Captain had been appointed with two others to look into the careless placement of timber, impeding traffic in this vital area). As the men talked, the Captain would pick up the delicate smoker's companion, lean over the fire, and snatch a glowing ember with which to light his pipe.

CURRENCY AND HISTORIC REENACTMENTS   During the summer of 2012, one of Neill's field students uncovered an unusual artifact that received a flurry of publicity in virtually every local paper. It was an old silver coin, a Spanish real dated 1689. The real was an accepted and common form of currency, used for commerce in colonial America when there was a very limited supply of English and American hard currency. The following summer, three more coins were discovered, each dating from the early 1700s—two Irish and one German. While the Spanish real was the most frequently used foreign currency, coins from other countries were also accepted as payment, as the later finding shows. We now had archaeological evidence supporting the existence of a robust commercial enterprise on our property over three hundred years ago.[38]

From time to time here in today's South Berwick, the town sponsors events that show-case life as it was in the early days. Harvey and I always attend these reenactments, hoping to broaden our understanding of the early settlers. For one such event, a replica of a gunda-low was brought to the shores at the base of the Hamilton House, close to the site of the old wharves of Pipe Stave Landing, the remains of which can still be seen today. The gundalow, a shallow-draft vessel anywhere from thirty to sixty feet in length, was used throughout Maine and New Hampshire during the seventeenth and eighteenth centuries for loading and unloading goods from the oceangoing vessels arriving from all over the world.

Walking on the decks of the replica we listened to the chorus of sea shanties like "Haul Away, Joe," with its rhythmic refrain "Way haul away, we'll haul away together," typically sung as a device for the sailors to coordinate their labors. These reenactments offer a glimpse into the past. I could easily envision ships sailing in with the tides, arriving with products from around the world, allowing me to further understand how the Spencer tavern would have thrived so near the undoubtedly brisk traffic at Pipe Stave Landing.[39]

Later, in the summer of 2013, the field students unearthed a discovery even more exciting than the coins, at least for me, if not for the local papers. In one of the pits they

1a

1b

2b

2a

3a

3b

1. German copper two-
schilling coin (1727).
2. Irish Hibernia copper
halfpenny (1723).
3. Spanish silver real
cobb coin (1689).
For each coin: (a) obverse
(b) reverse. Coins not
shown at actual size.

uncovered a stone foundation just ten feet west of our current house. When I first saw those beautifully dressed, very heavy granite stones, I was transported back hundreds of years. I could picture the workmen carefully stacking them by hand, creating a solid underpinning for the building to come.

For Neill, the archaeologist, this discovery presented ever more questions. Was this granite foundation part of the original Georgian home the Captain built and that was reproduced around 1795? If so, then what did the foundation under the two-story railroad house addition belong to? Or was it the foundation of the Captain's blacksmith shop? Or even the Spencer dairy? Or was this foundation part of the Spencer home built in the latter part of the seventeenth century?

Gazing down at the granite stones of the foundation walls, it was easy to conjure up the dim light of the main hall of the Spencer house. As the light filters through the diamond-shaped glass of the casement windows, I can imagine Humphrey descending the stairs, thinking about his day at the tavern.

HUMPHREY SPENCER, INNHOLDER The elder William Spencer purchased this land in the middle of the seventeenth century and upon his death in 1696 willed the property to his nephew Humphrey.[40] Humphrey also inherited his uncle's indentured servant Moses Spencer, a cousin. As Humphrey did not marry until 1701, the extra set of hands would have proven helpful once his tavern opened for business, three years after he inherited the property. The two-story house left to him in his uncle's will was ideally situated for its probable use as a tavern. The property starts just a few feet up from the road we now call Old Fields Road, at the convergence of several convenient roadways connecting Berwick to other towns in Maine, New Hampshire, and Boston. At the end of the 1600s, it was also perfectly centered in the Upper Parish of Kittery (where the three towns of Berwick, South Berwick, and North Berwick sit today), so travelers would have passed right by the property on their way north, to Wells and Portland (then known as Falmouth), and on up to Canada.

Aside from the many travelers on foot or horseback who would have passed directly in front of the house, just down the hill about five hundred yards Pipe Stave Landing was a bustle of activity as the men unloaded cargo from the local and overseas merchant vessels anchored at a section of the river known locally as Deep Hole for its unusual depth. Those laboring at the wharves could no doubt have been counted on to climb the hill leading to the property, hungry and thirsty at midday. I can also picture the officers of the various ships disembarking and coming up the rise of the hill to Humphrey's tavern, ready to share their tales of the high seas and exchange their Spanish reales for a meal and a bed.

Following the British tradition, taverns in colonial America also served as inns. The tavern keeper was responsible not only for feeding and providing drink to his patrons but also for providing beds to weary travelers. Here at the tavern, local men would come to read the news provided by the broadsides and newspapers or to have the articles read to them by others, as illiteracy was quite high in those years.[41] Here, too, they would find out the latest prices for their hay or potatoes, discuss (or perhaps argue about) whether one should remain loyal to the British king, gossip a bit, and maybe enjoy a fine roasted joint and a pudding. All the while partaking in strong drink.

As I stand at our tavern table, chopping herbs and vegetables for the sauce to accompany tonight's leg of venison, I watch Harvey constantly maneuvering the spit to ensure that the lean joint does not dry out, and I think about Humphrey Spencer's early days as innholder. Given the amount of labor involved in running a successful tavern, I expect that he and his servant Moses were busy indeed. It must have been a welcome addition when in 1701, following a yearlong courtship, Humphrey married Mary, the daughter of John Cutts, a storekeeper in Portsmouth, New Hampshire. Mary certainly would have been prepared to aid Humphrey in his duties, having undoubtedly acquired a number of useful skills while assisting her father in his Portsmouth store.

Thinking about the Spencers and their tavern, I want to know what life was like, not only for Humphrey and Mary but also for every inhabitant of the District of Maine at the close of the seventeenth century and the beginning of the eighteenth. I still cannot imagine how they managed to get through those long years of conflict with the Wabanaki Indians of Maine and New Hampshire.

Ambrose ⊠ Gibbons. 1630.

o well

Vineyard

Chadbourne's Mill.

James Stackpole

granted to Tho. Canney 1656

Tho. Hobbs --

Sylvanus Nock.

Jas. Grant 1656

David Hamilton

Henry Nock Wyer

Eleazer Nock

Henry Hobbs

Sligo

Henry Magown 1656 Berry Weymouth 1708

Nawichawannock River

Little Johns Falls

XXXX

John Bradstreet

Ashanbedick

"Parker's Field"

Cem. Jas. Stackpole John Wade Jeremiah Wise

200 acres granted to Thomas Spencer, 1652

Oldest House in Maine --

100 rods by 320, estimated

XIX. 342

⊠ "Old Fields" Site of Gar. Spencer.

Dan! Goodwin

B. Nason to H. Spencer VII. 65

88 rods

Pipe Stave Landing

200 acres granted to Richard Nason. Willed to sons, Benjamin and Baker

T. Etherington 12 acres Y.D. John Wm "

J. Gatin 12 acres IV. 84 Wincoll Jr. Hearle

Francis Harlow VII. 48 R. Lord XV. 107

R. Lo VIII R.

Alexander Maxwell, 1656. John Neal. Nathan Lord John Cooper in succession.

School House -- ▪

▪ Richard Nason.

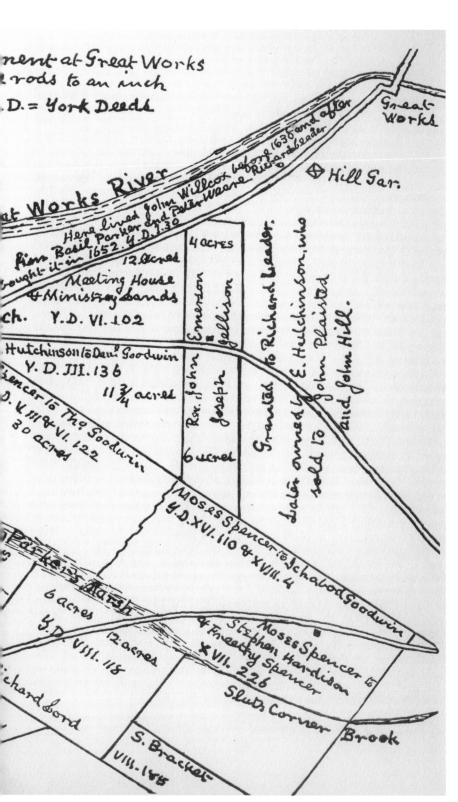

ment at Great Works
rods to an inch
D. = York Deeds

Great
Works

at Works River

Here lived John Willcox before 1638 and after
Rev. Basil Parker and Peter Weare Richard Leader
bought it in 1652. Y.D.I.30

⊕ Hill Gar.

12 acres
Meeting House
& Ministry Lands

4 acres

ch. Y.D. VI. 102

Emerson Jellison

Granted to Richard Leader

Later owned by E. Hutchinson, who
sold to John Plaisted
and John Hill.

Hutchinson to Danl Goodwin
Y. D. III. 136

11 ¾ acres

Rev. John
Joseph

Spencer to Thos Goodwin
D. V. 111 & VI. 122
30 acres

6 acres

Moses Spencer to Ichabod Goodwin
Y.D. XVI. 110 & XVIII. 4

Parker's Marsh

6 acres
Y. D. VSII. 118

Moses Spencer to
Stephen Hardison
& Timothy Spencer
XVII. 226

12 acres

Slut's Corner
Brook

Richard Lord

S. Bracket
VIII. 1845

Map drawn by author and historian Everett Stackpole for his publication The First Permanent Settlement in Maine. *In the middle, just to the left of the centerfold, is marked "Old Fields" Site of Spencer Gar[rison]. Pipe Stave Landing at far left.*

Commerce and Conflict in Berwick

Harvey and I have discovered that living in a town with a population of less than eight thousand means you get to know the people at the local food market, the bank, and the post office (despite their reputation, Mainers can be quite loquacious). Not only does Maine truly have some of the cleanest air in the country, but the pharmacist in our town will deliver your prescription when you are too ill to pick it up. We have come to enjoy South Berwick's small-town atmosphere, its proximity to beautiful beaches and mountains, and, perhaps most important, the town's far remove from the hurried pace of a mid-Atlantic lifestyle. And, remarkably, we are able to enjoy all these benefits while still living less than an hour and a half from the big-city culture of Boston. Of course, at the time of the Spencers and Goodwins, Boston was a more than three-day journey by horse.[42]

The area where Berwick is located attracted a good number of English settlers during the seventeenth century. Similar to other Early American towns that had ready access to roads and waterways, Berwick was a vibrant commercial center, but it had one additional significant advantage: it was blessed with a number of steep waterfalls. These falls gave its early settlers a great source of energy—water power. One of the most prominent falls in the area, known as Rocky Gorge, is just about a mile east of the Spencer property. In the mid-1600s, the men of Berwick established a sawmill at the gorge, creating what was possibly the first overshot water-powered site in America.[43] This powerful mill served as one of the principal drivers of the town's growth.

Humphrey Spencer's uncle would have undoubtedly recognized the area's potential when he chose to settle at Old Fields. Aside from the falls, the numerous landings established along the Newichawannock provided settlers access to a quicker and easier form of travel than the existing dirt roads, crude extensions of the original Indian pathways. The elder William would have also realized the benefits offered by the deep waters along the Newichawannock.

The wharves at Pipe Stave Landing played an important role in the region's commercial trade of the time. The depth of the river supported the two-masted brigs capable of crossing the Atlantic, allowing the neighboring sawmills to export their lumber to England, boosting one of the area's major sources of income.

Moreover, Pipe Stave Landing was just ten miles west of Portsmouth, New Hampshire, which was founded on the banks of the Piscataqua River. As the Newichawannock River flows directly into the Piscataqua, which empties into the Atlantic, Berwick had direct access to this important gateway that offered uninterrupted commerce throughout the long New England winters as the river's waters never froze. Its swift currents afforded year round access to ships transporting Berwick's lumber and pipe, or barrel, staves (thus the name of the landing) to Boston, cities along the mid-Atlantic, the southern colonies, and points beyond. Of course the importation of goods was equally beneficial.

To Berwick's deep waters came ships from around the world, oceangoing vessels with everything needed in a growing community: hardware and flatware; leather, cloth, and finished dry goods; salt, refined sugar, wine, raisins and citrus; coffee and tea; molasses; and, regrettably, I learned, slaves. I couldn't imagine my beloved adopted state being involved in the purchase and enslavement of fellow human beings. This was a part of Massachusetts, after all, *not* Virginia. Yet when I did some research into slavery in colonial New England I was surprised to discover that slavery did, in fact, exist as far north as the District of Maine until the end of the eighteenth century. It appears that ownership of slaves ceased to exist in Massachusetts by the time of the 1790 census, but until then those same ships bringing luxury foods and manufactured items to New England were involved in this inhumane but lucrative trade.

It is worth noting that citizens living in the earliest settlements of Kittery had access to extravagances that settlers in the Midwest would not enjoy until the mid-nineteenth century. An ordinary farmer like the Goodwins' neighbor Benjamin Gerrish could borrow a horse, ride to Kittery, and come back with coffee, sugar, tea, and perhaps even that broadcloth coat that settlers in Springfield didn't have until over a half century later.[44] Townsmen could easily purchase or barter goods such as clothing, building materials, cider, meat, and potatoes. Recognizing these benefits, many men and their families continued to settle by the banks of the Newichawannock, hoping to improve their own financial well-being—ambitious men such as Humphrey Spencer and Captain Goodwin.

A farmer isolated from populated areas like Kittery spent all the hours of the day tilling the soil to grow the crops necessary to feed his family and livestock. Maintaining his self-sufficient lifestyle meant the rural farmer had no time to spend on other pursuits as did his urban counterparts. The gentlemen farmers in Berwick, on the other hand, often engaged in additional income-producing activities such as operating taverns, blacksmith shops, or mills. They used this additional income not only to increase their lands or expand their other businesses but also, based on the evidence of the items found in our trash pit, to acquire luxury items such as the lovely set of China export porcelain that was probably purchased by the Captain for his wife, Elizabeth. The economy of Berwick was expanding, and it seems that those first Goodwins of Old Fields benefited. County records show us that the General, the Captain's son, was able to purchase additional land to advance his commercial interests in timber, while the inventories of both the Spencer and Goodwin families show us that Humphrey and the Captain could afford indentured servants and slaves to assist with the labor-intensive tasks of life in colonial New England.

HARDSHIPS For the gentlemen farmers of Berwick, life was certainly less arduous than for New Englanders on more isolated farms, but their seventeenth- and early-eighteenth-century existence could hardly be considered carefree. Outside of tending the fields and doing chores, which included dairying, feeding the farm animals, washing clothes, cooking, and baking, their lives scarcely allowed for much recreation. And even routine tasks such as the obligatory trimming of lighted candles every fifteen minutes to prevent smoking seems burdensome from the perspective of the twenty-first century.

Moreover, when picturing their daily lives, we must consider the rather inhospitable climate of northern New England. Long, dark winters meant that much of the day was spent simply trying to stay warm, *warm* being a relative term. Many diarists of the times wrote how water brought indoors during the winter would freeze overnight. In the winter months, typically from October through May, a midsized home could go through upward of forty cords of wood. One cord is a stack of wood measuring four feet by four feet by eight feet, so forty cords would run the length of just over a hundred and six yards. Picture a football field and you get a sense of the enormity of the job at hand just to cut and transport the fuel needed to stay warm and cook the food.

Both the demanding labor and the winter chill proved manageable for those tough early settlers, yet in the late 1600s and early 1700s there was a precipitous fall in the population of the District of Maine. Clearly, there was a far more serious threat causing these otherwise hearty colonists to flee.

CONFLICT WITH THE INDIANS   Intermittently from 1675 into the 1720s there was a series of wars, major and minor, between the British settlers and the Wabanaki, who were aided and encouraged by that traditional British enemy, France. King Philip's War began in 1675, ending one year later in 1676, followed by King William's War, from 1688 to 1697, and finally Queen Anne's War, from 1702 to 1713. Less formal warfare began again a decade later with the war known as Father Rale's War, 1722 to 1725. Finally the conflicts were concluded with the French and Indian War, 1754 to 1763.

These ongoing conflicts disrupted the lives and certainly affected the psyches of early Mainers.[45] Life here was insecure to say the least; many families, especially those who lived north of Wells, simply left, leaving behind deserted homesteads and diminished towns.[46]

The antagonism that developed between the British settlers and the Native Americans was perhaps inevitable. As their numbers declined, the Wabanaki felt increasingly vulnerable. The French, as the historic enemy of the British, capitalized on the situation and incited the Indians to attack the English colonists. In close proximity to eastern Canada where the French had settled, Massachusetts and its District of Maine became the easiest and most logical target of French and Indian aggression. Thus, for almost fifty years these

A 19th-century rendering of King Philip, the leader of the native Wampanoag after whom the first war was named. The Native American leader had adopted a British name when relations with the British were friendlier.

KING PHILIP

early settlers of the northeastern colonies, many innocent of egregious acts against the native population, were kidnapped, tortured, and murdered. No one living in Maine during that time could have felt safe.

The lives of Humphrey and Mary Spencer coincided with these fearful times. Every day must have been fraught with uncertainty. A settler going out in the morning to his field might never return. If he did, he might come home for dinner to find his family kidnapped and his house destroyed. In 1690, during that same raid in which Hetty Goodwin was captured, Humphrey's uncle barely escaped with his life when a war party of Wabanaki attacked a sawmill at a nearby pond. During that same joint assault by French troops and Wabanaki warriors, the entire estate of Humphrey Chadbourne, valued at more than £1,700 in 1667, was burned to the ground.[47] A prominent Berwick citizen and one of the wealthiest men in Massachusetts, Chadbourne had built a homestead that included his home (over 2,500 square feet), a barn, a dairy, and a second house where it's thought the servants slept.[48]

To cope with the threat of attacks, residents who stayed in the area built garrisons. These fortified structures or secured complexes of buildings provided some safety during the frequent raids. The William Spencer Garrison was one such defensive site, offering protection for hundreds of Berwick's citizens. High above today's Salmon Falls River, the William Spencer Garrison would have afforded a great vantage point for spotting advancing war parties. According to local historian Stackpole, the Spencer compound, named for Humphrey's uncle, was "built before 1675." Given the frequency of the raids during the French and Indian offensives, the garrison most likely served as a refuge numerous times well before Humphrey received that first liquor license. Based on our research, Neill, Harvey, and I believe that William Spencer's compound was the largest in Berwick. We know it was capable of housing up to a hundred residents at a time for in 1711, the garrison sheltered ten families, thirteen men, and four soldiers.[49]

Here within the confines of the compound, the citizens of Berwick had earlier held off the horrific attacks of 1690, when almost all the homes in the town were destroyed and many of the inhabitants, including our brave Mehitable, were either captured or killed.[50] The following year, the Spencer Garrison of Berwick again afforded its citizens a safe haven when the Wabanaki appeared near the sawmill of Rocky Gorge, just about a mile from Old Fields. One of the three men who managed to escape was William Spencer himself.

At the time Humphrey Spencer inherited the property, around 1696, there was a house large enough to also serve as a tavern, as well as a dairy and other outbuildings; the Spencer complex of buildings could have housed up to a hundred people, if under somewhat crowded conditions. I can only wonder how many times the Spencers opened their doors to frightened citizens of Berwick in those terrifying years between 1675 and 1723.

FRIGHTFUL TIMES Today is one of those perfect days of early June, the kind of day I was looking forward to when we made our decision to move to Maine. The sun is bright, the humidity low, and the temperature comfortably warm. I am thoroughly enjoying the soft breeze as I take my brisk walk down Vaughan Lane to the river. The wind picks up and the sudden gust causes the pine needles to dance, casting lively shadows that add to my pleasure. But what is that darker shape I see? I think it was a heron rising slowly from the river, but I imagine the fear that such a sudden movement might have caused those who walked here before me. Fear must have been a constant companion of Humphrey and Mary Spencer as they served their patrons in the first decade of the eighteenth century. Every inhabitant of Berwick undoubtedly understood that each day could be their last during the precarious years of Queen Anne's War.

I can't help thinking about those who weren't able to reach Spencer's safe haven. One night in 1703, during the first year of Queen Anne's War, not everyone from the town made it to this property when the enemy attacked. That night, outside the garrison, one man was killed, another wounded, and three women were taken captive.[51] In 1704 a woman was killed at the nearby Andrew Neal Garrison, and in 1707, returning home from services at the meetinghouse that once stood on today's South Road (originally called *the road to York*), James Ferguson and his wife were murdered by a war party of Wabanaki. My walk just took me up South Road past the charming eighteenth-century parson's house located next to the site of the old meetinghouse, only a few hundred yards from our home. Our proximity to the site where the Fergusons were murdered makes it all too easy for me to imagine how vulnerable the inhabitants must have felt. Following the route of the unfortunate Fergusons, I take the path from where the meetinghouse once stood and turn left at Old Fields. I imagine walking in Mary Spencer's shoes as she returns home after Sunday service. I can feel her senses heightened, ever watchful.

How Mary lived with the constant fear she must have felt while gathering greens for a midday soup or quickly running out to the dairy building to bring back a block of butter is inconceivable to me; yet she and her husband persevered. Unlike many who fled to the safety of Boston or towns farther to the south, Humphrey and Mary Spencer stayed in the area and kept their tavern going throughout the war. In fact, when Humphrey died in 1712, Mary had the means to spend the substantial sum of £37 on the funeral service, suggesting that despite all, the tavern had remained quite busy.[52]

On the day of Humphrey's funeral, the silent pallbearers would not have had far to go, as the town burial ground was just a couple of hundred yards away, on Vine Street. Upon returning to the Spencer home—now hung with black crepe—the mourners would have been offered a sufficient quantity of alcoholic beverages, a tradition brought over from England; Mary would have made certain of it. And with the help of her servants and neighbors there would have been more than enough food to feed everyone. Among the dishes offered would likely have been the colonial standard—a hearty meat pie.

MEAT PIE: A DISH WORTHY OF THE FUNERAL SERVICE OF AN INNHOLDER
Meat pies were quite fashionable in early America, as the first colonists brought their traditional British cooking with them. If you look through eighteenth-century cookbooks or modern culinary books with discussions of eighteenth-century cooking, you will find a plethora of recipes for chicken pies, pigeon pies, pork pies, game pies, and pasties, the sheer number indicating their popularity. One reason for the appeal was the airtight casing that acted as a preservative. An uncut meat pie could keep for days.

During a recent visit to Colonial Williamsburg, Harvey and I had enjoyed an excellent game pie, whetting our appetites and motivating me to create our own version. Soon after that trip, we decided to use venison we had recently purchased in New York, and I began researching historic recipes. I ran into some difficulties, as virtually every recipe I found had a different methodology. For example, one recipe said to cook all of the ingredients, including the venison, beforehand; another advised just to brown the main protein and vegetables; then a third said to marinate the meat and vegetables; while yet another marinated only the meat. Then, of the various other conflicting instructions, you could cube, mince, or grind the meat; or you could leave the meat or poultry whole, requiring, of course, a gigantic pastry cover; and, if using a fowl, it would have to be boned first. Then there were as many options for your crust, or *coffin*, as it was often called. You could use hot water crust, short crust, puff pastry, or quick puff pastry.

By this time, I was thoroughly confused.

The Colonial Williamsburg version that we had recently enjoyed seemed to have had everything cooked in advance before being assembled under the piecrust lid, and often the taverns at Williamsburg serve twenty-first century adaptations of eighteenth-century recipes, rendering them inadequate for my purposes.[53] *The Williamsburg Cookbook* itself contains numerous historic recipes that were later adapted, sometimes as late as the 1930s. So, while delicious, their meat pie was too modernized to give me the authentic taste I was hoping to achieve, and the resulting pie would also not have had the requisite airtight casing. I wanted to stay as close as possible not only to ingredients that would have been available in the late 1600s and throughout the 1700s but also to the cooking methods used to assemble a particular dish at that time.

I should acknowledge that I readily took advantage of the conveniences of our electric refrigerator and oven. Over time, though, Harvey and I began to solely use the brick hearth and Dutch oven for our recipes from the eighteenth century. Unfortunately, we have not come up with a reliable replacement for our refrigerator.

After reading about ten recipes, many by authors from earlier eras, and trying to absorb the culinary philosophy underlying their various methods, I eventually came up with my own version of a late-seventeenth-century venison pie.

As an experiment, I made two pies. I cooked one pie in the electric oven, and Harvey baked the second in the brick oven. Both were wonderful, with perhaps a slight nod to the brick-oven version, its crust a little crisper and the interior contents significantly more moist. I served the pies, one slice of each per person, with some additional carrots, boiled and buttered, and we finished with a light dessert of syllabub, a frothy British milk-based dessert flavored with wine or liquor.

I do wonder if Mary Spencer (or more probably her servants), was as exhausted as I was after preparing this rather elaborate yet common meal. I imagine not, as her stamina was no doubt far greater than mine. Nevertheless, I do not think that venison pie was often on the menu at their seventeenth-century tavern. A less labor-intensive, undemanding spit-roasted venison would have certainly pleased their regular patrons. I also venture a guess that such a meat pie was rarely, if ever, served by a typical colonial New England woman cooking for her own family. A more usual home-cooked meal at the time would have involved a soup or a piece of meat that had simmered in a pot hanging from the crane, perhaps with a pudding encased in a floured cloth and submerged in the liquid; these one-pot boiled dinners were exceedingly common at the time. They needed no laborious prep-arations and very little attention while cooking, thus freeing up the housewife (and any servants she may have had) for other duties.

A WIDOW RENEWS THE TAVERN LICENSE Now widowed with three children to raise, Mary might have had trouble surviving if she hadn't been the widow of an innholder. Humphrey's will specified that their son, William, was to inherit the tavern upon his twenty-first birthday, fourteen years hence. In the interim, Mary was able to renew the liquor license in her name and continue running her husband's tavern until her son could take over.

Sharon V. Salinger, author of *Taverns and Drinking in Early America*, notes that many of the traditions of English tavern life were transported to the colonies. She speculates that those men responsible for regulating British taverns—the number of which was carefully controlled both in England and in the colonies through the regulated dispersal of innholder licenses—understood that it was more beneficial to society if a widow could sustain herself.[54] I am sure that this was also on the minds of the town leaders of New England, who, furthermore, would have recognized the central role these taverns played in colonial life. Ensuring the continuity of these early taverns must have been a primary concern of those in charge of granting the licenses.

Clearly, Mary Spencer was equal to the task of preserving order at her tavern, as the town was willing to renew her license year after year. This woman took care of her three children, ran the homestead, and from 1712 until 1722, when she remarried, she found the time to properly manage the Spencer Tavern at Old Fields. Upon her marriage to a Mr. Joseph Moulton, Mary rented the tavern to a Mr. Frost until William came of age and was finally able to take over the family business.

When I learned that Mary was granted her first license in 1712, I found the arrangement a bit odd, to say the least. Women were not allowed to drink in a tavern, yet the innholder's widow was granted permission to run one! I wondered if the widow was also exempt from the laws banning women from drinking in taverns; and, if so, might Mary have helped herself to the occasional drink or two with her patrons? After all, the tavern was her home.

It appears that the young William Spencer did not inherit the business acumen of either his father or his mother. Presumably in need of money, William sold sixty acres of family land to a Benjamin Hodson just one year after taking over the reins of the property. We also know that in 1729 he had to borrow money from the town of Berwick to pay his annual tax—a tax of ten shillings.[55] Then in 1734 he sold two acres of his Long Marsh meadow to Ichabod Goodwin, the Captain. By 1740, three townsmen—John Hooper, Moses Butler, and Benjamin Nason—took William Spencer to court for nonpayment of debt. That same year, William sold the nineteen-acre property with its main house and outbuildings to the

Captain, the first Goodwin to dwell at Old Fields. As mentioned earlier, the documents stipulated that William retained the right to occupy the home for another two years, sharing some of the space with his mother and her second husband, Joseph Moulton. So it was not until 1742 that the last Spencer to live at Old Fields moved out, after selling our first Ichabod another twenty-acre parcel of land.

Venison Pie

Makes two 8-inch pies

FILLING

2½ pounds venison, cut in ¼ inch cubes*
Red wine, enough to cover
Salt to taste
2 carrots, sliced thinly
1 onion, sliced thinly
½ pound bacon lardons,[56] cut in ½ inch cubes

Marinate the venison in red wine at room temperature for 4 hours. After 4 hours drain, reserving marinade for gravy. Add salt to taste and combine with the carrots, onion, and lardons.

I used a loin cut, but will try a shoulder next time as the tougher cut should stay more moist.

GRAVY

4 cups good beef stock, reduced to 2½ cups (homemade, preferably)
¾ cup reserved marinade, reduced to ¼ cup
Red currant jelly to taste—I used about 2 tablespoons

Combine all ingredients. If you prefer a slightly thicker gravy, you could prepare a roux [57] and then add the reduced beef stock and marinade.

PASTRY CRUST

6 cups pastry flour

   (a low-protein flour results in a more tender crust)

1½ teaspoons salt

10 ounces butter, cubed

6 ounces leaf lard,[58] cubed

1 cup ice water mixed with 1 egg

About 1 cup dried beans or pie weights

Mix the flour and salt. Cut in the butter and lard. Slowly stir in the water-egg mixture and stir until the dough comes together.

Rest the dough in a very cool place (or refrigerator) for at least 1 hour.

Cut into 4 pieces. Roll each piece between 2 sheets of parchment paper until it is about ⅛ inch thick. Prick the dough and then let it rest again for around half an hour.

Preheat oven to 450F.

Line 2 pie pans with pastry crust and place parchment paper on top, then add the beans (many recipes today call for pie weights[59]) and bake for about 10 minutes.

Remove the paper and beans (or weights) and bake 5 minutes longer.

ASSEMBLE THE PIES

Fill the 2 crusts with the venison mixture. Top with the 2 remaining pieces of crust. Pinch or fold edges to seal.

Bake for about 2 hours, lowering oven to 375F after 30 minutes. You may need to cover the top crust with parchment paper if it starts to become too brown. The total cooking time will depend on the cut and age of the meat you use, with young venison possibly needing 30 minutes less, and older meat possibly requiring 30 minutes more.

When the pies are done, reheat gravy, cut a 1-inch circle of crust from the lid, and slowly pour half the gravy into each pie. Replace the lid and let the pie rest for about 15 minutes.

Serve with red currant jelly on the side.

I recommend trying the jelly with a little piece of the baked top crust. It adds another flavorful element to the meal.

The First Goodwins
Arrive at Old Fields

In a 1740 document, our Captain, the new proprietor of the Spencer homestead, is referred to as "gentleman," clearly a step up from his classification as "blacksmith" recorded three years earlier in another document. He is taking the helm at a much calmer time than that of the Spencers. The three main and most terrifying wars with the French and the Indians were over; the British had, as of yet, refrained from antagonizing the Americans sufficiently to set off a rebellion against their king; and the population of colonial New England was growing rapidly.[60]

Ichabod and Elizabeth Goodwin had been married just over a decade when they purchased the Spencer estate on July 24 in 1740. Elizabeth Scammon was only eighteen on August 25, 1729—the day she entered into the "marriage state"[61] with the twenty-nine-year-old Ichabod. The couple were married by Berwick's Reverend Jeremiah Wise at the meetinghouse on Old South Road.

The purchase of the Spencer property, including the tavern, a blacksmith shop, and the landing just "about 100 rods from the great Newichawannock that flows directly into the Piscataqua River, out into the Atlantic and over to England" would require almost all of their savings, £600—or about $100,000 in today's dollars.[62] It appears that Ichabod might have taken out a loan to purchase this substantial piece of property.

And so eleven years after standing in front of Reverend Wise, Ichabod and Elizabeth would start to think about their move just down the street from where they were married. Happily, in 1741, the year before the Goodwins moved to Old Fields, Dominicus was born. Elizabeth and the Captain had just suffered the loss of their third son, named Ichabod after his father. This was a most difficult loss, as they had already suffered the deaths of two other children—their first son, also named Ichabod, had died before he was two years old and soon after another son died before his first birthday. Raising a child past infancy was no small task at that time. Without vaccines, sanitation, or antibiotics, newborns often did not survive illnesses such as measles or mumps, let alone now-uncommon scourges like diphtheria and whooping cough.

Dominicus was the first son to survive infancy. Then, the year following their move to Old Fields, Elizabeth gave birth to one more son, the third of her boys to be christened Ichabod. This Ichabod lived to the age of eighty-six and was one of the first Mainers to be promoted to the rank of major general. He was also the second Ichabod Goodwin to head the Old Fields homestead and the one after whom our house was named.

AN OLD OXCART TRAIL   In 2012, during the second summer of our dig, Neill beckoned Harvey and me outside to show us what is still one of my favorite of his findings. Through a maze of undergrowth and small trees on the western border of the property, Neill pointed out the remains of an old roadbed, one whose footprint is a trail of ruts on either side of mounded grass. What we were looking at is an early section of Old Fields Road (known as *the road to Kittery*), over which oxcarts traveled, likely as early as the seventeenth century, creating those deeply cut ruts over years of use. Talk about being transported. I always feel a strong connection to an early eighteenth-century Berwick as I walk along that rutted trail imprinted by oxen almost three hundred years ago.

Elizabeth and Ichabod, along with their three young children, would have traveled this furrowed road when they moved to the former Spencer property in 1742. Turning off the main road at the junction of Old Fields Road and Vine Street, where our circular driveway now begins, the oxcart would have headed up the path and stopped just outside the keeping room door near the granite hitching post (one day Harvey and I hope to discover the meaning of the letters *BS* carved into the post that still stands).

As I believe that the home Elizabeth Goodwin moved into in 1742 was the newly built early Georgian house, the model for the one in which Harvey and I currently live, the keeping room we so enjoy today is very similar to the one Elizabeth would have seen when she first got to Old Fields. Was she as excited as we were as her eyes fell upon that vast walk-in hearth? I have a feeling that the answer must be a resounding yes. Elizabeth knew they would be running a tavern—like Humphrey before him, her husband had been granted a license to serve alcohol the year they arrived at Old Fields—so a fireplace with the potential to roast a whole lamb or huge joints of beef was a definite benefit—in fact, a necessity for a tavern serving countless midday dinners.

She would have surveyed the large keeping room, which originally had a small partitioned-off section on the northern wall for what I believe was the buttery (where butter would have been churned and dairy products stored, as it was protected from the heat of the fire). In that corner, she must have been pleased with the generously proportioned hutch she had instructed be built with its numerous shelves for the pewterware, glasses, tankards, and utensils she would need to prepare meals for the many patrons who would be arriving. Harvey and I use the hutch in a similar way, though we don't have any patrons to serve, of course. On the lower shelf of the hutch is a charming remnant of the past, a depression that, according to an architectural historian who visited soon after we moved in, was created by an apple-coring apparatus, one available in the colonies as early as 1750.[63]

Upon closer examination of the hearth, she would have noted the crane, sturdy enough to hold the largest of Dutch ovens for the many one-pot boiled dinners she would serve, the ample room for several trivets, upon one of which she could keep a kettle of simmering water, and a place to fry smaller cuts of meat or johnnycakes for the family breakfast. Just above the mantel the new homeowner would find a built-in storage cabinet, perfect for keeping food items away from any critters that may have set up residence for winter. Then,

peering into the depths of the fireplace, Elizabeth would have found the vast beehive oven on the right side of the back wall.

This brick oven was ideal for the quantities of sturdy Rye 'n' Injun bread that would have been served to fill up the travelers who had stayed in the tavern overnight and would need a substantial meal before continuing on their journeys. The young housewife might have had her servants help start those quintessential New England loaves the night before so that they would slowly rise in the cooling room overnight, allowing the bread's flavor to develop, or simply to make sure the bread would be ready for the first meal of the day. In the morning, the help would have descended the back staircase from the attic or a second-floor bedroom to revive the coals of the banked fire, punch down the dough for its next rise, and start preparing the foods planned for the day.

Rye 'n' Injun Bread
Too Authentic for My Taste, but Not for Harvey's
Adapted from Sandra L. Oliver's Saltwater Foodways [64]
Makes 1 loaf

Due to blights and the expense of importing goods to New England during the eighteenth century, wheat was a scarce commodity. To compensate, corn-meal, combined with equal parts rye flour, was substituted for all, or most, of the wheat required for yeast breads. It was because of the cornmeal and its association with the Indians that this bread was given its name. (Despite the perjorative history of the word *injun* the recipe maintains its historic name in cookbooks both new and old.) In wealthier households and later in the century when wheat became more readily available, the ratio was one-third cornmeal, one-third rye flour, and one-third wheat flour; therefore it was often referred to as *thirded bread*. The result of the latter proportions was a somewhat less heavy product. To accommodate our modern palates, I went with the "thirded" version.

SPONGE

3 cups warm water (about 110F)

½ cup molasses

1 tablespoon dry yeast

3 cups whole wheat flour

Combine the water, molasses, and yeast in a small bowl. Let stand for about 10 minutes, until foamy. Stir in the flour and beat until smooth.

PREPARE THE CORNMEAL

3 cups cornmeal

2 tablespoons salt

2 to 3 cups vigorously boiling water

Mix the cornmeal and salt in a large bowl. Add the boiling water. Stir and let stand for 20 minutes, until cooled to no more than 110F.

ASSEMBLE THE BREAD

3 cups rye flour

1 cup or more whole wheat flour

Take the prepared sponge and fold in the rye flour, one cup at a time. Then fold in the prepared cornmeal.

Dust a board with an additional ½ cup or so of wheat flour, turn out the dough onto the floured board, and knead thoroughly until there is some spring to the dough when you press with a finger. It will still be rather sticky.

Cover with a damp cloth and leave to rise until the dough doubles in bulk. Divide into 2 pieces, knead, and shape into round loaves. Put on a baking sheet that has been sprinkled with cornmeal. Let rise again until doubled.

Preheat oven to 375F.

Place the baking sheet with loaves in the oven, leave 15 minutes, and then lower heat to 325F. If you are using a beehive oven, the temperature should drop after about 15 minutes. If it still seems too hot, remove the door for 5 or 10 minutes to release some heat.

Bake for 50 minutes.

The resulting loaves were still quite heavy, heavier than I had imagined, so I am grateful that I opted for the thirded version, with some wheat.

To be truthful, I still was not fond of the bread, leaving Harvey, with the more tolerant palate, to make sure our labor did not go to waste. Undoubtedly, though, it would have kept the patrons at the Goodwin Tavern full.

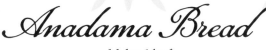

Anadama Bread
Makes 1 loaf

Happily, there is an alternative for those who never come to embrace Rye 'n' Injun bread. Anadama is a bread that originated on the North Shore of Boston in the late nineteenth century.[65] It includes many of the same ingredients—flour, cornmeal, molasses, and yeast—but not the coarse rye flour.

1 cup whole wheat flour
2 ½ cups bread flour
¾ cup cornmeal
1 tablespoon salt
1½ teaspoons instant yeast
2 tablespoons softened butter
3 tablespoons molasses*

Mix the flours, cornmeal, salt, and yeast. Add the melted butter and molasses. Then slowly add 1 to 1½ cups warm water, no more than 100F, until a soft dough has formed. You may need a bit more water.

Knead for about 15 minutes. Shape into a ball, place in a bowl, and cover loosely with plastic wrap.

Let the dough rise until doubled in bulk. In my cool kitchen it took 2 hours.

Preheat oven to 350F.

Turn the dough out of the bowl and place in a well-greased 9 ½-inch loaf pan. Let rise again, until about doubled. Brush with water and bake about 45 minutes to an hour.

Cool on a wire rack.

A trick I use for getting a precise measurement of molasses is to first coat the measuring spoon with oil. This prevents the molasses from sticking to the spoon.

BARTERING IN BERWICK By the late winter of 1743, the Goodwins would have already been at Old Fields for at least a few months. Elizabeth was due to give birth that May to her fourth child to survive infancy and the first Ichabod who would grow up to be an adult. I can just imagine all the things on her mind. In the past few months, she had overseen the setting up of their new home and the opening of their tavern for business, and also had to ensure that her family had enough provisions for the long New England winter. It would still be many months before the early lambs would be ready to butcher for the table or the first crops of spring could be harvested (here in South Berwick we usually don't see any spring green until the end of April). Anticipating the familiar depletion of food supplies, the Captain would likely have accepted food in exchange for his blacksmithing services.

An elaborate bartering system had developed in colonial New England and was a major component of our early economy. A result of the scarcity of currency of any origin in early America, bartering was an important method by which the colonists exchanged goods and services.

In the archives of the Maine Historical Society there is a fascinating diary written in 1791 by Benjamin Gerrish, the same neighbor who borrowed a horse to ride to Kittery. A contemporary of the General, Gerrish was a local farmer who lived on today's Brattle Street, less than half a mile up the road from Old Fields. The first diary entry is dated January 1, 1791, and the last, October 23, just before Gerrish boarded a ship bound for the Caribbean in search of work. During this voyage, he lost his life, so the diary spans only ten months. [66]

Despite covering less than a year's worth of activity, the daily entries shed light on how a community such as Berwick was able to thrive through a complex system of interdependency. The diary focuses mainly on the weather, clearly a major concern for a farmer, but also comments on Gerrish's health or his wife's and the deaths (or "excets") of various neighbors. Most revealing are his descriptions of the exchange of food, tools, and labor among himself and his neighbors. As with most colonists in early New England, Gerrish most likely had very little hard currency, so bartering became a necessity. In fact, rarely is actual money discussed, other than when the farmer buys a few specialty items from a store, often traveling to Kittery for sugar and tea.

Fortuitously, this lack of coinage turned into an asset for many communities as townspeople learned to rely on one another. In entry after entry, Gerrish chronicles working for neighbors, or neighbors laboring for him, as well as trading the use of tools and animals for food and furnishings—an excellent system, considering the shortage of labor and the expense of purchasing every piece of equipment that might be needed. The great cost of acquiring and maintaining a horse, even more so a pair of oxen, meant that the ability to borrow these extremely useful animals was a real advantage for farmers such as Gerrish.[67] Think how much he saved by borrowing the Goodwin horse rather than having to buy, stable, and feed one of his own.

The lives of these eighteenth-century villagers were connected in other ways as well. With the ever-present danger of fire, all townspeople were required to have a fire bucket such as the one we saw that summer at the antique show in Concord. These buckets were no doubt more effective in a city, where within a few minutes of hearing, "Fire!" a large number of men could appear, ready to assist. Yet even in smaller, rural towns where the houses were farther apart, a few neighbors, fire buckets in hand, would certainly be helpful.

TOWNSMEN OF MANY HATS Moreover, most town populations were too small to have much specialization of labor. As a result, each townsman donned many hats—much as men and women do today in smaller communities. In the eighteenth century men of Berwick volunteered or were selected for municipal duties. Not only was the Captain chosen in 1762 to work with two other townsmen to improve the traffic to and from the important boat landing of Quamphegan, but the Captain and the General both served as sheriff and each was chosen to serve as deacon of the First Congregational Church.

Of course, Elizabeth and her daughters were no less busy than their menfolk, even if their duties took them no farther than the barn or kitchen garden. Women of New England would labor alone or alongside their servants to keep up with the endless chores of a seventeenth- or eighteenth-century household. In addition to her daily and weekly duties, the colonial wife bore numerous offspring and tended to the sick. Given the number of diseases that plagued our forebears over two centuries ago—serious illnesses such as typhus, dysentery, smallpox, and yellow fever—we can assume that this latter task alone would take up a considerable portion of a woman's day.

Before joining the auction business founded by my father-in-law, my own roles as part-time teacher, mother, and to a trivial extent a semi-homesteader preserving fruits and vegetables from our large garden and collecting wood for the woodstove were more than enough to juggle; I couldn't imagine also having to make the lye for soap and melt tallow for candles. The chore I would have faced with the most dread would have been the weekly laundering of clothing and bed linens.

Each week, an entire day was set aside for dealing with the laundry. First, the water would be drawn from the well and the fire prepared in the hearth. Once the water was heated, the week's laundry would be put in to soak, loosening some of the soil.[68] The soaked clothes were then placed in a separate pot of hot water, this one containing lye for the actual cleaning. After soaking in lye, the laundry went into a pot of fresh water to rinse out every trace of the very caustic soap. Next came the wringing, which often required two people for larger items such as sheets. Then everything was hung to dry, outdoors on nice days and all around the kitchen when weather did not permit. Finally, every item would be ironed by an implement that needed to be reheated every few minutes to be effective. Once a week, every week, the women of New England faced this colossal task. I cannot imagine how they did it week in, week out, especially as I get annoyed just folding three loads of clothes taken from my electric dryer.

Clearly, these early New Englanders deserve their reputation as men *and* women of great industry.

AN INNHOLDER'S DAY IS NEVER DONE   Living in the same house as men and women who managed to survive in much more difficult times, I am constantly comparing my life to theirs. Like those before us, Harvey and I wake up before the sun rises and work seven days a week; well, at least we did from 1993 through 2012, when we were still actively running our auction houses. Nonetheless, I am acutely aware of how easy our existence is compared to the lives of those who lived more than 250 years ago.

Inspired by our power outage that first spring, Harvey and I started to try to live part of our lives without some of the conveniences of today, specifically electricity and the Internet. Our new routine involved turning down the thermostat (no, we did not give up central heating altogether!) and feeding the fire on cold winter days when the high is ten degrees Fahrenheit, cooking with the spit and forgoing the ease of our modern stove, and foraging for dandelion greens in early spring instead of getting in the car and driving to the grocery store for salad fixings. But even when we partially replicate those earlier times, I still know a day in my life cannot even begin to resemble one of theirs.

As I began to delve into documentary sources online, I found a fascinating website— GenealogyBank.com.[69] The site is a trove of historic news articles from an archive of over seven thousand newspapers, some as early as 1704. Focusing on Massachusetts, New Hampshire, and Maine, and using a variety of key words, I located hundreds of articles about both major and minor events specifically related to the Captain and the General, primarily between 1704 and 1829.

While scanning through newspaper advertisements placed during the time that our first Ichabod lived at Old Fields, between 1742 and 1777, I came across the Captain's name mentioned in an advertisement from the *Boston Post-Boy* in October 1745:

> *There will be a Proprietors Meeting…at the House of Ichabod Goodwin in said Berwick, Innholder, upon Tuesday the Nineteenth day of November…at Ten of the Clock Forenoon to raise money…in building a Meeting-House…And those delinquent Proprietors that have not paid their Part of the Tax are desired to make Speedy Pay, or they may expect Penalty of the Law.*[70]

So in addition to running the inn, our first Ichabod also collected taxes on behalf of the British king—a most onerous task in any century but especially so prior to the Declaration of Independence, these taxes being one of the principal complaints of the early colonists. Regardless of the unpleasantness of the task, being appointed tax collector in the service of King George III was an honor and reflected the community's trust in one's character.

In 1745 the Goodwins had five children—the General would have been two years old and baby Samuel just a few months old—and just thinking about what the day of that meeting might have entailed for Elizabeth made me tired. I can also imagine the anxiety felt by those in attendance. Ichabod in his role as astute "innholder" likely would have served a nice rum punch to improve the mood in the room. Paying taxes has never been a pleasant pastime, so perhaps a tavern would be just the right venue for such activities today?

Once the proprietors' meeting had been concluded, a midday meal might have been served, and the men, now of good spirit, would likely have discussed current events. As it was late in 1745, those in attendance might have asked the Goodwins' neighbor William Chadbourne to repeat his tale of the siege of Louisburg, a successful military operation completed at the end of June of that year, one of which the men of Berwick would have been most proud. Chadbourne, along with 149 of his fellow townsmen, formed the regiment that joined Lieutenant Colonel William Pepperrell's expedition to try to take the French fortress at Louisburg, one mistakenly judged as having a strong defense. The men from Berwick helped to quickly capture thirty of the enemy's cannons, leading to the swift surrender of the French commander, Louis Du Pont Duchambon. Pepperrell's York County Regiment and the remainder of the colonial forces from Massachusetts gave the British an important victory over the French in the competition for North American territory.[71] And given the unexpected swiftness of their triumph, I can almost hear the loud banging of the walking sticks as Chadbourne's audience applauded the exploits of their militiamen.

An earlier advertisement, from an October 1743 issue of the *Boston Post-Boy*, informed the proprietors of Berwick that they were to meet at the home of Ichabod Goodwin, innholder, to vote on several "Articles," and to pay taxes "on the Building of the Meeting-House" and "for several large Bridges already built."[72] According to a notice placed in the same paper a year later, the townsmen were to meet again at the Goodwin Tavern to pay their share of charges for their own "Defence."[73] Then, in 1745, was the advertisement publicizing that additional money needed to be raised for the Berwick meetinghouse. These advertisements indicate that, aside from being places where men would congregate and gather the news of the day, taverns were also used as meeting rooms for municipal functions.

At this time innholders were respected members of the community and were often called upon to serve significant roles in their towns. The qualifications required to obtain a license to serve alcohol were many. An innholder had to be a gentleman of means, one who was successful in his business dealings and known for his strict disciplinary character. The men who governed these towns were determined to avoid the disorderly conduct that often accompanied the consumption of alcohol. The innholder was expected to maintain order among his patrons and get results at the various town meetings held on his premises.

Keeping those men in attendance happy could not have been an easy task, especially as each of the advertisements I found described the Captain's role at the meetings as essentially the money collector. Elizabeth would have also had an important role in preparing the meal and keeping the children from getting underfoot. There is nothing like a fine roast followed by a pudding for maintaining a contented crowd.

INDIAN PUDDING TO FILL UP THE CHILDREN AND KEEP THE PATRONS HAPPY
I can easily imagine Elizabeth making this pudding before any of the meetings advertised at the Goodwin Tavern, to keep her children quiet. It would also serve to feed the men who had been obliged to attend. An easy and filling dish, Indian pudding must have been a staple of taverns across New England.

Named for the association of cornmeal with the Native Americans, Indian pudding is a dessert of milk, cornmeal, and some form of sugar. It takes almost no time to prepare and was therefore a very common dish in early New England households. In fact, one article I came across suggested that John and Abigail Adams served it quite often, but prior to the main course, to fill up the children.[74] The anecdote may be apocryphal, but since appetizer, meat or fish, and dessert courses were all served at the same time, parents may have spooned the pudding onto a child's plate at the start in the hope of stretching farther the more expensive components of their midday meal.

Today, Indian pudding is not especially popular, possibly because its appearance and somewhat lumpy texture are not the most appetizing. Nevertheless, Harvey and I have been enjoying this dessert for years and find it comforting on a cold winter evening.

Similar to various versions of today's popular recipes, yesteryear's can differ to some degree on ingredients and their quantities. How much sugar, salt, spices, and fat can vary from author to author, so I was not surprised to find conflicting opinions on how much sweetener to use, or whether to use only milk, or milk mixed with cream or butter. Nevertheless, I do not think I have ever seen modern recipes in which measurements diverge as dramatically as I found in those eighteenth-century sources for an Indian pudding. One recipe calls for a ratio of six cups of milk to seven tablespoons (or less than one-half cup) of cornmeal, while a second version said to scald six cups of milk and add *two cups* of cornmeal. The latter would be a most filling pudding, to say the least.

One online source gave instructions to bake the pudding in a pan sitting in front of hot coals;[75] another said to boil the pudding in a pot hanging from a crane over the coals;[76] and a third recipe said to place the pudding in a moderately heated brick oven.[77] Obviously, there are any number of ways to get an Indian pudding from raw to cooked state, the determining factor being a mix of your family tradition, budget, and available equipment.

Indian Pudding

A tradional Bennett recipe adapted from various sources

Serves 6–8

3 cups milk	1 tablespoon butter
⅔ cup cornmeal	⅓ cup molasses
½ teaspoon salt	⅙ cup maple syrup
⅔ teaspoon ginger	⅙ cup sorghum syrup
½ teaspoon cinnamon	1 egg, lightly beaten
½ teaspoon nutmeg	1 additional cup milk

Heat brick oven to around 400F (or a conventional oven to 350F) and grease a 2-quart casserole.

Scald the milk and slowly whisk in the cornmeal. Over very low heat, stir continually until nice and thick. Add all remaining ingredients other than the additional cup of milk. Pour into a casserole and place uncovered in the oven.

After approximately 45 minutes, pour the additional 1 cup of milk on top and then bake for about another 3 hours if you are using the brick oven. If using the modern oven, bake for about another 1½ to 2 hours.

Regardless of the oven, you want the top to be browned and crustlike and the liquid to be thoroughly absorbed.

When serving, heavy cream is traditionally poured over the pudding, a fine substitute for the vanilla ice cream that for years has been the customary topping for Harvey and me.

You will note that I use a mix of sweeteners. I found some historic recipes that called for sorghum, which has a similar flavor to molasses but is a bit lighter. I also added some maple syrup, assuming that a thrifty New England housewife would have had it on hand, as tapping the trees for sap was a skill they would have learned from the Indians.[78]

When deciding between ovens, if you have a choice, know that the brick oven adds a slight smoky nuance and a somewhat more concentrated flavor than my usual gas-oven version.

Despite its decidedly homely appearance, I highly recommend this rustic dessert, with or without the brick oven.

A Late-Spring Dinner
at the Goodwin Tavern

As I indulge in my new favorite pastime, imagining my Ichabods, I am in the keeping room, tending to the cast-iron pot hanging from the old crane. It is the fall of 2012 and this is only the second time we are using the crane to cook a soup in our enormous hearth. How many times, I can't help wondering, had Elizabeth Goodwin attended to this same task?

The soup is based on a recipe from the Colonial Williamsburg website. I occasionally stir as the beef and barley gently, very gently simmer in my homemade broth filled with vegetables. The aroma is unlike any Harvey or I have ever encountered, and I have made dozens and dozens of soups—always from scratch—yet prior to that day, with the one exception of a modern rendition of minestrone, my soups were always cooked on our modern stovetop and never over an open flame.

"This soup is astonishing," Harvey exclaims upon sampling his first sip. "When can we make the next one?" he then asks while happily finishing every drop in his stoneware bowl. That soup was just the first of many eighteenth-century boiled dinners to come.

Now that we had made our first hearth-cooked soup, we were ready to try other historic dishes. And as we were starting to reduce our workload (we were a few months away from declaring ourselves officially semi-retired in January of 2013), Harvey and I had more time to indulge in our passions. Inspired by the exceptionally appetizing hearth-cooked soup, we embarked on a journey into eighteenth-century foods, trying to re-create the earlier tastes by using not only historic recipes but also the cooking methods of the 1700s.

By the following spring, after experimenting with a few more single dishes, I decided it was time for a more elaborate, multicourse meal—one straight out of the eighteenth century—to celebrate the coming of spring. After gathering my half dozen or so historic recipe cookbooks and searching the Internet's vast resources on early British and American cookery, I began to put together the menu. After having lived at Old Fields for over eight years, we saw this occasion as our first proper eighteenth-century spring dinner in our home. I wanted to create a tavern dinner the Goodwins might have served to their patrons, making use of ingredients available in late April.

I decided on parsnips, a popular vegetable dug out of the ground just after the winter thaw, and a salad—or sallat as it was called then—made from early greens and the first shoots of the herbs from our kitchen garden—both would have provided a welcome change from the winter diet of cabbage, dried string beans, and pickled vegetables. Now was also the time to finish the stored potatoes, saving enough to use as seed potatoes for spring planting. Many families in Maine also raised sheep, and the Goodwins were no exception, so an early-born lamb could have been served at the tavern by late April. Then, based on Neill's archaeological findings, I decided on oysters to start. And to finish, apples, as Elizabeth would have wanted to use the last of her store of dried apples from the orchard planted by Humphrey Spencer just before his death. Of course, cream from their dairy cows would have been used atop the apples, a suitable dessert for this fine tavern dinner:

GRILLED OYSTERS WITH HORSERADISH SAUCE

ROAST LEG OF SPRING LAMB

FIRED POTATO PUDDING

SPRING-DUG PARSNIPS IN BUTTER SAUCE

SALLAT WITH VINAIGRETTE

BAKED DRIED APPLES WITH CREAM

For our first attempt at preparing a complete eighteenth-century meal, Harvey and I invited Sandy and Carl, a couple we are very fond of and who appreciate good food as much as we do. Sandy also happens to be a professional photographer, and when I told her about the cooking component of this book, she generously offered to do a photo shoot of any of the colonial meals I would be preparing. I gladly acquiesced for this evening, but with one stipulation: she and her husband would have to join us in eating the results!

We chose a Wednesday in late April for what I hoped would be a photogenic as well as an appetizing meal. The day came quickly and I began to gather the ingredients, all carefully chosen from as many local producers as possible, while the dandelions came from our own, pesticide-free backyard. I was most excited about the lamb, the centerpiece of the menu. It was supplied by our favorite local farmer, Mary Patridge, who delivered the lamb to our door the day before the shoot. Mary started out by raising some of the finest poultry we have ever tasted anywhere, France included; she then ventured into new pastures and had bottle-fed this Dorset-cross animal for the first five months of its life. After the lamb had been weaned, it was grass-fed and then put on organic grain. I could picture a Goodwin child raising a lamb in a similar fashion if the animal's mother had not survived the birthing.

With the dinner scheduled for around six o'clock, we placed the lamb on the spit at two-thirty, having estimated the cooking time to be two hours and allowing time for the lamb to rest and to be photographed. Within fifteen minutes, the aroma of the roasting leg began wafting through our home, whetting our appetites for the meal we were about to share. Given the most unspringlike temperature of forty-five degrees, we were also enjoying the warmth of the cooking fire blazing in the keeping room hearth.

Harvey was responsible for the critical job of turning the lamb on the spit every five or ten minutes for two hours. In between turns he was also tasked with setting the dining room table, using our eighteenth-century-style dishes and linens, along with the antique glasses and flatware. I had spent the morning preparing the side dishes and polishing silverware; in the afternoon, I laid out serving platters and bowls and put the finishing touches on what I hoped would be an authentically and aesthetically arranged eighteenth-century sallat. By three o'clock, when Sandy was due to arrive, the lamb was cooking beautifully, and everything else was ready for the photo shoot.

Sandy arrived on schedule and began carrying all her equipment into the house. The year before she had been the photographer for an article on our home for *Early Homes* magazine,[79] so I was somewhat familiar with the process. I knew I should be on call for assistance as a stylist or for additional ideas and opinions; and as expected, I soon found myself involved in the rearrangement of the belongings of my entire home, or so it felt at the time.

Tables and chairs were moved from one spot to another, sometimes to another room. Glasses were rotated by minuscule amounts to catch the fading light, or because they looked better in the frame. Even the food had to be positioned just so on the dishes. For the first photograph, we placed the salad course—the first dish to be subjected to the photographer's scrutiny—on the table in the dining room. Not content, Sandy had me move the dish to the gateleg table in the keeping room. To my eye, the new placement worked well, but to Sandy's artistic sensibility it still was not perfect. The tavern table also proved inadequate, and eventually we wound up placing the dish on the floor. Sandy finally got her desired shot. The other dishes followed a similar trajectory, all with great results.

After three hours of arranging, rearranging, and rearranging again, Sandy finished her shoot, and we could eat. According to the eighteenth-century chef Charles Carter and others of the period, I imagine that Ichabod would have initially set out the first course of oysters, sallat, parsnips, as well as a soup, and maybe a boiled fowl. Some patrons may have sat in chairs placed around the table, but for many it was standing room only. After the first course, the rest of the food would have been brought out to the table. Perhaps a joint of roasted meat, accompanied by beans or barley, would have been presented alongside the sweet, such as our apples with cream. In addition, there would likely have been a ham, possibly a roast goose, a relish or sauce, and maybe some gingerbread or a pudding. In those days, it seems they needed to consume more calories than we do, particularly in these northern, colder climes as just staying warm required an inordinate number of calories.[80]

I chose to serve the meal in a modern fashion, with an appetizer followed by an entrée, and then the dessert, rather than in the eighteenth-century manner. For our meal, we began in the keeping room, where Harvey tossed raw oysters onto the eighteenth-century-style grill we had set up in the hearth over a bed of glowing coals. As the shells opened a tad, we quickly removed the oysters with tongs and placed them on a platter, where they were greedily consumed by all. The delicacy of the just warmed-through shellfish was unquestionably enhanced by the light smoke of the fireplace. I may never eat a raw oyster again.

For the main course, as we refer to it these days, we moved to the dining room. Here we feasted on the roasted lamb with its pan juices, together with the parsnips, sallat, and a potato pudding. Farmer Mary's lamb was rich-tasting, with a proper amount of fat adding

to the flavors. The essence of the pan sauce was extraordinary and the five-and-a-half-pound leg fed the four of us with plenty of leftovers for the still-exhausted cooks the following day. The parsnips—one of those underappreciated vegetables, but a great favorite of the eighteenth-century cook—were quite tasty, with an earthy sweetness reminiscent of a carrot prepared with a touch of honey. The salad was excellent, the soft texture of the boiled eggs contrasting with the crispness of the greens and radishes. The potato pudding may have been the most surprising dish of all. Picture, if you can, a dish of mashed potatoes that has been enhanced by savory meat drippings and a hint of smoke. Incredible.

As we ate, the early-evening light streamed in, filtered through the old hemlocks just outside the west-facing windows. The silver-green needles of the hemlocks cast lively shadows, dancing from the ever-present breeze off the river and providing a constantly changing landscape on the tabletop and across the antique delft tiles surrounding the fireplace. At times like this, the play of light turns the fireplace surround into a delicate Japanese brush painting. The fire Harvey had built in our "modernized" nineteenth-century-style fireplace added one more critical element to the ambience of the evening. For the four of us feasting around the dining table, the finest entertainment of the evening was provided by the wonderful flavors of those eighteenth-century dishes.

After dinner we withdrew (hence the English term *drawing room*) to the parlour. There at the tea table, we savored the unique flavor of dried apples that had been soaked in rum and then baked with spices and a touch of apple juice. We offered our guests a cocktail prepared with the rum I had used for soaking the apples, garnished with lemon peel and served over ice. This was perhaps not something they would have served in the eighteenth century, yet I believe the Captain's tavern-goers would have happily imbibed this newfangled drink. Then again, those frugal New Englanders would likely have found a similar way to make good use of the leftover rum.

By evening's end, as we enjoyed the last of the apples, we lit the candles, allowing the peaceful quiet of the darkened room to work its magic as our retreat into a world of long ago came to an end. After our guests left, Harvey and I retired upstairs. With the flavors of the lamb and parsnips still fresh in our minds, we eagerly discussed when the next hearth-cooked meal would be. Given the ten-day forecast, however—yes, yes, another of our twenty-first-century advantages—we knew that we could not attempt another hearth meal anytime soon, not with the daytime highs predicted between seventy-five and eighty degrees, as our flue does not draw properly when the outside temperature is over sixty. The keeping room fills with smoke after a half hour or so. Despite having consulted professional chimney sweeps and historians in the hope that they could help us understand the problem, we have yet to determine the cause of the smoke. Our next historic cooking exercise would have to wait for the fall and cooler temperatures.

A Late-Spring Dinner

GRILLED OYSTERS WITH HORSERADISH SAUCE
Serves 4–6

2 dozen oysters, unshucked
6 tablespoons white horseradish, freshly grated or bottled
1 tablespoon heavy cream

Prepare a fire in the fireplace and place a grill rack over the flames. Wait until the fire has died down, and you have a nice bed of hot coals. You may also use an outdoor charcoal grill.

While waiting, prepare the sauce by mixing the horseradish and heavy cream in a small bowl.

Place as many oysters as can fit on the grill surface. As soon as each has opened, about 1 to 3 minutes, remove from fire, place on platter and eat while hot, with a little of the sauce if desired.

ROAST LEG OF SPRING LAMB
Serves 6

5–6 pound bone-in leg of lamb
Salt, to taste
8 tablespoons butter, softened
A few sprigs fresh rosemary

Ever since Neill uncovered three skewers in the cellar foundation, we have enjoyed the knowledge that we use the same tools when roasting meat on our spit as the Goodwins did. In fact, there is not much difference between cooking a lamb today versus two hundred years ago.

Harvey roasted the joint using the spit in the hearth, set in front of the fire, and I refrained from any continental touches such as garlic or anchovies.

Approximately 1½ to 2 hours prior to starting the roast, prepare a fire a bit wider than the spit. Before cooking, the fire needs to reach a certain level of maturity with moderate to high flames and a good bed of coals.

Salt the lamb generously.

Insert the spit through the length of the meat and push two skewers, one at a time, through the meat until each connects with one of the skewer holes of the spit. Try to visualize the placement of the holes on the spit, line up the skewer, poke it into the meat and wiggle it around until you find the spot. This step is truly one of the most challenging aspects to hearth-roasting and one that has never gotten any easier, even after all of these years.

Set your pair of andirons in front of the fire when it is ready. Place the spit with the skewered meat onto the top support of each andiron and place a large roasting pan beneath to catch the drippings.

Baste the lamb with softened butter every so often, using a long-handled brush.

While roasting turn the spit one-quarter turn every 5 to 10 minutes. Add wood to fire as necessary and reposition the andirons if the cooking slows down or the surface becomes too brown. Total roasting time about 2 hours.

After 45 minutes remove the pan with the drippings. While still hot, add the rosemary.

After removing the dripping pan I placed the pan of fired potatoes below the meat to absorb the meat drippings, giving the potato dish a savory and mouth-watering flavor.

Continue roasting and turning the lamb until done, with an internal temperature of 135F. Let the meat rest for 15 to 20 minutes.

Reheat the pan drippings. Carve the lamb and serve with the drippings.

I quickly learned that these historic cookery projects are labor-intensive and need last-minute adjustments to succeed. Perhaps due to the lamb's exclusive diet of milk in the first few months of its life, it finished cooking about a half hour ahead of schedule, taking only an hour and a half instead of the two hours I was planning for. As a result, the potato pudding cooking underneath the lamb did not have sufficient time to turn the appetizing golden brown I had anticipated. With the photo shoot in mind, I decided to press our twenty-first-century oven into service.

FIRED POTATO PUDDING
Serves 6–8

6 large potatoes, not peeled
¾ cup milk, warmed
¼ cup heavy cream, warmed
Salt to taste—I used about 1½ teaspoons
4 tablespoons butter, room temperature
2 eggs, well beaten

While the lamb is roasting, start the potato pudding by preparing traditional mashed potatoes. Place the whole potatoes in a pot and cover with coldwater. Bring to a boil and cook for about 40 minutes or until easily pierced with a fork.

As soon as they are not too hot to handle, peel the potatoes and mash with the warm milk. Add the salt and butter, stir in the beaten eggs, then spoon into a fireproof pan (I used stainless-steel-lined copper).

About 45 minutes after the lamb has begun roasting, place the pan with the potatoes under the roast and as close to the coals as possible. Bake for at least 1 hour. The potatoes can continue cooking after the lamb has been removed for its resting period.

I had to place the potato pudding under the broiler to achieve the desired golden top in time for the photo shoot. Our tender little lamb was done about thirty minutes ahead of schedule, just in time to photograph the grilling oysters before it got too dark. If the potato dish had stayed on the fire while the lamb had its twenty-minute-plus rest, I am sure the surface would have browned properly.

PARSNIPS IN BUTTER SAUCE
Adapted from Dining at Monticello, *edited by Damon Lee Fowler*
Serves 6–8

8 medium parsnips, lightly scraped
1 teaspoon salt, or to taste
4 tablespoons Madeira
5 or 6 tablespoons butter (to taste)

Put the parsnips in a single layer at the bottom of a saucepan. Cover with cold water and add about 1 teaspoon salt. Bring to a boil. Simmer about 20 minutes or until tender. Drain the parsnips, reserving the water. Remove the parsnips to a serving bowl.

Boil the reserved water until reduced to about 3 tablespoons.

Add the Madeira to the water.

Over very low heat, so the mixture does not separate, swirl the butter into the water-and-wine reduction, one tablespoon at a time. When all the butter has been incorporated, taste to see if additional salt is needed.

Pour over the parsnips and serve.

HISTORIC SALADS

One might think of the chef's salad prominent today on countless restaurant lunch menus as a relatively recent concept, so I was surprised to learn that this salad, originally known as a *salmagundi*, was quite common in the eighteenth century. Composed of mixed greens with assorted vegetables, hard-boiled eggs, and another protein (such as poached chicken), it would have been dressed with a vinaigrette that invariably included "good" olive oil shipped from Spain. "Only in the most elite enclaves within the Spanish colonies was this expensive import used for cooking. In the English and French settlements, olive oil was reserved almost exclusively for salad dressing."[81]

In fact, as I researched historic recipes, I came to appreciate the extensive variety of herbs and spices incorporated into many of the salads. You will find not only the more obvious herbs such as parsley, sage, and thyme, and spices such as cinnamon and ginger, but also a far greater diversity than expected, including lovage, marjoram, savory, borage, nutmeg, coriander, cloves, and flower waters.[82]

SALLAT
Serves 6

Assorted greens: young romaine
    leaves, baby dandelion greens
4 tablespoons chopped parsley
Chives, a handful, snipped
6 radishes, thinly sliced
Scallions, approx. 6, slivered
Whites of 2 hard-boiled goose eggs
    or of 6 extra-large chicken eggs; reserve yolks (for vinaigrette, opposite)

Arrange the platter so that the romaine leaves and other greens serve as foundation. Rim the edge with radishes, placing the remaining ingredients in concentric circles inside the radish border, ending with the egg whites in the center and the scallions placed around the whites.

Serve with vinaigrette.

VINAIGRETTE
Makes about half a cup

1 teaspoon salt
2 tablespoons apple cider vinegar
1 teaspoon powdered sugar
2 teaspoons fresh thyme leaves
8 tablespoons extra-virgin olive oil
Hard-boiled yolks of 2 goose eggs or of 4 extra-large chicken eggs
2 teaspoons cold water

Mix the salt and vinegar. Add the sugar and thyme. Beat in the olive oil, 1 tablespoon at a time. Gently mash the egg yolks with the water and stir into the vinaigrette.

Pour into sauceboat and serve with the sallat.

BAKED DRIED APPLES WITH CREAM
Serves 6–8

6 ounces dried apple rings
1 quart light rum
½ teaspoon nutmeg
1 teaspoon cinnamon
½ teaspoon allspice, ground
⅓ cup apple juice
Heavy cream, to taste

Soak the apples in the rum for 24 to 36 hours, until they are fairly soft.

Preheat oven to 375F.

Drain the rum from the apples, reserving the liquid, if you like, for a rum punch (see recipe in chapter 8).

Add the spices and apple juice to the apples. Place the mixture in a baking pan and bake uncovered for 30 minutes.

Cool to room temperature and serve with a sauceboat of heavy cream.

GOODWIN FAMILY RECIPES

With time to spend on our new passion for historic cooking, I began poring over historic recipes in dozens of published sources. As a foodie, I relished the task, but nothing compared to the delight I felt when some Goodwin family recipes were discovered among their papers at the Dartmouth College Library. There was a recipe for clam chowder—a cherished New England favorite—that is pretty close to how we make the soup today, as well as one for potted beef or seafood, a centuries-old method for storing these foods over the winter months. From these recipes I learned how the Goodwins corned their beef and cured their own bacon. Although I have an unwavering fondness for the slab bacon Harvey and I order by mail from Edwards, of Surry, Virginia, one day I plan to try this early Goodwin recipe for curing beef, dated August 30, 1799:

> *To acommon* [sic] *leg one ounce of salt peeter* [sic] *one pint molasses one pint of pork fatt* [sic]. *If the leg is one larger ad* [sic] *in proportion together with one quart of water or nearly that to a leg if you put them in a tub where they will be covered it will save the trouble of Basting* [sic] *two months in this liquor is short time anough* [sic] *for the legs to stay before smoking them.*[83]

This recipe also provides some insight into the state of grammar and spelling at the end of the eighteenth century, or at least as used by the author of this particular recipe. I recall how William Goodwin, the Goodwin descendant who read aloud entries from the General's military diary to the Maine Historical Society, commented on his ancestor's poor spelling, although spelling was in flux into the nineteenth century. This explains why we find correspondence written by the well-educated Abigail Adams, wife of our second president, in which she wonders if two things had "an eaquil quantity of Steel."[84] Also note the capital *S* used for a common noun at the end of the sentence, a practice long out of fashion.

> *After the meal's end, Sandy's*
> *husband sat by the fire in the keeping*
> *room. I could not help but imagine*
> *the General seated there in front of*
> *the hearth, glass of Madeira in hand,*
> *similarly enjoying the warmth.*

1750-1766: *Runaway Slaves, Heirlooms, and Conflict with England*

In the spring of 2013, not long after our photo-shoot dinner, I was browsing Genealogy-Bank's newspaper archives when I found an ad placed by the Captain in 1750. The notice announced a reward for the return of his Indian slave SaraJohn. A week or so later, I found an earlier ad, from 1748, also placed by our first Ichabod. This one offered a reward for a "Negro Man" named Pompey. Later I uncovered yet a third ad from July 1750, one month after the escape of SaraJohn. It seems that Pompey had been captured after running away in 1748, only to flee once more two years later; this time, according to the ad offering a reward, Pompey was accompanied by William Nason, an indentured white servant.

By the time I found these advertisements, I was already aware from the Captain's inventory that he owned slaves, yet my conscience was troubled anew when reading about the high rewards offered by the Captain for his runaway slaves—ranging from £4 to £10.[85] My research continued to strengthen my knowledge of Ichabod as someone who viewed his fellow man as commercial property, and valuable property at that.

These advertisements revealed details about the types of clothing worn by the Captain's wife and Pompey, as well as clues about the Captain's character. According to the first ad, from 1750, when she escaped, SaraJohn took with her a "silk Crape Gown," presumably one of Elizabeth's.[86] As SaraJohn was described as "fat thick short" in the ad, maybe the Captain's wife had the same build; or it is possible that SaraJohn planned on bartering the dress for food or transport. The 1748 ad placed when Pompey ran away for the first time (we presume) described him as dressed in "Trowsers, a homespun Jacket and a check'd Woolen shirt."[87] The ad went on to state that Pompey had on "a pair of Pot-hooks." At first, I didn't think anything of the description as I excitedly presented my latest find to Neill.

Though distressed by the nature of the ad, I was happy to have more specifics on the Goodwins until alarm bells went off as Neill explained that a pot hook, besides being a device for hanging a pot over a fire, was also devised as a punishment for slaves. These iron collars often had two or three protruding spikes. When placed around a person's neck, the pot hook rendered its wearer unable to lie down, and anyone who got too close was in danger of being gouged by the spikes.

The third advertisement I found on the website, placed by the Captain when Pompey ran away a second time, described the runaway as having "one of his Ears cut."[88] Together, these advertisements paint an unsavory picture of the Captain. His last will and testament, dated 1777 (see below), lists the names of three slaves—Bash, Philis & her child—but SaraJohn and Pompey do not appear in this document. Either, they had not been captured after 1750 or had died by 1777. I like to think they had gained their freedom.

WAR WOUNDS AND A FAMILY TREASURE   It was 2008 and the house was finally furnished. Harvey and I had been at Old Fields for almost four years. While we were still working too much I made sure to steal a few hours whenever possible to escape into the world of the Ichabods. The Goodwins' lives continued to unfold as I discovered new details every week through my research.

One of my favorite "finds" while researching the Goodwins was a 1982 article in the *Lewiston Evening Journal* in which Elizabeth Hayes Goodwin (the last Goodwin to live at Old Fields and the daughter of William Allen Hayes Goodwin, who authored the letter to her describing the fire) was interviewed. In 1958, Elizabeth had sold the General Goodwin House and had taken on the role of caretaker and tour guide at the Sarah Orne Jewett home (less than two miles away, in what is now the center of South Berwick). By the time she was interviewed for the article, Elizabeth was living at a retirement home. In the piece, she reminisced about Old Fields, her family, and her past and described the wonderful friendship she had had with Jewett; Elizabeth told how on her way to Berwick Academy in the mornings she would visit the noted author and get caught up in the fascinating stories shared by Jewett, making her late for school.

Elizabeth also described family heirlooms, mentioning a silver wedding cup whose first inscription is dated 1729, with the names of her great-great-great-grandparents Captain Ichabod Goodwin and Elizabeth Scammon.[89] Sadly, the cup has since been sold. Ever hopeful to find this Goodwin family treasure, Harvey and I have asked countless antique dealers to keep an eye open for the cup; and, of course, we scan all our Google alerts involving Ichabod Goodwin. Two other heirlooms mentioned, and likewise sold, are a powder horn and a sword that Elizabeth tells us was carried by Captain Ichabod Goodwin in the Battle of Carillon—at Fort Carillon, better known today as Fort Ticonderoga.

Prior to the battle in 1758, the Captain was involved in raising a militia to join other colonial and British troops in the attack against the strategically placed fort. Marching into battle alongside the Captain was his fifteen-year-old son, soon to be our General. The engagement ended in an ignominious defeat for the British and their colonial militia. It was a most fearsome fight. Right from the start, fortune was not on the side of the American and British soldiers. Before the real fight had even begun, British Brigadier General Howe was mortally wounded in a brief exchange of fire. With the early loss of Howe, command fell to Major General Abercrombie, who appears to have been quite inept at logistics, leading to a significant loss of morale among the troops.[90] Abercrombie continued to charge the French fortifications, sending more and more reserves to be slaughtered in the same manner. Ultimately, two thousand British and colonial soldiers were killed or wounded, over fifty of them from New England militias, who lost five captains and a colonel.[91] Our Captain was evidently among those wounded, as witnessed by the £4.10 sent by the colony of Massachusetts to Ichabod in 1764. This amount, according to Neill, was needed to help with "lingering effects" of the Captain's battle wounds.[92]

Each time I place the cleaned skewers back on their nail next to the mantel in the keeping room, I am reminded of the Goodwin family treasure mentioned by Elizabeth Scammon. I can easily imagine the sword hanging in its place of pride over this same mantel—the Captain's sword that had been carried in the ill-fated battle at Fort Carillon.

THE STAMP ACT Taverns in Colonial New England were busy institutions. Every town had at least one, and many towns like Berwick had more. Townsmen first heard the day's news at their local tavern through rumor, newspapers, or the eighteenth-century version of our modern-day flyer—broad*sheets* were printed on both sides with topical news, while broad*sides*, in contrast, were printed on only one side. Most often, broadsheets or broadsides warned of an arsonist nearby or announced some new regulation, whether a tax imposed by the British king or a restriction on the serving of drink in taverns. In the years immediately prior to the Revolutionary War, these printed sheets were effectively used by the Committees of Correspondence, groups formed by Samuel Adams to ensure that the colonists were informed of British actions. To coordinate efforts against the British Crown, these committees printed numerous broadsides and -sheets and dispersed them to taverns in every city and town throughout the colonies.

The local tavern was where most of the male colonists would have first heard news of the detested Stamp Act. Word of the new tax burden imposed by King George III and his legislators would have spread quickly, the Committees of Correspondence using the vast network of taverns almost as effectively as the Internet. I can imagine many heated conversations, as the men unified against the English king, voices rising as the levels of rum punch in the quite-sizable punch bowls were reduced.

Issued on March 22, 1765, and to go into effect in November of that same year, the act decreed that every document, every license, every newspaper, even playing cards, was to be taxed. The purchase of any item on the list would require payment of a tax to obtain the mandatory stamp that would authorize the purchase. Understandably, the new act roused the colonists to unify against the oppressive measures. They believed they had invested enough of their own "blood and treasure" as we say today, and felt that the king was just looking to enrich himself and his lords.

While the king defended the Stamp Act, maintaining the need to replenish his treasury after the costly wars with the French and the Native Americans, he finally agreed to repeal the hated Stamp Act in March 1766 in response to the colonists petitions and protests. As expected, however, the British proclaimed additional directives and levied new taxes, including one that eventually resulted in the famed Tea Party in 1773, an event forever ingrained in the imagination of so many American schoolchildren. It seemed that the tyranny of King George III would never end and that the colonists would need to take more drastic steps to secure their rights as Englishmen.

A FINE RUM PUNCH WITH WHICH TO CELEBRATE NEW ENGLAND'S DEFIANCE OF KING GEORGE III   The time we spent experimenting with historic punch recipes was definitely not a chore. After reading a number of historical sources for ideas, we discovered that these drinks were quite watered down. Although the spirits were around ninety proof, they were diluted with any variety of mixers. Somewhat to our surprise, the variations were remarkably appealing to our twenty-first-century tastes. After some very enjoyable afternoons spent educating ourselves on historical mixology—never before five o'clock, of course—we decided on the following proportions.

Rum Punch

*A variation on the eighteenth-century recipe
for Philadelphia Fish-House Punch* [93]
Serves 12–16

Peel from 6 lemons
1 cup sugar
1 cup lemon juice (squeezed from about 6 lemons)
20 ounces rum*
10 ounces cognac
60 ounces water

First make an oleo-saccharum, a mix of muddled citrus peel and sugar: peel the 6 lemons with a vegetable peeler (trying to get as little pith as possible).

Put the peels in a bowl with the sugar, muddle well, and let sit for 1 to 2 hours.

Juice the peeled lemons, using more lemons if necessary to yield 8 ounces of juice. Set aside.

After the oleo-saccharum sits for up to 2 hours, combine it with the other ingredients.

Strain to remove the lemon peel from the punch.

Add ice and serve.

I should note that it was not common to use ice in drinks until the nineteenth century, but I really prefer my alcoholic beverages icy cold, unless, of course, it is a traditionally warm drink like hot buttered rum, perfect on a raw winter evening by the fire.

*You will often find recipes for rum punch, or even rum-based cocktails, using a combination of rums, and we have followed suit. We used a combination of Old Ipswich Tavern Style Rum (by Turkey Shore Distilleries) and a dark rum. Both kinds of rum were produced in the eighteenth century, although in New England light rum was the more prevalent version. For me, it is like mixing sweeteners in desserts like gingerbread, in which a bit of molasses brings out the ginger, but using all molasses would be too strong. Here, the light-colored Ipswich rum is a little dry and is balanced by the richer, almost sweet darker rum.

War with Britain

One of many things I embrace about our home is the daily awareness that we are living in a house filled with history, in a town that witnessed the struggles of our Founding Fathers. It is this historical aspect, the idea that I could live surrounded by American history, that affected me so greatly while looking at that photo of the keeping room in *American Farmhouses*. Then when I found a document placing our Captain Ichabod at the Provincial Congress of Watertown, I was able to directly connect the Goodwins to a major event in the early history of our country. I could vividly imagine a young Lieutenant Colonel Goodwin discussing the area's vulnerable seacoast with fellow patriots Samuel Adams or John Hancock at the Congress in Massachusetts. I now felt I could experience history more intimately through their stories.

In the years between the repeal of the provocative Stamp Act in 1766 and the first battles at Lexington and Concord in 1775, the British king and his Parliament continued to enrage the American colonists by imposing additional laws and taxes. One of the most ill-considered decisions on the part of the king was to send British troops to occupy Boston in 1768. An important consequence of that decision was the unification of the thirteen disparate colonies. The British occupation of one city was seen as a significant threat to every city and town throughout the colonies. Citizens of Massachusetts, including the townspeople of Berwick, were uncomfortably aware of the vulnerability posed by their coastline and its exposure to the formidable British navy.

In 1775 over a hundred leading citizens from the ten counties of Massachusetts, plus York County in the District of Maine, convened in Watertown, Massachusetts, to declare their support for their brethren in Boston—a meeting that became known as the Second

Provincial Congress. In attendance were men who would gain fame during the Revolutionary War, including such notable figures as Samuel Adams, John Hancock, and Joseph Warren.[94] Also present was our own General, the younger Ichabod, who had been chosen by the men of Berwick to represent their town.

In May of 1775, Ichabod would have saddled his horse; bade farewell to his wife, two young sons, and baby daughter; and begun the eighty-mile journey to Watertown. Today that trip takes Harvey and me an hour and three-quarters, whereas Ichabod would have needed four to five days to reach his destination.

More than seven weeks passed before the General returned to Berwick. This separation was not the longest he and Molly would endure during the General's periodic deployments between 1775 and 1779, as recorded in *Massachusetts Soldiers and Sailors of the Revolutionary War*.[95] Those years when their lives became caught up in the Revolutionary War could not have been easy on the young couple.

When thinking about the Goodwins, Harvey and I often find ourselves comparing their lives to scenes from the HBO series *John Adams*, an excellent adaptation of David McCullough's highly regarded biography. One of the early themes in the series is the impact the Revolutionary War had on the relationship of John and Abigail Adams. In 1774 and again in 1775, Adams was called to the Continental Congress of Philadelphia, a journey of at least fifteen days by horseback. Then, after serving in Philadelphia for four successive years, he traveled to Paris in 1778 as a diplomatic envoy, serving overseas for the remaining six years of the war. The couple was not reunited until 1784.

This enforced separation made a huge impression on me. Harvey and I thrive on each other's company, and it pains me to imagine the poignant moments of leave-taking during these times. Watching the series again, I begin to think of how the war must have impacted the General and Molly.

THE SECOND MASSACHUSETTS PROVINCIAL CONGRESS   For fifty days in 1775, from May 31 through July 19, the Provincial Congress worked to resolve many issues, including printing passes for safe passage into and out of occupied Boston, forbidding the killing of sheep, whose wool was necessary for an ample supply of coats for the Continental Army, and advising George Washington on how they planned to provide for the sick and wounded—this task was assigned to a three-man committee that included our Ichabod.[96] I found the level of detail, especially concerning the wool, rather forward-thinking.

Each delegate in attendance was there to express support and pledge defense for the colonists of Boston living under British occupation. The petition offered by Ichabod Goodwin on behalf of his fellow citizens of Berwick reflected the town's concerns of what looked like inevitable war with Britain—the Massachusetts colony was determined to declare war if necessary. The declaration reads, in part:

> *The petition of the Freeholders and Inhabitants of the town of Berwick in the county of York in town meetings convened humbly showeth: That the harbors of York and Kittery within the said county lie open to our now known enemies and the lives and properties of the inhabitants thereof and the neighboring Towns along the sea coast exposed to the ravages and depredations of the enemy and the remaining part of the inhabitants of this and the neighboring Towns labor under the disagreeable situation for a scant of arms and ammunition, of being incapable to defend themselves, wives, children and properties should a descent be made by the King's troops on this coast, which they have the greatest reason to fear will inevitably be the cost. Your petitioners therefore humbly pray this Honorable House in their great wisdom to take the premises into consideration and that they would dispatch one or more of the companies in the service of the Colony in order to guard and defend this coast and enable them by raising more troops in the service of the Colony in some measure to defend themselves.[97]*

As the delegates traveled back to their hometowns, stopping in taverns along the way, they would have spread the news of their unanimous opposition to the British.

Once preparations for war began, everyone in Berwick was quite busy, including our second Ichabod, who in February of 1775 had been chosen lieutenant colonel of the Second York Regiment, the same regiment led by William Pepperrell almost twenty years before on the march to Fort Carillon. He was involved with obtaining firearms and delivering them to the commissary, paying up to £3 per weapon that met the specifications—gun barrels with a length of three feet nine inches, and a blade not less than eighteen inches. Ichabod was also in charge of receiving and delivering articles of clothing donated to the Massachusetts Board of War and was authorized to dispense up to £300 in exchange for such donations as shoes, stockings, and shirts.[98] Many of these articles of clothing were sewn by the women of Berwick, one of their important contributions to the war effort.

The younger Ichabod and his fellow townsmen began to see themselves as a separate nation, no longer British citizens, but fellow Americans. This shift in sentiment was brought home to Harvey and me when we found a 1774 document that the older Ichabod had

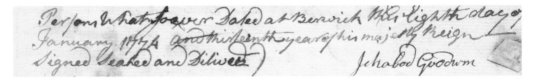

signed in the "thirteenth year of his majesty reign" (of King George III). Then two years later on July 1, 1776, the Berwick town clerk, A. H. Marshall, signed the town's "Declaration of Independence," wherein it is declared:

> Should the Cont'l Congress for the safety of the Colonies declare themselves independent of Great Britain, we, the inhabitants of said town will solemnly engage with our lives and fortunes to support them and that Col. Ichabod Goodwin be served a copy of this vote.[99]

1776: THE FIRST YEAR OF THE WAR   To help ensure the safety of the maritime region and beyond, Berwick did indeed send many men to fight for independence from England, contributing even more than its required quota of soldiers. Ivory Hovey, the Goodwins' neighbor and a physician, was appointed Acting Surgeon in Colonel Scammon's battalion, to which Captain Philip Hubbard of Berwick also belonged.[100] Troops from this small northern town were present at the Battle of Bunker Hill near Boston. They defended Kittery Point in Maine and fought in the Northern Campaign in Quebec, eventually joining with other militias in Providence, Springfield, and West Point. Berwick's men were also among those troops who suffered through the long winter at the encampment at Valley Forge, Pennsylvania. Some even marched south to Virginia to participate in the final battle at Yorktown.

The first significant battles following the July Fourth declaration took place in the state of New York, in or near Manhattan. At the end of August, Washington and his troops had been defeated at the Battle of Long Island and by mid-September the British occupied Manhattan. The Continental Army abandoned New York and retreated to New Jersey, eventually moving into Pennsylvania.

That year there was not a single American victory, major or minor, over the British other than a few skirmishes with the Native Americans, from August through the last week of

December. News from the battlefront reported only British successes throughout New York State, New Jersey, and Rhode Island.

At the close of a cold, icy December, a despondent Washington and his demoralized army were near Trenton, New Jersey, a little over sixty miles from the British-occupied city of New York. It was there in Trenton that a major battle was fought and won on December 26. Such a decisive American victory not only improved the morale of the young citizenry, it also helped encourage much-needed enlistments for the beleaguered army.

THE SISKIN COLLECTION OF COLONIAL-ERA LETTERS   On October 7, 2005, just short of one year after our move into our historic house in Maine, Harvey and I had the good fortune to auction a collection of envelopes, or covers, mailed between 1663 and 1799, many of which still contained their letters. This fascinating holding had been the property of Ed and Jean Siskin. Of the roughly two thousand envelopes available for sale in the public domain, the Siskins had managed to assemble about one-third of them over a period of twenty-five years.[101] Their goal was to document the development of mail service in the colonies prior to, during, and just after the Revolutionary War. The collection ends with the postwar period of George Washington's administration.

I am hardly an avid postal historian like Harvey, who is riveted by postal rates and mail routes. Rather, my interest was with the letters themselves, written by ordinary men discussing events of the time. I found the details about the war especially engrossing, most notably the descriptions by soldiers who had actually participated in the various campaigns.

One of these Siskin letters provides an eyewitness account of the battle that was fought at Trenton, albeit from the British point of view.[102] The author, a British lieutenant colonel and a member of the British Parliament by the name of J. Maitland, discusses the battle that had just taken place. The letter was addressed to the Earl of Lauderdale, Maitland's father. The writer places the blame for their significant defeat on the commanding officer, a Hessian named Rall (or, as Maitland wrote, "Raul") who, in the narrator's opinion, blithely decided to take no steps to prepare his men despite numerous warnings of Washington's planned attack. It seems the Hessian assumed the American general would never travel with his army in such disadvantageous weather. During the "surprise" attack, Rall himself was killed and hundreds of his Hessian troops were captured.

This resounding victory at the end of 1776 gave the Americans the much-needed encouragement to continue the fight.

Bruswick N.J. febr 18th
1777

My Lord

It is a long while since I wrot to your
whic is owing to my hardly ever having
time and very seldome Papers. we
Ended our Campaign Nobly and went
into a Sort of winter Quarters and would
have been very Comfortable. had it not been for
the too much Security of a Hessian Colonel
his name was Raul, he was Quarterd at
Trentown on Delaware with three Regiments
of Hessians, he was informed from all
sides that he was to be attacked the
next morning but nothing could bring

A 1777 letter written by the Earl of
Maitland to his father, the Earl
of Lauderdale, blaming the British
defeat at the Battle of Trenton on
a Hessian officer named "Raul."

1777: THE BATTLE OF SARATOGA AND ITS AFTERMATH The second year of the war brought mostly bleak reports to the rebellious colonies, with one notable exception.

That same year also found the Captain in failing health, and by mid-November the first Ichabod to live at Old Fields had died, but not before witnessing another decisive American victory when Washington again managed to reverse the downward spiral in early fall at the Battle of Saratoga, in New York.

The American troops were under the command of the major generals Horatio Gates, Benjamin Lincoln, and Benedict Arnold (who at this point was still a patriot). After several skirmishes and two main battles—on September 18 and October 7—the British army found itself surrounded by October 13. Four days later their general surrendered.

The campaign at Saratoga is widely considered the turning point of the war. While the details of the fighting are intriguing, I am more fascinated by the unusual set of conditions surrounding the British surrender—conditions I cannot imagine being negotiated today. The British commander desperately wanted to avoid the shame of imprisonment, particularly for himself and his officers, so he asked that the 2,400 Hessian mercenaries and 3,400 British soldiers under his command be sent back to Britain. Strangely enough, Washington agreed, and our then Lieutenant Colonel Goodwin, soon to be a major general, was directly involved with the aftermath.[103]

THE GENERAL AND THE SO-CALLED SOLDIERS OF THE CONVENTION Never one to impose harsh treatment upon prisoners of war, Washington agreed to the British terms but added a stipulation that none of the British soldiers being released could fight in future battles on American soil. To enforce this stipulation, Washington insisted that the British provide a list of the names of all of their officers. Without this list, Washington could not monitor if the defeated British officers were being sent back to fight the Americans.

It was also suspected that the British would surreptitiously replace their officers fighting in France with those from the regiment defeated at Saratoga. Those officers who had been fighting on French soil could then be shipped here, providing more manpower against Washington's army.[104] (An enemy during the French and Indian War, France officially became an important American ally after signing a treaty in February 1778, a treaty that Benjamin Franklin had been negotiating throughout 1777.)

When it became clear that the British general had no intention of providing the requisite list, Washington and Congress (perhaps now regretting the too-favorable terms of surrender) revoked the negotiated terms of surrender, called *convention* terms. By this point, however, the prisoners had already begun the march from Saratoga to Boston with the understanding that in Boston they would board ships back to Britain, thus avoiding the ignominious fate of other prisoners of war.

By January 1778 Washington had almost six thousand prisoners on his hands. The British regiment having finally arrived in Boston, the captives were sorely in need of housing. Barracks were constructed outside of Boston in Winter Hill and Prospect Hill—two areas of present-day Somerville, Massachusetts—and in April, Ichabod was given command of the two sites. He was not only responsible for the well-being and behavior of the prisoners, but of equal importance, he was accountable to the people of Cambridge. Still bitter after the British burned Charlestown, just a few miles away, in 1775, they were most unhappy with the presence of these prisoners. The conditions under which Ichabod first took control were deplorable for everyone involved.

Ichabod's military journal, found on the Maine Historical Society website, offers a fascinating first-person account, as well as insight into the challenges of his command at this time.[105] Each day, starting on April 16, 1778, and ending on June 24 of the same year, Lieutenant Colonel Goodwin wrote an entry from his headquarters in Cambridge detailing the oversight of the two prisoners-of-war facilities. He had to contend with escaped prisoners, disorderly British officers, his own unruly, often inebriated troops, and the ever-present threat of smallpox.

This last problem was of particular concern as this disease had significantly impacted troop levels. In the ten weeks Ichabod kept the journal, he frequently mentioned actions taken to prevent the deadly disease from spreading, immediately quarantining any man showing symptoms.

In another entry, Ichabod described being informed that the provisions delivered that day were not fit for consumption. To avoid this problem in the future, Ichabod ordered the captain on duty to inspect all food directly upon delivery and to demand a proper substitution should any item be deemed unfit for use.

Despite Ichabod's best efforts, his prisoners complained of poor accommodations, insufficient meat, and a severe lack of wood for heat. These complaints were no doubt valid as such shortages existed throughout the colonies at this time, yet the imprisoned British officers under Ichabod's care were afforded much better food and lodging than even most colonists. In fact, the British officers had relatively spacious quarters, and some even had their own servants to wait upon them. Certainly, none received such ill treatment as patriot Ethan Allen. From a letter written by Benjamin Franklin, along with other plenipotentiaries, and sent to the English Lord of the Treasury, we learn that "Col Ethan Allen was dragged in chains from Canada to England, from England to Ireland, from Ireland to Carolina and from thence to New-York."[106] The letter goes on to complain that two-thirds of those Americans imprisoned at Fort Washington in Manhattan, New York, had perished under the most cruel conditions.

Ichabod also had to contend with the unruly behavior of his own soldiers as well as that of the British and Hessian prisoners. The disorderly conduct was often due to overconsumption of alcohol and resulted in much damage to the nearby town of Cambridge. To relieve the suffering townspeople, Ichabod authorized harsh punishments for anyone involved in the destruction of property.

In his journal, Lieutenant Colonel Goodwin notes that General Washington had implemented a strict protocol by which the enemy officers were to be treated. Goodwin points out that "officers should Enjoy every Reasonable indulgen[ce] and limits sufficiently Extencive [sic] for their Riding for the[ir] Amusement."[107] I found it hard to believe that the British officers were allowed the relative freedom to go into town.

Upon finishing the last entry in the military journal, dated June 24, 1778, I felt I had a good sense of the younger Ichabod's voice and character. It is obvious that he diligently attended to the needs of his prisoners. I also got the sense that our thoughtful Ichabod was most concerned with providing a fair trial for any soldier—British or American—accused of wrongdoing.

These Prisoners of Convention remained imprisoned outside Boston until November, when they were marched to Charlottesville, Virginia, and then moved one last time back north to Lancaster, Pennsylvania. It should be noted that they were not chained as the unfortunate Ethan Allen.

PENOBSCOT CAMPAIGN The deciding triumph of the Battle of Saratoga notwithstanding, the war continued.

In 1778 there were several attacks by the Iroquois Confederacy, a British ally, in New York and Pennsylvania. With so many men deployed in the Continental Army or enlisting in state militias, the women and children left behind on isolated farms or in small villages in the north were especially vulnerable. George Washington was convinced that the only way to prevent further assaults was to organize a punishing counterattack, so in late March 1779, under the direction of Congress, Washington ordered General John Sullivan to lead a scorched-earth expedition against the Iroquois nations in the Finger Lakes region of western New York.[108]

Serving in numerous key battles during the Revolutionary War, General Sullivan was not only a well-regarded officer at the time, but here in Maine and New Hampshire he is justly famous today.[109] Born just three years before the younger Ichabod, Sullivan grew up in Berwick in the area known as Pine Hill.

After considerable delay Sullivan and his men finally set off for New York. As they had with the Battle of Trenton, the Siskin letters provided Harvey and me with colorful first-hand accounts of the pending expedition. One of our favorite letters contains this excerpt written by Captain William Pierce, Sullivan's evidently quite-educated aide-de-camp. It offers a rather dramatic characterization of the proposed operation:

> *We have an Army collected for the purpose of a secret Expedition, tho' every body knows it. I cannot consistent with my office, give you any intelligence of our rout; let it suffice that we shall have innumerable difficulties to encounter with Savages, Wildernesses, Rocks & Mountains, such as would stagger the persevering spirit of a Hannibal; if compelled to retreat (but the Devil, why should I introduce such a word?) we should run a hazard equal with Genophon when he retreated through three Hostile Countries with 10,000 men.[110]*

By the conclusion of the campaign in mid-September, forty Iroquois villages, along with their farmlands and their crops, had been completely destroyed. The Iroquois warriors suffered significant losses in the one major battle at Newtown in New York, but the aftermath was more devastating. As a result of Washington's order to destroy all of their crops and any shelters on their land, an additional five thousand members of their nation—men, women, and children—died of cold and starvation in the winter of 1779–1780.

At the same time as the Sullivan Expedition, Ichabod was in upstate Maine near what is now the town of Castine, at the confluence of Penobscot Bay and the Bagaduce River. There, under the orders of General Wadsworth, he took part in the famed, and ill-fated, Penobscot Campaign—a joint maneuver of the navy and the Massachusetts militia to regain control of coastal Maine from the British. Although not too familiar to those of us with just a passing knowledge of the Revolutionary War, this campaign is well known in the annals of military history as not only a major naval expedition but also the largest American naval defeat prior to Pearl Harbor.

Placed in charge of the Massachusetts artillery regiment was a Lieutenant Colonel Paul Revere, the same Revere who had alerted the Massachusetts colonists that the British were coming on his famed ride through Lexington and Concord. Another noted officer at Penobscot was Brigadier General Peleg Wadsworth, grandfather of the well-known poet and the only high-ranking officer to exit the campaign with his reputation intact. And on July 5, 1779, Colonel Ichabod Goodwin was assigned responsibility for the "general return of officers and men for equipments." In military terms this meant that Ichabod was responsible for keeping track of muster (enlistment) rolls, guns, and uniforms and ensuring that the men on the list were appropriately trained and equipped.[111] At the time of the campaign, our Ichabod was already a colonel, having advanced to the rank in 1778.

The campaign began on July 24 at Boothbay Harbor, and initially all went well. The navy conducted several successful assaults against the British ships while the ground forces laid siege on the British deployed at Fort George. On August 13, however, the American commander called for a rapid evacuation when the formidable British naval warships were seen arriving as reinforcements. But the retreat was not successful.

The entire naval fleet that participated, forty-three ships in all, was destroyed (with the exception of one captured ship), and over four hundred and seventy American sailors were killed or taken prisoner. Meanwhile, on land there was great disarray and a severe shortage of food and supplies as Ichabod and his fellow soldiers retreated to Boston. General Wadsworth facilitated the best possible withdrawal for his troops, yet the Massachusetts militia still suffered great losses, given the lack of equipment and provisions for meals.[112]

In 1780 General Wadsworth again issued direct orders to Ichabod, sending him and his troops to Pownalborough and Fort Western (near the site of the ignominious defeat the year before) to secure the Kennebec River. In the words of the famous poet's grandfather, Ichabod was "to ensure no harm be done to the cattle or to the inhabitants of the area."[113] As a good commander, he realized that food spoilage, as much as enemy fire, could devastate an army. As Napoleon Bonaparte wisely noted, an army travels on it stomach.

Massachusetts Soldiers and Sailors of the Revolutionary War chronicles military activity through 1781 and yet there is no record of Ichabod being deployed after 1780 (it was also in that year that the the Governor of Massachusetts appointed Ichabod to enlist two hundred men from York County in the Continental Army.)[114] As most of the fighting after the Penobscot Campaign took place in the southern half of the newly formed country, Ichabod might have returned to Old Fields as his services may no longer have been needed.

As Harvey and I climb the winding stairs to the master's bedroom each night, we feel it a privilege to walk in the footsteps of Ichabod and Molly. We are reminded of those many committed Americans who set aside their own needs to attend to political and military obligations far from their homes. These men left their farms, their livelihoods, their families, and all that was familiar to face the powerful British army and an unyielding British king. Thanks to these patriots, we live in a country that gave birth to a new form of government, one that would guarantee a life of liberty for those early Americans and for the generations that would come after. We are thankful to have benefited from their efforts and their legacy. Of course, we are aware that in those days, a life of liberty was meant for white men only (and only those not indentured).

The slaves, Native Americans, and women would have to wait.

STEWED RUMP OF BEEF FOR A HUSBAND ON FURLOUGH FROM WAR   I like to imagine the joyful occasion of Ichabod's return to Old Fields after his two assignments in 1780. I am certain something special was on the menu his first night home. But for most of those war-time meals, with Molly's increased responsibilities and the scarcity of ingredients like sugar, coffee, and meat, the common—and thrifty—one-pot boiled dinner was surely found on the table for many of those midday meals. With those restrictions in mind, Harvey and I decided to re-create, as faithfully as we were able, an eighteenth-century stewed rump of beef with carrots, potatoes, and turnips.

As usual, I needed an authentic recipe in a comprehensible language and format, that was relatively easy to make. I found many historic recipes for stewed rump of beef and after reading more than a handful, I started to get a sense of how such a relatively simple dish would have been an obvious choice for the hardworking women and servants of the Goodwin household. I do like to think, however, that Molly would have prepared a somewhat more elaborate version of this one-dish dinner for this special occasion.

So I pulled lists of ingredients from my various sources, focusing on the recipes from Colonial Williamsburg's History Is Served website, *Martha Washington's Booke of Cookery*, and *The Complete Practical Cook* by Charles Carter, an eighteenth-century chef, and came up

with a recipe above and beyond what I perceived to be the typically plain, often overcooked, boiled beef and vegetables that would have been prepared by the average colonial house-wife. I chose to include more meat, taking the additional time to brown it prior to boiling (although I get the feeling that browning was not a common step for the average colonial-era housewife given the extra effort and time). One slight difference from my sources was the cut of beef. Following my butcher's suggestion, I used a piece of chuck roast—a fattier cut—as it would be less dry than the rump.

When gathering the ingredients for these historic dishes, I try to use as many local foods as possible, seeking out farmers who raise their own vegetables, fruits, and heritage-breed meats, and using herbs from our own garden. By selecting ingredients from these homegrown sources, I hope to achieve flavors not that different from those enjoyed by our New England predecessors.

As is my usual practice, even for my modern cookery, I make the cooking stocks from scratch, just as Elizabeth and Molly would have done. The Goodwin women had easy access to spirits and spices from around the world, so I can rationalize my use of items like red wine and cloves.

After assembling the ingredients, the next step in preparing any hearth-cooked meal is, of course, to start the fire. This step needs to be done at least one hour ahead of cooking so that the bricks of the hearth will have time to absorb and radiate the fire's heat, in essence becoming a facsimile of today's convection oven.

As simple as browning seems, whenever I do this step I end up with grayish beef or pale chicken that has basically boiled in the hot fat and turned into a watery mixture. I have tried to brown protein in smaller batches in very hot fat to ensure that the meat doesn't steam, thinking quantity might be the issue, but the result is always the same—that anemic-looking meat sitting in a wet puddle.

I was, therefore, intrigued when I found one eighteenth-century chef who had a dif-ferent method for browning the beef. His instructions call for roasting the red meat or fowl on the spit over a hot fire. Genius. The meat browned perfectly. For those of you with an electric oven, I found another source that says you can brown meat by broiling it. I have yet to try this myself, but the effect may be similar to roasting, achieving the same carameliza-tion—which is the point, after all.

We had already cooked a few dishes using our huge cast-iron pot hung from the crane, so we were not entirely surprised at how perfectly the meat and vegetables of the stew cooked. There was just the right amount of slow simmering over four hours. The incredible aroma of the slow-cooking stew that floated throughout our old home was also neither a new experience nor one we will ever tire of. We were amazed by the incredible flavor of this simple hearth-cooked, one-pot meal. The beef retained all of its meaty essence while at the same time creating a wonderfully savory broth. Likewise, the individual flavors of the vegetables were preserved and the dish as a whole was much more appetizing than its homely name implies.

Of course, such a heavy meal called for a relatively light dessert. Our choice was ice cream, a refreshing dish that was in fact invented early enough that Thomas Jefferson was able to serve the frozen confection in his gracious dining room at Monticello toward the end of the eighteenth century, and according to a website on all things Mount Vernon, George Washington had a "Cream Machine for Ice" as of 1784.[115] We believe, therefore, that we are justified in our choice of dessert, and although the ice cream we devoured was store-bought, it was still purchased at a local café that orders its products from a small dairy in Vermont that uses no preservatives.

Alas for the eighteenth-century Goodwins and other New Englanders, ice cream was not enjoyed until well into the next century. Given the expense of stocking an icehouse, especially in the summer months, when the confection would be most desirable, only the wealthiest of colonists—men such as George Washington, who had an icehouse built at Mount Vernon—would have been able to enjoy a frozen dessert. However, as patented ice cream makers came into use in the mid-nineteenth century and freezers and dry ice by 1930, I imagine that at some point in the late nineteenth or early twentieth century, later generations of the family might have enjoyed this frozen treat in our home.

In fact, the same architectural historian who told us about the addition of the bay window in our study, told Harvey and me that our house likely had an icebox where our pantry is now located, in the ca 1870 two-story addition. The historian also pointed out the proximity of our still functioning nineteenth-century dumbwaiter to where the icebox might have been located. The cut-out in our kitchen floor (covered by a wooden "lid" when not in use) leads directly to the dumbwaiter resting in the cellar. I had read once that ice was commonly stored in a house's cooler cellar, so the Goodwins might have used this apparatus to bring ice up in order to restock the icebox. This convinced me that Elizabeth Hayes Goodwin, who left Old Fields in 1958, would have been able to enjoy ice cream at home at the turn of the last century when she was a little girl about five-years old.

Stewed Rump of Beef

Serves 6–8

5 pounds rump beef or chuck roast

1 quart beef stock, preferably homemade

1 pint red wine

2 onions, very thinly sliced

6 carrots, sliced about ½ inch thick

3 stalks celery, diced

4 medium potatoes, peeled and sliced ½ inch thick

3 cloves garlic, very finely minced

3 cloves, ground—I just take the seed head from the
    stem and crush between my fingers

4 tablespoons chopped parsley

4 sprigs thyme

Salt, to taste

Brown the meat on a spit, or broil in an electric oven, until all surfaces are caramelized, then cut into 1½-inch cubes.

Place the beef in a cast-iron Dutch oven or any stewing pot if cooking on a stovetop. Add the liquids, vegetables, garlic, cloves, herbs, and salt.

Hang the Dutch oven on a crane over hot coals. Bring the liquid to a boil. Adjust the height of the pot (i.e., its distance from coals) as needed to maintain a slow simmer, and cook for 3 to 4 hours until meat and vegetables are tender.

If you are cooking on a stove, place the stew pot on the stovetop, bring the liquid to a boil, and then reduce heat and simmer as per hearth-cooking instructions above.

Remove the pot from heat and let the meat sit in its broth for 30 minutes.

Serve the meat with its broth and the vegetables.

The War Ends

Records of military regiments of Massachusetts show a distinct reduction in troops beginning in 1779. This scaling down continued through 1780, with even more divisions disbanded after January 1, 1781. We know that a small number of the state's remaining regiments continued to be active throughout 1781. In late October of that year, some Maine militias assisted in the final battle at Yorktown in Virginia, witnessing the end of the war when the British surrendered on October 19. Initial peace negotiations began in April 1782, but the Treaty of Paris was not ratified until 1784—America in January and England in April.

Following the turbulent years of the Revolutionary War, men like Ichabod returned to their homes and families and struggled to reestablish their financial well-being. The first few years following the Treaty of Paris were difficult, due not only to a weakened economy but also to the arduous task of creating a union out of thirteen disparate entities. At times, it appeared that the union might not last at all, with one segment of the population or another always in rebellion against the new rules and new forms of governance.

Of course, the union did hold. A new constitution was written and ratified, and those sentiments first expressed in the Declaration of Independence continued to bind the people of the young country together. They would be celebrated for hundreds of years to come.

CELEBRATING THE FOURTH OF JULY   Since the very beginnings of our country, the Declaration of Independence has been memorialized each July, celebrated as early as 1777, when an official dinner was planned by the Continental Congress. Throughout the war years, however, our new country was probably not always able to celebrate the day with such "handsome entertainment."[116] In 1781, the last year of the fighting, Massachusetts declared July 4 a state holiday, and by 1784 festivities would have been especially elaborate, given the ratification of the treaty. With his military duties over, we know that Ichabod was home in Berwick in 1784. There is no doubt in my mind that he would have made sure that his family did not miss the celebration.

In neighboring Portsmouth, a detailed article about the day's festivities was written up in the *New-Hampshire Gazette* on July 10, 1784, including a description of "a discharge of thirteen cannon" and "festivity, which ought to have animated every real friend to America."[117] As the Fourth of July was on a Sunday that year, the paper noted that the "gentlemen" (no women, I suppose) gathered at the fort on Monday, no doubt dressed somewhat formally for the occasion. (The "fort" would have been Fort William and Mary, later renamed Fort Constitution, a beautiful spot overlooking the Piscataqua River.) If that day's temperature was anything like the 106 degrees reported the following week in Boston's *Massachusetts Spy*, these gentlemen likely commented (a bit unhappily) about the atypical heat.[118]

The ceremony began at one o'clock in the afternoon of Monday, July 5, with the firing of the cannon, and continued with a "handsome entertainment," drinking, and toasting. The attendees toasted George Washington, fallen heroes, peace, agriculture, and on and on. I imagine that a great deal of alcohol was consumed in a relatively short period of time. Such a scene must have been found in just about every town and city throughout this newly independent country.

Harvey and I have created our own tradition to mark the Fourth, an especially meaningful day for us given that we live in the home of someone who actually participated in the struggle for our country's existence. We begin in the late afternoon with our customary holiday glass of Madeira in the parlour. I first set out our glasses on our round tea table, one that is probably not that different from the tea table listed in Ichabod and Molly's inventory. Then, to honor the occasion, Harvey brings in the oldest Madeira we own; this year, 2013—our ninth summer in our house—it is a bottle from 1834, the year that the fourth Ichabod to live at Old Fields was just fifteen years old.

We first raise our glasses to all the generations of Goodwins, who among them would have observed over 150 Independence Days—from the first peacetime celebration in 1784 until the last Goodwin moved out in 1958—in this house and possibly in this very room, at least after our house was built to replace the original, which burned in the fire. Over the years, on this, our national Day of Independence, they likely discussed whoever the current president was—for the earliest Goodwins, George Washington, John Adams, and Thomas

Jefferson. Later, the Goodwins of the twentieth century would have talked about the administrations of Franklin Roosevelt, Harry Truman, and Dwight Eisenhower.

The family likely would have discussed an ongoing war and the loved ones who had been called to the fight, be it the War of 1812, the Civil War, or one of the two world wars in the first half of the twentieth century. I can also picture the Goodwins choosing to chat about a more pleasant subject. If it were 1868, they might have talked about how well the Berwick Academy Club had performed that July Fourth morning at the National Game in a baseball match against the Eons.[119] In 1872, just four Independence Days later, the discussion might have centered on the construction of the impressive new railroad extension that allowed one to board the train in South Berwick, have dinner in the West Ossipee Mountains in New Hampshire, and be back "at half past five o'clock the same evening … ready for tea."[120] I would enjoy such a day myself, if only a passenger train still came into town.

Each July Fourth Harvey and I cook a proper Yankee dinner. This year we decided to prepare a popular early New England meal of salt-cod fish cakes, turnips, and baked beans, all washed down with a hearty local ale. After the main course, we enjoy a not-quite-eighteenth-century but still very traditional New England dessert, strawberry ice cream. After cleaning up, we honor a long-standing Bennett tradition by watching the HBO series about our second president, John Adams—something we have done every Fourth of July since 2009. We watch only Part II, with the dramatic scenes leading up to, and including, the unanimous vote by all thirteen colonies declaring their independence. Even after multiple viewings, Harvey and I still find ourselves deeply moved when, finally, each delegate rises from his chair and votes "Aye."

Our evening concludes in the master's bedroom, where the west-facing windows allow us to catch a glimpse of the fireworks display from over the hills of Rollinsford, New Hampshire. This is a perfect follow-up to the film, as it was John Adams, after all, who promoted the idea of "illuminations" (or fireworks) as a fitting way to commemorate this important day.

INDEPENDENCE DAY SALT-COD FISH CAKES It never ceases to amaze me how even the simplest cooking task, like soaking salt cod, has what seems like an infinite variety of options. You might be instructed to soak it for twenty-four hours, changing the water hourly. Others suggest soaking the cod for as long as forty-eight hours, or even seventy-two. Alternatively, you can leave the cod in cold water for as little as six hours, changing the water every hour or two. You can also choose to keep the piece whole or cut the cod into three or four pieces prior to soaking.

Once it has soaked, you have the option either to place the salted cod in water already brought to a simmer and then cook it for fifteen minutes, or to place the piece(s) in cold water, *then* bring it to a simmer and immediately remove it from the heat.

The ratio of salt cod to mashed potatoes also varies considerably. You can use one pound of cod to one pound of potatoes, or one pound of cod to two pounds of potatoes; or, one website gave a ratio of one-quarter pound of salt cod to one pound of potatoes, trying to replicate the old-time coddie—a Baltimore variation of a fish cake served on saltines with a dab of mustard that Harvey and I remember nostalgically from our Baltimore childhoods, a tasty treat neither of us had thought about for many, many years.

Add spices, suggests one recipe; just onion, instructs another.

As I frequently do when trying to remain true to the eighteenth century, I referred to Sandra L. Oliver's *Saltwater Foodways*. In her book Oliver compiles various historic recipes from the eighteenth and nineteenth centuries and adapts them for today's cook.[121]

While I try to adhere as closely as possible to authentic historic recipes, I usually improvise a bit, combining elements from the various recipes. Given the proximity of the French province of Quebec, I can imagine there was some influence of French-Canadian cooking on Mainers. I found one historic recipe, written by a French-Canadian chef, that used milk instead of water. With that in mind I chose to simmer the salt cod in half milk and half water, milk being the liquid of choice in the French recipe I referenced. I also increased the amount of cod in proportion to the potatoes, as I believe wealthier families like the Goodwins would have preferred more fish than starch.

While preparing the fish cakes, I set aside some of the cod and potato to make coddies in the proportions suggested—one-quarter pound cod to one pound potato. Fried in a half inch of oil, the cakes actually resembled that long-ago treat, one Harvey and I had not had in about fifty years. For the two of us, it was a wonderful bit of nostalgia. We both recalled the spinning leather-topped metal stools, the canisters of pretzel rods, and the nozzled levers that dispensed the flavored fountain sodas of the local drugstore. But best of all were their coddies—those fried cakes carefully placed on a saltine cracker, drowned in mustard, and topped with a second saltine, mustard oozing through the perforations.

I have to say, Harvey and I were once more amazed by how enjoyable an eighteenth-century recipe can be to our twenty-first-century palates.

Salt-Cod Fish Cakes

Makes nine 3-inch cakes

1 pound salt cod, cut in three pieces
Mixture half milk, half water, enough to cover cod, plus additional ½ cup
½ onion
1 pound potatoes, peeled and quartered
3 tablespoons butter, plus another 3 tablespoons
3 tablespoons bacon drippings

Soak the cod for approximately 6 hours in cold water, (due to time constraints I was only able to soak the cod for 5 hours and the result was perfectly satisfactory). Change water every 2 hours, then drain.

Place the mixture of half milk and half water in a clean saucepan and bring to a simmer. Add the cod and simmer gently for 15 minutes. Never let the cod come to a boil (every recipe mentioned this important point). Let cool.

While the cod is simmering, boil the potatoes until soft enough to pierce with a fork. Mash with ½ cup milk and 3 tablespoons butter. Set aside.

When the cod is cool enough to handle, flake it between fingers. Mix thoroughly with potatoes, form into 3-inch cakes, and sauté in hot bacon drippings. I did not have sufficient bacon drippings, so I supplemented them with butter (as Oliver suggests in her recipe). In total, I probably used about 6 tablespoons of fat for the frying.

SLAVERY IN MASSACHUSETTS COMES TO AN END There was one bit of local news in 1784 that I found worthy of note. The *New-Hampshire Gazette* ran an ad placed by a Jedediah Goodwin, a cousin of the Captain, offering a "handsome reward" for his runaway "indented" servant, a sixteen-year-old boy related to William Nason—the Captain's own indentured servant, who I mentioned had run away with Ichabod's slave Pompey in 1750.[122] The Nason mentioned in the 1784 ad had "the fore finger of his left hand" cut off. Could it be that the two Goodwin cousins shared a leaning toward ill treatment of the humans they regarded as their property?

In 1783, the year before Jedediah placed his ad, the Massachusetts Supreme Court ruled in favor of a slave who sued his owner for his freedom. This Supreme Court decision effectively abolished slavery; however, the trade was not ruled illegal by the state until 1788; by 1790 the Massachusetts census had no listing of slaves among the populace (the British by contrast did not pass the Abolition of Slavery Act until 1833).

RATIFICATION OF THE CONSTITUTION The cold was insufferable in the fall of 1786. By mid-November, the St. George River in Warren, Maine, a town not two hundred miles north of Boston, was frozen solid, the ice already thick enough to bear the weight of horse-drawn sleighs. Monday, December 4, was bitterly cold, and a fierce snow began to fall throughout much of New England. On Friday of that same week, another powerful snow-storm hit, and the citizens of Boston were incapable of leaving their homes. The snow was six feet deep by the time the second storm finally ended.[123] Given the almost ten feet of snow that fell during the first three months of 2015, many Bostonians today can certainly relate to the experience of those early citizens of Boston.

There were other kinds of storms raging in Massachusetts in 1786. The years imme-diately following the war were ones of hardship for most Americans. The loss of income due to British interference with trade was incalculable, and the lack of manpower due to the casualties of war meant there was little, if any, surplus farm production that could be sold.

Beset by a depressed economy that was exacerbated by a lack of hard currency, the rural farmers of Massachusetts began protesting the collection of taxes they could ill afford. In August, their protests kept the county court from convening for the purpose of collecting the money. Led by Daniel Shays, these organized protests spread into numerous towns and cities of the commonwealth. In January 1787, Massachusetts governor Bowdoin called upon the militia to get involved. Within a short period, Shays' Rebellion was crushed, giv-ing the governor a chance to demonstrate the power of his administration.

A staunch Federalist, Ichabod was probably supportive of the governor's actions and was doubtless relieved to learn of the quick and decisive victory over the insurgent farmers. As the Federalists were not known to be a party to seek revenge, the governor offered clem-ency to the leaders of the rebellion.

By 1787, influential men such as Alexander Hamilton, George Washington, and James Madison were calling for a constitutional convention. They realized that the Articles of Confederation were far too weak to keep the country unified and strong enough to defend itself. In May of that year, a new constitution was drafted, and by September the majority of the delegates had signed the document. The revised document attempted to create a balance between a strong national government and a modicum of states' rights. It stipulated that only the powers specifically enumerated would be enforced by the federal administration, and that all other powers were to remain in the hands of the individual states. Nine states needed to ratify the Constitution before it could go into effect, and in December Delaware became the first state to do so.

Then in February 1788, Massachusetts became the sixth state to ratify the Constitution. As noted in an article in *The Massachusetts Gazette* of Portland, Berwick's "most respectable inhabitants ... met at a respectable house in the town, to testify their satisfaction" with the ratification.[124] Unsurprisingly, we find our General among this elite group of citizens. "For the sake of decorum," he was charged with presiding over the group as they read through the document, ensuring that each man be allowed to express his point of view with regard to the new Constitution. Being firm believers in a strong central government, the Federalists in attendance—the General among them—would certainly have viewed the revision as a distinct improvement over the terms laid out in the old Articles of Confederation.

By June of that same year, New Hampshire became the ninth state to ratify the constitution, allowing the new draft to become operational.

1789: THE FIRST INAUGURATION AND THANKSGIVING MADE OFFICIAL In April of the following year our country's first president was inaugurated. One of Washington's initial acts in office was to declare a national holiday, an official day of Thanksgiving to be held each year on November 26. Prior to Washington's signing of the proclamation, each of the thirteen colonies had designated a different calendar day for their Thanksgiving, and that calendar day would change from year to year even within the same colony (although in 1777, all thirteen colonies did celebrate on the same day—December 13). I also noticed that each year Massachusetts would observe their day of Thanksgiving far earlier than the rest of the nation. According to the diary kept by Colonel Samuel Pierce of Dorchester, Massachusetts, however, there was not an official celebration in Massachusetts until January 30, 1779. Pierce also notes that Thanksgiving fell on a different date each year.

On this twenty-first-century Thanksgiving Day in 2014, Harvey and I are in the dining room as the late-afternoon light of winter is quickly fading, the skies leaden with the threat of snow. We are relaxing after the task of getting our feast to the table. Friends will soon arrive and we will gather around the table. Harvey will begin to fire off a string of puns, a familiar scene to anyone who knows him. My husband loves to make people laugh, and his mind is ever on the lookout for a word that can be turned into a pun. As Harvey tells me, it is in his gene pool, noting that his paternal grandfather was quite the punster himself. I like to think that laughter also often accompanied holiday meals at the Goodwin table. As a man familiar with the courts, judges, and trials, perhaps Ichabod may have recounted the story about a certain Judge Smith, one that also involves a turn of phrase:

> *A spark being brought before a magistrate, on a charge of horse-stealing, the justice, the moment he saw him, exclaimed, I see a villain in your countenance. It is the first time, said the prisoner, very coolly, that I knew my countenance was a looking-glass.*[125]

Thinking back on our day, we marvel again at the sheer number of hours it would have taken to prepare such a meal on a feast day nearly two centuries ago. On the first national Thanksgiving Day in 1789, the Goodwin family would still have been in their original house, likely gathered in their dining room, a room that until just recently was the more informal parlour. Here they would have sat down to a festive dinner and offered toasts as these new Americans so often did at *any* celebration commemorating their history. Based on our own experiences, we are acutely aware of just how early a Goodwin servant must have risen to tend the fire in time to cook the turkey for the family's midday dinner. We have no difficulty placing ourselves in their shoes, and by our tenth Thanksgiving at Old Fields, we were quite prepared to face the six hours of labor-intensive cooking involved in roasting the turkey in front of the fire. Someone must lift and turn the iron spit every six to eight minutes (for a twenty-pound bird, that would be at least fifty turns or more). This prevents one side of the turkey from scorching while the other side cools down. In our world, that spit-turner—or human clock-jack [126]—is Harvey.

I therefore propose one more toast, to my husband, Harvey, without whom the hearth-roasted turkey would not be possible. After all, he is the sole family member who dutifully prepares the fire each Thanksgiving and faithfully turns that spit for the requisite period of time. We obviously realize how much easier it would be simply to turn the oven knob to 350 degrees, plus or minus, as we do for the majority of our everyday meals. Nevertheless, with every bite of the spit-roasted turkey, juicy with a shatteringly crisp, deep-golden skin, we acknowledge that the results are well worth Harvey's efforts. Of course, that is easy for me to say as I am not the one lifting an iron spit holding a twenty-pound bird.

PROSPERITY RETURNS By 1790, the uncertainties of wartime were past and the newly independent country was experiencing a period of economic expansion. As the editors of the *New-Hampshire Spy* confidently declared:

> *It is worthy of contemplation how rapidly the people of this country are extricating themselves from the calamities and burdens of the late war. Many towns that were laid waste by the ravages of the enemy, are now restored to their former size and prosperity.*[127]

Less than ten years after the Revolutionary War, the country experienced renewed wealth through innovation and experimentation. There was a revival of manufacturing, and novel methods were being developed to increase production. While Harvey and I are reading today about the newfangled driverless car, in 1790 the General would have been reading an article on a new hulling machine invented by yet another neighbor named Chadbourne.[128] A "valuable improvement" as described under the heading "Manufactures" in the December issue of the *Cumberland Gazette*,[129] this expensive machine not only hulled peas—which I know to be a rather slow process when done by hand—but also pearled barley (barley being a valued food source in both medicine and "cookery," as the article informs us).

The resultant product was seen as equal to the quite costly imported version, and the advertisement encourages its readers to "prefer" this manufacture to a "foreign one." Clearly, a young United States was making sure the balance of trade was favorably weighted to exports rather than imports, a nationalistic stance somewhat out of balance in our twenty-first century. Yet again, Berwick served as a microcosm reflecting the larger stories of our American history.

As the populace of New England and England looked to machines to help reduce its workload, another labor issue was at the forefront and conversations regarding slavery became ever more heated. In 1787 the Society for the Abolition of Slavery formed in England and began proselytizing against the inhuman trade.[130] By 1790 readers of the *New-Hampshire Spy* learned of a similar society being formed in Richmond, Virginia.[131] That same year, the first federally issued census does not list any slaves in Massachusetts, which at the time still included Maine.[132] The seeds of emancipation had been sown, and times were changing. The human rights issue left unaddressed when independence was declared from England was now being wrestled with.

LOCAL NEWS: GOSSIP AND MURDER I am sitting in the General's study with Maine's local paper, *Foster's Daily Democrat*, in front of me. There are stories about a fire, a sex scandal, and a local man imprisoned for tax evasion, not the sort of reading I prefer on a Saturday morning. In fact, I tend to skip over these stories on most days. This leads me to just one of the many things I love about Maine.

A common stereotype regarding residents of Maine is their decided lack of loquaciousness. My experience has been exactly the opposite. Neighbors, shopkeepers, repairmen— all seem quite happy to take ten or fifteen minutes out of their undoubtedly busy day to talk about the weather, a local author whose lecture they have just attended, or their camp in the summer. What they do not spend much of their time on is something I might call *town gossip*, though perhaps they do not mind reading a sensational story now and then; not too different from news readers in Berwick centuries ago, judging by the large number of long-winded articles I found dating between February and October in 1792, reporting on the murder of a Moses Gubtail and the ensuing trial of one Joshua Abbot.

The articles describe the confrontation between these two Berwick residents on February 7, 1792. The subsequent trial, with two thousand people in attendance, was covered by the *New Hampshire Gazetteer* in Portland, Boston's *American Apollo*, and the *Massachusetts Spy* in faraway Worcester, Massachusetts. The reporting of the disturbing details of this sensational crime, with a short conclusion mentioning the verdict, was especially elaborate in the *American Apollo*.[133] It seems that Moses Gubtail arrived at the home of the accused, Joshua Abbot, demanding to borrow a flax break (a tool used to separate fibers of the flax from its inner core) that Abbot himself had borrowed from a neighbor. Benjamin Gubtail, the brother of the deceased, was at the home of the accused when Moses arrived. Joshua responded that he had not yet completed his cleaning of the flax and so would not turn it over. Moses became enraged and shouted that Joshua would have finished with it if not "for his dam'd old bitch of a wife." Infuriated at this uncalled-for attack on Mrs. Abbot, Joshua ordered Moses to leave. Instead, according to Benjamin, Moses refused to leave and continued with his shouting. Joshua eventually picked up an oaken plank and struck the intruder on his head. After being hit, Moses returned home where, later that night, he lost first the use of his arm, then of his leg, then his speech, and was soon unable to move. By two o'clock in the morning he was dead.

The *Apollo* concludes with the trial, where "the defence was pathetic and learned," and that the "Jury returned their verdict, after being out *eight hours*, that the prisoner was

'Guilty of Murder.' *Sentence of Death* was pronounced against him." Abbot was sentenced to be executed on the sixth of September. By "pathetic and learned," was the paper suggesting that an educated lawyer might not be the right advocate? And was eight hours emphasized in italics because the jury took a long time to decide? Or was that length of time considered too short? I do know that the *New Hampshire Gazetteer* reported that the lawyers for Joshua Abbot took four hours to present their defense, speaking passionately and knowledgeably about the law.[134] So I am concluding that the Boston paper may have preferred a less lawyerly presentation by less educated men.

The story did not end as the verdict dictated, for just before the execution was to take place, the "Supreme Executive of Massachusetts" (who that year would have been John Hancock) issued a pardon. The people of Berwick were in attendance at the meetinghouse when they heard the news as part of that day's sermon, given by the Reverend Matthew Merriam. Later in my research I discovered a printed version of the reverend's sermon advertised for sale in an issue of the *Oracle of the Day* dated July 27, 1793.[135] I cannot imagine a religious sermon being advertised in the local paper today, let alone someone paying for it.

But I can imagine the day of the sermon announcing the pardon, as the shocked citizens of Berwick exited Reverend Merriam's Congregational Church during the noon break. They would likely have gone to Haggens's tavern, the Goodwins' tavern having closed after 1769. That is strange to imagine today, as many areas still maintain the blue law banning the sale of liquor on Sunday, the Christian Sabbath day; yet in the eighteenth century, taverns were encouraged to be built near the unheated meetinghouses, where their fireplaces would provide chilled churchgoers a welcome opportunity to thaw out their fingers and toes. Abbot's friends and neighbors, even those who normally avoided idle chatter, would undoubtedly have been in animated discussions on this surprising and happy outcome for their fellow townsman.

FIRST PETITION FOR INDEPENDENCE   By 1790 all thirteen states had ratified the new Constitution, yet there were still times when it seemed that the fabric holding the states—or even the towns within those states—together might fray. In fact, through my research on the Goodwins, I learned that New England had threatened to secede from the union in the early years of the republic (something I had never learned in school); and in 1792, the same year in which Gubtail was killed over a flax break, residents of York County in the District of Maine held a convention to discuss separating from Massachusetts. As Berwick's representative for the District of Maine, Ichabod was present at the convention and played a key role as president of the council that voted on the measure.[136]

Some of those attending the meeting offered a compelling case for Maine to be its own state. Their reasons included the distance that residents of Maine had to travel to attend to obligatory governmental affairs in Boston. Also, they argued, New Hampshire physically cut the District of Maine off from the rest of the state. In addition, most citizens believed that Maine deserved to be its own state merely for the fact that its population was greater than five other regions that had been assigned statehood—Rhode Island, Delaware, Georgia, Vermont, and Kentucky. But despite the strong case for statehood, that year the nays outweighed the yeas, and Maine continued as a district within the state of Massachusetts.

In 1792 Ichabod authored the statement declaring York County's resolution not to secede from Massachusetts, writing:

> *Considering our present government, being mild and perfectly agreeable to us, we cheerfully submit to its constitutional rules and regulations; and we are of opinion, that it will not be for the interest of the county of York to be separated from that Government, with whom we have for a long time been connected, and risk our honor and happiness on that part from which at present we have nothing to build our future hopes upon; Therefore would recommend it to you to instruct your Representatives at the next General Court, to oppose the Separation, if brought forward.*[137]

Eventually, in 1820, the District of Maine did break with Massachusetts, becoming the twenty-third state of the union, partly for the very same reasons that had failed to convince the citizens to secede almost three decades earlier.

1794 map of the Province of Maine by Samuel Lewis. First settled in the early 1600s, Maine remained a separate colony until the 1650s, when it became a part of the Massachusetts Bay Colony.

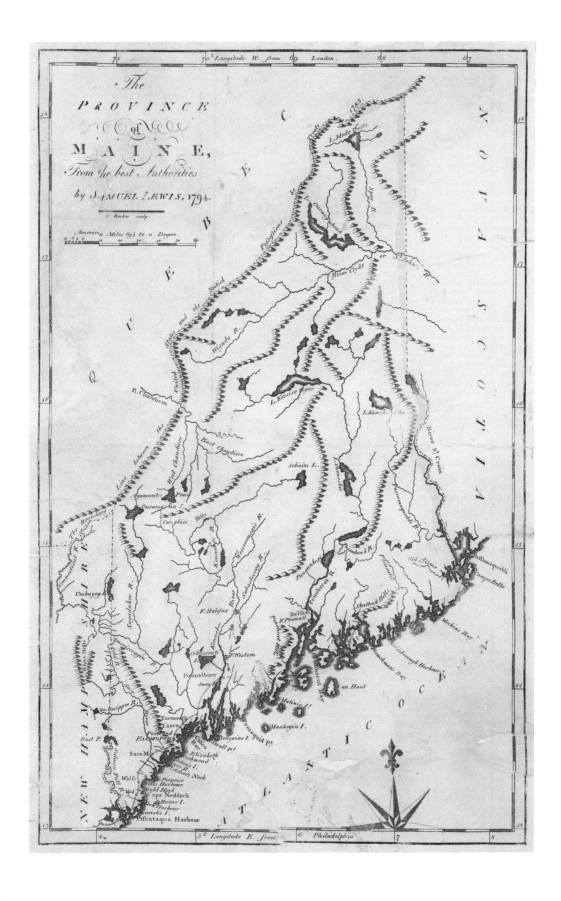

The
PROVINCE
of
MAINE,
From the best Authorities
by SAMUEL LEWIS, 1794.

W. Barker sculp.

American Miles 69½ to a Degree.

1794: A Conflagration and the Close of a Century

After independence was won, President Washington and the Congress were under constant pressure to create a viable nation. They had to ensure that the new country, with its weak military and struggling economy, would not become embroiled in the perennial conflicts between France and England. At the end of the eighteenth century, Congress and the new president struggled with matters large and small, from establishing a banking system to declaring a national day of Thanksgiving. At the same time, the General and his family were dealing with their own difficulties at home.

We know from William Allen Hayes Goodwin's letter to his daughter, Elizabeth, that Molly and Ichabod's house was destroyed in a fire "around 1795." William writes in the letter that the fire occurred on a night that his great-grandfather came "home late from court." The General, possibly weary after an unexpectedly long court session, might have neglected to bank the fire properly, or perhaps it was a servant who forgot to do the final check before retiring for the night. The General's daughter Sally (nine years old at the time of the fire), related to her great-nephew how they "brought up milk pans from the dairy."[138] We also know from Sally's recollections that the family was able to save some furnishings from the fire. Aside from the mirrors she mentions, I like to think that the tea table we found in the attic of the Hamilton House is one of those cherished belongings. I can see Molly and her then seventeen-year-old daughter Abigail frantically carrying the table out through the wide double doors. Brock Jobe, the author of *New England Furniture*, had dated their table to between 1760 and 1790, and his caption noted that the tea table had been in the General Goodwin House for generations.[139] It therefore seems likely that the table was purchased prior to the conflagration and, having been saved that night, remained with the family until

1958, the year Elizabeth Hayes Goodwin sold her ancestral home and donated some furniture and artifacts to Historic New England.

Regardless of the cause of the fire, the family story recounts that the General needed to rebuild and did so in a fashion "precisely like the old" house with a pediment whose style was no longer used in the 1790s and sash windows somewhat smaller than the fashion at the close of the eighteenth century.[140] Both Harvey and I continue to think it odd that the General rebuilt his house in the outdated architectural style of the first house.

During our first years at Old Fields, we had fun trying to solve these mysteries. Every tidbit uncovered in my research or Neill's archeological work helped us fill in the pieces. I remember being thrilled when I found a mention of our house in a book entitled *Maine Forms of Architecture*.[141] Denys Myers, the author of the chapter in which our house is included, dates the construction of the current General Ichabod Goodwin House to around 1797, confirming the Goodwin family lore. Myers goes on to echo our own sentiments when he states that it seems odd, although not unheard of, to build such an old-fashioned structure at the end of the eighteenth century. He notes the anachronistically small windows and mentions that the pediment was reminiscent of those made in the 1730s, or not long thereafter. The discrepancy between the style of our house and its presumed construction date led the author to write:

> *Dating houses from stylistic evidence alone, however, does not work well where vernacular examples are concerned…. Be that as it may, it is somewhat refreshing to find an example like the Goodwin House that may well, for a change be earlier than the date given.*[142]

While heeding the architectural historian's caveat, I did not doubt that there had been an earlier house that needed to be rebuilt after burning down in a fire, but I was not 100 percent certain that the original structure had been entirely destroyed by the fire and a completely new one erected in its place.

My skepticism was reinforced as we learned more about architectural developments at the end of the eighteenth century. Despite the fact that around 1750, maybe 1760 at the latest, a brick oven was almost always placed outside the hearth (some with their own flues), our beehive oven is located inside the back wall of the hearth. You can undoubtedly imagine the dangers of reaching over the hearth's open flames to place your breads or other baked dishes inside the oven's obscured opening at the back, dangers that Harvey recognizes from firsthand experience.

Placing the oven outside the hearth significantly increased the safety of the person preparing the meals, as Harvey likes to point out, so there would be no logical explanation not to include this design in the rebuild. With that in mind, we came to firmly believe that our hearth, at a minimum, had survived the destruction. Then in 2010 our carpenter noted some scorched boards along the northeast staircase off the keeping room, where he had discovered the redware fragment. This led us to speculate that some part of the first house, in addition to the hearth, had survived. But given that there is no sign of fire in the attic and given the physics of fire, we believe that the upper section was completely rebuilt.

In early 2013, when Harvey and I began to embrace a more semi-retired lifestyle we both became involved in the local historical society, and I finally had time to study the holdings of the various local archives around South Berwick. The extra time bore fruit, and in September 2013, on GenealogyBank's website, I found a news article in *The Newhampshire and Vermont Journal*, describing an event that took place on May 20, 1794:

> *On Saturday last, the dwelling house of Gen. Goodwin of Berwick was consumed by fire, with almost every article of his household furniture; it is conjectured this unfortunate accident was occasioned by a spark alighting from the chimney on the roof of the house, which before timely assistance could be afforded, baffled the art of man to save the building.*[143]

Rather a fanciful way of saying that the house burned down before the firefighters could arrive on the scene. Now we knew the actual date of the fire—1794, not 1795—and that the extent of the destruction went beyond an isolated section of the house; though nothing in the article precludes the possibility of some section surviving, it does suggest the attic would have had to be completely rebuilt. The reporter states that the house was "consumed by fire, with almost every article of his household furniture," and yet our house has an old-fashioned hearth in the keeping room and when it was rebuilt it originally had an outdated fireplace in the dining room, both of which likely survived the fire.

Even with the newspaper article, there were still a number of missing puzzle pieces. Why would the rebuilt house include an outdated oven when an alternative design that so improved the plight of the cook had been developed? Harvey and I still believe the hearth with its "old-fashioned" beehive oven survived intact and was incorporated into the house that stands today. Furthermore, why was the original seventeenth-century Spencer house not included in the "exact replica" rebuild when the archaeological evidence indicates that both houses burned at the same time? Were they physically connected? And, of course, we have yet to find any documents that provide evidence of exactly when the original Georgian home (the one that burned) was constructed.

These questions weigh on my mind as we continue our search for evidence, both archaeological and documentary, to clarify some of the mysteries.

HOME IMPROVEMENTS AND SOME FESTIVITIES It seems that life continued to grow more comfortable for the Goodwin family at the end of the eighteenth century. One can imagine the General after the war focusing on his civic responsibilities and commercial interests, expanding on the wealth he had inherited from the Captain, while Molly indulged in some interior decorating.

As we had already learned, dining rooms became widespread in New England at the end of the eighteenth century. It is very likely that Molly remade their informal parlour into a dining room right after the house was rebuilt. I believe that these formal dining rooms, as they are today, were likely reserved for special festivities like a family wedding reception, or the Thanksgiving holiday, or for entertaining guests, whereas most family meals would probably still have been served in the keeping room—just as today many of us use our kitchen for everyday meals, often because it is simply more convenient to serve food in close proximity to where it is prepared. For families like the Goodwins, aside from the ease of dining in the keeping room by the cooking fire, the monumental labor and cost of maintaining a fire in these newly appointed rooms would have limited their use from mid-November through March.

Though it is conjecture that Molly converted the parlour into a designated dining room, evidence indicates that Molly or the General did have the fireplace in that room redesigned. Richard Irons, a well-known restorer of historic hearths who was responsible for the work at Nathaniel Hawthorne's House of Seven Gables, informed us that the fireplace currently in our dining room was originally much larger. Fairly soon after the Goodwins had completed their new home, it appears the family made the decision to redesign the dining room fireplace to reflect the latest in hearth design. The original larger and deeper hearth was replaced by the shallow design developed by Count Rumford, whose design is still favored today for its energy efficiency (in fact, the fireplace in our modern Baltimore home was constructed with the proportions of a Rumford design).

The restorer's observation made us question yet again what might have been leftover from the fire in 1794. Would Molly and the General have rebuilt a large, outdated hearth just to replace it a few years later with the newer, energy-efficient Rumford design already popular by the end of the eighteenth century? Or did the hearth in the informal parlour survive the flames, as we suspect the one in the keeping room did? Our house continually reveals new details that keep alive our desire to keep searching for clues to solve the remaining mysteries. Harvey has a fantasy that one day we will discover a diary from the General or Molly with a lengthy entry discussing that fateful day in 1794 and describing in detail the reconstruction that followed.

In the first years after the new house was built, an itinerant artist was commissioned by the Goodwins to stencil wall decorations—a popular stylistic detail at the time—in the master's bedchamber of their rebuilt home. Unfortunately, the artist's name is not known, but while reading a book on American wall painting by Nina Fletcher Little, I came across illustrations showcasing the work of the same unnamed itinerant artist known for his "dainty borders…on an uncrowded wall space."[144] Alongside other examples of this artist's work—including the King Hooper Mansion in Marblehead, Massachusetts; the house in Exeter, New Hampshire, of John Phillips, the founder of the still extant *Phillips Exeter Academy*; the Peter Farnum home in Francestown and the Governor Franklin Pierce Homestead in Hillsborough, both also in New Hampshire—was an illustration of a wall decoration in the Ichabod Goodwin House, "Courtesy, Miss Elizabeth Goodwin."[145]

I can see this itinerant artist now, traveling throughout New England with his large leather pack, bucket hanging from its side, and wooden boards protruding from the top. His sales pitch would have encouraged homeowners to let him stencil their walls in a manner just like the fancy, and much more expensive, wallpapers found in the manor houses of England. His payment likely would have been room and board and a small amount of hard currency to pay for his journey to the next place of work.

Regrettably, in 1985 the owner of Old Fields decided to paint the master bedroom and covered over the original stenciled door- and window frames and walls. Thankfully, he took a number of photographs to document the eighteenth-century ornamentation, leaving those snapshots behind for future owners to appreciate. From those images, we know that Molly chose a pattern of quarter fans in the Sheraton style to be stenciled around the doors and windows and had the walls painted a dusty rose color. The fans had black spokes radiating out from their points like a sun burst, against an orange-brown background. They are placed in each corner inside a lovely border of white with black stencil designs. The succeeding generations of the Goodwin family must have cherished this charming wall treatment for, despite the serious deterioration through the years, the stenciling was never painted over for almost two hundred years.

I would love to have had the stenciling as part of our bedroom and think it rather a shame that the owner chose to paint the room rather than restore the pattern to its original beauty. There are any number of preservationists who would have been able to touch up the stencil design, although perhaps the expense was prohibitive. I am assuming that today's artists would doubtless expect far more recompense than just a meal.

BERWICK CELEBRATES THE SWEARING-IN OF OUR SECOND PRESIDENT   John Adams was sworn in as the second president in 1797, the same year that the architectural historian who wrote about the house's anachronistic details, believes the General and Molly had their house rebuilt. George Washington had voluntarily stepped down after his two terms, proving the skeptics wrong and allowing for our democracy to take hold. Citizens of the young nation took pride in the smooth transition and marked the occasion with celebrations to honor John Adams's *nativity* (as the inaugural ceremony was referred to at the time). Thus, on the fourth day of March 1797, as the swearing-in took place, Berwick and her citizens along with other towns across the United States of America marked the occasion with a long day of festivities, the details of which are described in town records and contemporary newspaper accounts.

One particularly detailed article appeared on March 8 in the New Hampshire paper *Oracle of the Day*.[146] The unidentified writer describes how on that inauguration day, the residents of Berwick awoke at dawn to the chiming of church bells, the first signal that this day was special. If anyone slept through the resonant ringing, they surely would have been startled from their sleep by the roar of sixteen guns fired soon after. John Haggens, tavern keeper and owner of the grand home that would later become the birthplace of Sarah Orne Jewett, had planned a "sumptuous entertainment" to take place after the orations at the meetinghouse where seventy townsmen had assembled. After all had feasted at Haggens's tavern, more guns were fired, followed by more toasting and drinking. After toasts were given for such luminaries as George Washington and John Adams, and then the governor of

Massachusetts and the Marquis de Lafayette, the town president offered a toast to Ichabod, the orator of the day: "May he in literature shine for brightness …" Jonathan Hamilton and Dr. Hovey likewise proposed toasts but none spoke that day with quite the flourish of our General who in turn, offered these few words to his brethren:

> *The town of Berwick—May its prosperity and happiness be equal to the politeness and hospitality of its inhabitants, the virtue and beauty of its fair, and the liberality of the present company.*[147]

This festive day concluded with a "splendid ball" at Berwick Academy, which shone with many candles lit for this distinctive occasion. The *Oracle* concluded that "[u]nanimity of sentiment … did honor to that ancient and federal town."[148]

These photographs of the master bedroom were taken by a previous owner, prior to painting over the stenciled decorations. They show the extent of the deterioration by the mid-1980s. The ca 1797 stenciled patterns in General Ichabod Goodwin's master's bedchamber were painted by an itinerant artist whose name is not known.

1807–1829: Politics, a Son's Death, and an Important Visitor

Much had changed in the years since the inauguration in 1797. With the first presidential campaign of John Adams, political parties emerged as an enduring part of government in the newborn democracy. Unsurprisingly, the inevitable result was a polarization of the governed. Adams, a Federalist, believed in the necessity of a strong central government. Thomas Jefferson, nominated by the Republicans as a fierce opponent of such a centralized body, advocated instead for a robust system based on states' rights. When Adams ran for reelection, the proponents of a decentralized government prevailed and in 1800 Thomas Jefferson was elected our third president, winning again in 1804.

In 1807, during his second term, President Jefferson called for an embargo as a response to the British impressments not only of British deserters but also of Americans taken from American vessels. The embargo was a fiasco. On the other side of the Atlantic, the impediment of trade had no impact on the British economy it was meant to harm. British exports flourished as the English focused on developing commerce with South America, avoiding the embargo by smuggling goods into the United States via Canada. Lasting until March 1809—just three days before the end of Jefferson's presidency—the embargo crushed American export opportunities and triggered a depression that lasted until the culmination of the War of 1812. During this time the economy of New England, so dependent upon shipping and international trade, basically collapsed.

(Circular) Treasury Department
31st May 1808

Sir

Complaints have been frequently made that in several ports of the State of Massachusetts, the general embargo Bond was still taken from all coasting Vessells instead of requiring a special one on each Voyage. This practice causes great dissatisfaction in those Districts where the Law has been carried into effect; and I had expected that my circular Letter of the 7th of April was calculated to remove every doubt as to the course to be pursued in regard to those Vessels whose employment is not confined to Bays, Sounds, Rivers and Lakes.

I am very respectfully
Sir
your obedt. servt.
Albert Gallatin

Joseph Wilson Esq
Collector
Marblehead.

An 1808 handwritten document signed by Albert Gallatin (treasurer under President Thomas Jefferson), that discusses the trade embargo with the British. This embargo negatively impacted New England.

THE JONATHAN HAMILTON ESTATE   Hamilton's estate, directly across the street from Old Fields, was among the countless New England households that endured significant financial setbacks in those terrible years of hardship between 1807 and 1814. Having died rather young in 1802, Hamilton, fortunately, was not alive to see his land sold off.

One of Berwick's wealthiest citizens, Hamilton had been enormously successful as an importer, a merchant, and a shipbuilder. His sons did not share the same success. An advertisement placed in 1810 by one of his sons, Oliver Hamilton, announced the auction of his father's house, along with all of the outbuildings and land, even his store in Portsmouth.[149] An article about the Hamilton family published on the website of the Old Berwick Historical Society points out that the tax assessment for Oliver's property diminished with each successive year between 1807 and 1812.[150] Perhaps the sons did not inherit their father's good business sense, or quite likely, they were unfortunate enough to be the heads of a shipping empire right around the time of Jefferson's embargo. The decision to pay for the building of two new ships during the embargo—one in 1808 and the other in 1810—turned out not to be a wise choice.

Olive, the daughter of Jonathan and Mary Hamilton, and her husband, Joshua Haven, eventually purchased the estate in 1811 for $4,000. The couple ran the estate until 1815, but during those difficult years for the New England economy, they were unable to revive the family fortune. In turn, the Havens were forced to sell the property in 1815.[151]

Hamilton's holdings changed hands twice more. One transfer took place in 1839 when the General's cousin Alpheus tried his luck with the Hamilton property. Alpheus had a plan. He gave up on the shipping industry and instead worked the land as a farm, raising sheep and growing apples, corn, and beans. He was successful for a while, but by 1877 it had to be admitted that the rocky soil of Maine was incapable of competing with the newly established farming industry of the Midwest. The descendants of Alpheus Goodwin found themselves unable to pay their bills. This time, Jonathan Hamilton's lovely home was abandoned and fell into a state of disrepair. Saddened by the decay, a local resident stepped in at the end of the nineteenth century to revive what was, for her, an important part of her town's history.

In 1898, Sarah Orne Jewett, the famed writer and an ardent devotee of South Berwick, the town in which she was born, contacted the Tysons. The two wealthy Tyson women—Emily, a widow of the president of the Baltimore and Ohio Railroad, and her stepdaughter Elise—were good friends of Jewett and resided in Boston, a city oft-frequented by the author.

The pair were persuaded by Jewett to purchase the Hamilton estate, thus saving it from certain ruin. Soon the two women set about restoring the house, the outbuildings, and the grounds, decorating the interior in the then-popular Colonial Revival style. Today the Hamilton House, along with the Tyson gardens and cottage, is one of the feature properties of Historic New England and a wonderful landmark for the town.

POLITICS BECOMES PERSONAL When the nonpartisan Washington stepped down after serving two terms, he established the precedent that no American president would serve more than eight years, with the lone exception of Franklin Delano Roosevelt, who remained in office for a partial fourth term during the perilous years of World War II. With the election of the second president, the country was divided into two major political parties—the Federalists and the Republicans—another precedent that would last into the twenty-first century. The General, our second Ichabod, sided with the soon-to-be second president and remained a loyal Federalist. In 1792 he successfully ran for representative of his party in the General Court of the District of Maine; and then, in 1793, Massachusetts governor John Hancock appointed him high sheriff of York County. I suspect that the General's experiences running the two prison barracks outside Boston during the Revolutionary War proved useful while he was serving as high sheriff from 1793 through 1820 (aside from one unpleasant interruption), the year Maine became an independent state.

Published in 1863, *A History of the Law, the Courts, and the Lawyers of Maine*, by William Willis, includes a section on the General that is over three and a half pages long and leaves the reader with a sympathetic impression of a man of noble character. Willis mentions the General's birth on what he called the family's "ancestral farm." Willis also describes the younger Ichabod's journey to Fort Ticonderoga (called Fort Carillon at the time) with his father, the Captain, during the French and Indian War, and comments on the unexpected break in Ichabod's twenty-five-plus-year tenure as high sheriff, noting the grace with which the General handled the situation. Willis concludes with the death of the by-then "corpulent" eighty-six-year-old man.[152]

Willis explains that with the return of peace after the Revolutionary War various official positions were bestowed upon those who had devoted themselves to the cause of independence as a way of acknowledging their service; hence the appointment of Ichabod to the office of sheriff of York County, still a part of Massachusetts, in 1793. Willis then elaborates on how partisan divides led to Ichabod's removal for one term in 1811.

Similar to today, the political atmosphere was fiercely partisan at the beginning of the nineteenth century. (A number of newspaper articles published in 1814 described the political schisms that were plaguing the country while we were still engaged in the War of 1812. The states might have been better served working together for their common cause.) In 1811, the Federalist governor of Massachusetts, Christopher Gore, lost to Elbridge Gerry of the Republican Party. Once in office Governor Gerry, somewhat famous for the term *gerrymander*,[153] quickly proceeded to remove many of the Federalist officeholders.[154] Our General was caught up in this sweep and was told he would be relinquishing his position to Colonel Lane that year. Willis's account describes how the General, after promptly meeting with his successor, magnanimously invited the colonel to spend the night at Old Fields.

By the next election the people of Massachusetts were unhappy with the strong-armed Republican governor and his crony Republican legislature and replaced him with a Federalist. Ichabod was immediately reinstated as sheriff. Upon hearing the news, Ichabod contacted Colonel Lane who, perhaps recalling the General's hospitable gesture, "proceeded in the kindest manner to perform the necessary duties of the occasion."[155]

PARTISANSHIP AND STATEHOOD While serving as sheriff in 1814, the General ran for public office, hoping to represent Berwick in the Massachusetts state congress. Ichabod lost the election by 50 votes, the electorate clearly favoring his Republican opponent, Benjamin Greene, who handily won with 137 votes. What caused this electoral shift in Berwick, where the Federalists had held sway for so long?

In 1814, Berwick—or, rather, South Berwick, as the southeastern corner of the town was rechristened that year—reflects yet again the issues concerning our young nation as a whole. South Berwick was established by carving out a section of what had been the larger town of Berwick prior to 1814. Based on contemporary news articles, some part of that decision may have stemmed from the desire of the Federalist party to create a reliable electorate for voting on issues such as trade with Britain.[156] In the second decade of the nineteenth century districts like South Berwick were being gerrymandered, just as today.

An 1814 news article from the *Boston Patriot* suggested that the Federalist-leaning Massachusetts state government had hoped that a newly formed South Berwick would join other towns in defiance of the federal government—at the time under the administration of James Madison, a Republican—by supporting a petition to eliminate the reinstituted embargo originally sponsored by the Republican president Thomas Jefferson.[157] Their hopes—

and perhaps their conscious redistricting efforts—were in vain. Not only did Republicans gain a majority in small towns like Berwick, but similar majorities were created in other states across America, as well as in Washington, D.C., our capital since 1790.

The conclusion of the War of 1812 in December of 1814 brought an end to the embargo and also provided the District of Maine with a legitimate rationale to once more request its independence. Massachusetts, the Mainers asserted, had evaded its responsibility to protect Maine's coastline from the British navy, possibly as a cost-saving measure. The farmers of interior Maine also felt overtaxed and that those officials dominating the government of Massachusetts only represented urban concerns, leaving the people of the District of Maine woefully underrepresented, reflecting a historic and never-ending divison between urban and rural populations.

It would take another six years, but on March 15, 1820, Maine was granted statehood.

A TRAGIC DEATH   In the summer of 1814, seventy-one-year-old Ichabod was still quite active in his role as major general. There were fierce battles in those final months of the War of 1812 with Britain, and Ichabod was responsible for the protection of the harbor at Kittery Point. On September 22 the major general dispatched two hundred infantry and fifty artillerists for the defense of the seaboard.[158] His son Dominicus, twenty-three at the time, was among the troops sent to fortify the breastworks of the harbor.[159]

The work was arduous, but the group accomplished its task in one day. On September 23 Dominicus was home again and despite being worn out from the preceding days at the harbor, the young man was determined to take a walk. I can imagine him enjoying the scenery at a time of year when Maine is at its most beautiful. While enjoying that stroll, Dominicus "fell, and died instantly," as reported in his obituary in the *Dartmouth Gazette.*[160] The second-youngest son of the General and Molly, the same obituary states, was a bright and well-loved young man. After graduating from Dartmouth College in 1811, he had gone on to pursue a law degree and had just been admitted to the bar the year before his father sent him to help defend the seacoast of Maine and New Hampshire.

As further testimony to the character of Ichabod and Molly's son, the *Dartmouth Gazette* printed a poem written by a former classmate of his at Dartmouth College entitled "To the Memory of Dominicus Goodwin, Esq."[161] The poem, while rather flowery (as was the style of the time) praises the boy's nobility, grace, and liberal mind. The other obituaries, likewise, note his intelligence, kindness, and promise.

Could exhaustion have caused so sudden a demise of such a young a man? After some research, I found articles mentioning an epidemic in 1814 of spotted fever, a disease we know today as typhus. This louse-borne illness is notorious for its prevalence among soldiers in wartime due to crowded conditions, an inability to wash clothes, and, yes, simple fatigue. Could it be that Dominicus was infected while at Kittery Point? We know that the pre-antibiotic world was precarious and deadly and such sudden deaths were not uncommon. And so, sadly, we find the General and Molly arranging another funeral service, just a few months after mourning the death of their oldest son, Ichabod, who had died in June of that same year, at the age of forty-four.

In honoring the memory of yet another beloved son, northern hospitality would have required that a substantial meal be offered at the Goodwin home after the funeral service. As I picture Molly mourning the loss of a child for the second time that year, I imagine that she might have preferred to prepare something that did not take much thought—a plain, everyday sort of dish, though maybe prepared in a slightly more elaborate way than usual. Perhaps a rustic chicken and dumplings with several large boiled puddings.

A MEAL IN MEMORY OF A DEAR SON   Following my now-familiar process of searching for a historic recipe that sounds both possible and appetizing, I turned as usual to my historic cookbooks and to the modern ones with historic recipes to find guidelines for making Molly's chicken, dumplings, and gingerbread pudding. As with previous meals, I started out thinking that the dishes would be pretty straightforward; then, the more I read, the more confusing it became. Some recipes called for a whole chicken, some required a cut-up fowl. Some said to brown the fowl and vegetables before poaching, others had no such instruction. Not surprisingly, the types of vegetables varied, as did the cooking times.

Finding a proper recipe for the dumplings was especially difficult. Almost every recipe included baking powder, but I know that baking powder did not exist until the mid-nineteenth century. Interestingly, each dumpling recipe that did omit the chemical leavening agent was different from the others. I was faced with choosing either a really basic recipe of flour, water, and salt, which sounded heavy and dull, or one with additional combinations involving eggs, fat, and milk, or milk *and* stock. Some dumplings were then simmered in the soup or stew, while others were to be boiled separately in water or chicken stock.

Faced with so many choices, I constructed a recipe based on several sources, devising my own version of this popular eighteenth-century dish.

Poached Chicken and Dumplings

Serves 6–8 (makes 15–20 dumplings)

POACHED CHICKEN

1 5- or 6-pound chicken, cut in quarters
1 quart chicken stock, preferably homemade
5 carrots, sliced about ⅓ inch thick
4 stalks celery, sliced thinly
1 onion, halved
3 sprigs parsley
Salt, to taste

Place chicken in a stockpot, or a cast-iron Dutch oven if using a fireplace. Add chicken stock plus water to cover. Slowly bring to a boil for about 15 minutes, intermittently skimming the surface until cloudy foam subsides.

Add the vegetables, parsley, and salt. Cook slowly on a crane over fire, or on the stovetop, keeping bubbles formed around the rim to a bare simmer.

Once the chicken is quite tender and falling off bones, about 1 hour, remove from heat. Place the chicken on a counter or cutting board, setting aside until cool enough to handle.

Strain the broth into a clean pot, reserving the vegetables.

Remove skin from the chicken and shred the meat into bite-size pieces. Place the shredded chicken and the vegetables back into the broth, cover, and set aside.

DUMPLINGS

1 tablespoon softened butter or
      other soft fat
1 cup water
1 teaspoon salt
2 cups flour
2 eggs, lightly beaten
½ cup heavy cream
Parsley to taste, chopped (for a garnish)

Boil water in a clean pot. Melt the butter in the boiling water. Then add salt and stir. Add the flour and stir again. Leave to cool.

Fold in the beaten eggs and mix to form a dough. Pinch off about 1 inch of the dough at a time and shape into balls.

Bring the chicken broth to a boil, then reduce heat to a simmer.

Drop the dumplings into the simmering broth with the chicken and vegetables and poach for 15 to 20 minutes.

Add ½ cup of the heavy cream and stir. Add the chopped parsley and serve.

I felt that cooking this dish over the fire was just as easy as using my stovetop—aside, of course, from the effort it took to prepare the bed of coals. The resulting flavor, however, was definitely superior.

STEAMED GINGER PUDDING

Adapted from Sandra L. Oliver's Saltwater Foodways
Serves 6

3½ cups flour
1½ teaspoons ginger
¼ teaspoon ground cloves
1 teaspoon baking soda
1 cup molasses
1¼ cups milk (Oliver states 1½ cups but I achieved the right consistency with less)
½ cup butter, melted

Sift the dry ingredients together in a mixing bowl.

In another bowl, mix the molasses with the milk. Add the melted butter. Add the wet ingredients to the dry and stir.

To steam the pudding, grease a large bowl or pudding basin and pour in the batter, leaving some room at the top for expansion. Cover with a well-dampened dish towel and tie cloth around the basin.

Place the basin in a large pot filled with enough water to come halfway up the sides of the basin. Bring water to a boil, then reduce heat, and keep at a simmer for 3 hours or longer, until pudding is firm enough to spoon into serving bowls. As the water evaporates, add boiling water to maintain a level halfway up the basin's sides.

The author of this recipe suggests steaming the pudding for three hours and serving. For me, the three hours did not begin to suffice for cooking the pudding to an edible stage. My version actually took closer to five hours, so I suggest that if you are planning to serve this dish for dessert on the evening you are preparing it, you might want to allow extra time. The pudding is equally good hot or cold; but you can easily reheat leftovers in a pan of hot water over a fire or in a few inches of water in a slow cooker. Alternatively you can remove the pudding from its basin and reheat in a microwave.

Here in the States, I believe we are missing out on this most comforting dish, for traditional English steamed pudding is rarely found on an American menu, not even during the winter holiday season.

1816: THE YEAR WITHOUT A SUMMER   The winter of 2014-2015 offered me some rather unwelcome insight into the frosty climate early New Englanders experienced during the years known as the "Little Ice Age"—a period of unusually cold weather, particularly between 1650 and 1715.[162] December 2014 was not too bad, but January was fairly chilly, and by February the nighttime temperatures were consistently dropping below zero. According to the weather forecasters, Eastern Canada had sent New England a polar vortex. While the thermostat may have said fifteen degrees, it felt like two with the windchill taken into account. On this particular morning, getting dressed for my regular exercise walk took a little longer. I put on my thermal leggings, wool socks, heavy knit pants, long-sleeve thermal undershirt, knit turtleneck sweater, a down coat, wool hat, and gloves. The exhausting ordeal took around ten minutes, and by the time I finished I felt five pounds heavier but prepared to face the bitter cold.

When Harvey and I first told our friends and family we were moving to Maine, invariably their initial response was, "But it's so cold." And every year since, when we return to Maryland at holiday time, our extreme winters are an unavoidable topic of discussion. To clarify, southern coastal Maine is actually not that cold. Here, the ocean keeps the temperatures of the easternmost portion of the state somewhat moderated, often only five degrees cooler than Baltimore (though nighttime temperatures average a good ten to fifteen degrees cooler). Also, Harvey and I prefer the cold to the mid-Atlantic summer heat and humidity. Yes, during the summer you can go swimming off the New Jersey coast without freezing—water temperatures along the mid-Atlantic in August average about seventy degrees, whereas in waters off the beaches around Portland, Maine, the temperature is usually just above sixty degrees. That ten-degree difference feels more significant than you might think, yet I still prefer Maine, where in the cooler months one has the option to add an extra layer of clothing or a comforter, as opposed to suffering the oppressive heat and humidity I recall in those midsummer days back in Maryland. However, if our first summer had been anything like the summer of 1816, Harvey and I might have considered fleeing, as so many Mainers did that year.

In an area used to about four months of frost-free days, there were less than two months that year; instead there was sleet, snow, and killing frosts throughout the summer months.[163] Snow fell for an hour and a half on Thursday, June 6, in Bangor, Maine. That evening it also snowed in Hallowell, Maine, where the snow continued on Friday and for over three hours on Saturday. Later that summer, the July 6 issue of the *Portsmouth Oracle* recorded eighteen inches of snow in Cabot, Vermont.[164] Alas, the summer of 1816 never did improve. There was frost in July and the ponds were iced over in August.

Of course the inhabitants of New England could not have known that the extreme cold was the result of an enormous volcanic eruption in what is today Indonesia.[165] The gases and particulates from the explosion were carried far and wide, blocking the sun in Northern Europe, Canada, and the northeastern region of the United States. As a result of the cold, thousands of Mainers fled, many of them to Ohio. Ichabod and Molly remained at Old Fields despite that strange summer. They had already endured the difficult years of war with Britain and Jefferson's embargo, so they were used to tough times. They had land and wealth, both of which undoubtedly contributed to their ability to survive that season and the loss of that all-important staple crop, corn.

1824: AN IMPORTANT VISTOR   Early in my research on the Goodwins I was excited to discover connections between South Berwick's famed resident Sarah Orne Jewett and two of the Goodwin women. In addition to her friendship with the young Elizabeth Goodwin, the novelist was quite close to Sophia Hayes Goodwin, the wife of the fourth Ichabod Goodwin to live at Old Fields. Based on her letters, Sophia (or "Lizzie," as she signed her letters held at the Dartmouth library) was quite the lively conversationalist.[166] Jewett was very proud of her town's history and was known to have spent a considerable amount of time interviewing the older Goodwin. Born in 1824, Sophia was twenty-five years her senior and would have been an invaluable source of South Berwick's earlier history. I can envision Jewett listening intently to Sophia's firsthand account of the exciting visit of Marie-Joseph-Paul-Yves-Roch-Gilbert du Motier, or more simply, the Marquis de Lafayette.

The legendary Frenchman who had joined the American effort against the British during the Revolutionary War retired from his position in the French legislature in 1824. That same year, President Monroe invited this former ally to return to America and travel the country to visit the young nation's citizenry. As the fiftieth anniversary of the signing of the Declaration of Independence drew near, American feelings of patriotism seemed to be fading considerably. Monroe had proposed this tour in the hopes of rekindling the patriotic fervor of his countrymen, reasoning that the many parades and banquets held to honor this great friend of the republic might provide the populace with a symbolic, as well as physical, reminder of their history.[167]

And so, in July 1824, this loyal comrade of George Washington sailed from France, disembarking at Staten Island, New York, on August 15. Throughout the remainder of that year, until September 7 of the following year, when he set sail for France, Lafayette traveled six thousand miles and visited every state in our new nation (twenty-four at the time). Everywhere he stopped, Lafayette found cheering crowds and festive ceremonies to celebrate his friendship with General Washington and his support for the American cause.

President Monroe had assessed the situation correctly. Viewing America's great ally riding in front of grand parades rallied the public. Crowds gathered everywhere to greet General Washington's important friend and military partner. Boston's *Columbian Centinel* describes one such parade with almost four thousand participants, with Lafayette at the head of the procession in his "splendid barouche."[168]

On June 24, 1825, after having spent the previous evening in Dover, New Hampshire, the marquis crossed the bridge connecting Rollinsford, New Hampshire, to South Berwick. As he arrived at the edge of town, Lafayette was welcomed by the men, women, and children of the community. In 1885, at the age of sixty-one, Sophia wrote a reminiscence of that special day in her notebook, which was later printed in the *Eastern Argus*. The article, entitled "The Visit of General Lafayette: A Childhood Reminiscence," begins:

> *I remember with great distinctness the visit of Gen. Lafayette to South Berwick,*
> *for I was then about twelve years old, a time of life when a visit of such impor-*
> *tance would make a great impression.*[169]

Given that Sophia was born in 1824, the memory could not have been her own. The article suggests that it was her mother's, though again the dating does not work. According to that spiral-bound collection of notes on Old Fields, it was Sophia's brother, John Lord Hayes, who had recalled being twelve years old at the time their distinguished visitor came to town.[170] This notebook has proven reliable in almost every detail, so I tend to believe it was the brother who had enthusiastically related his memory to his sister.

Such an exciting affair must certainly have been a significant event for the whole family. I can picture the scene unfolding. According to a contemporary newspaper article, we know that the bridge between Rollinsford and South Berwick was adorned with oak leaves with roses scattered about. An arch was built especially for the occasion and draped with evergreens. The women and girls were on one side of the road, wearing white and blue dresses; the men and boys on the opposite side, sporting hats inscribed "Welcome Lafayette."[171]

Judge Benjamin Greene delivered a speech proclaiming everyone's utmost appreciation for the marquis's service to America in its pursuit of independence. Greene then took his honored guest's arm and escorted Lafayette and his son, George Washington, to Mrs. Frost's tavern for a lavish breakfast. Sophia noted how handsome her father looked in his claret-colored frock as he served as master of ceremonies.

There was one exciting detail that Sophia was probably quite animated about while sharing the tale with her attentive audience. After the feast at Mrs. Frost's, the marquis was told that there was one more place he was to visit while in South Berwick. He was then taken to the home of Mrs. Cushing, a woman he had met while fighting the British so many years before. Evidently, poor Mrs. Cushing had not been informed until that morning of this unexpected honor and was embarrassed to have nothing to offer such an important visitor. She called on her friend Susan Lord Hayes, Sophia's mother, to see if she could help. As Susan was planning a party of her own that evening, she had just finished icing a plum cake, which she readily gave her friend. Mrs. Cushing was therefore able to offer the marquis a basket of "beautifully frosted plum cake" along with a glass of currant wine that she proudly declared was "made with her own hands."[172]

THE GENERAL'S FINAL YEARS AND BERWICK ACADEMY   Between 1826 and 1828, the General served as president of Berwick Academy. This important institution still stands today as one of the town's signature achievements and has been an economic anchor for the growth of South Berwick over the last two centuries.

At the end of the preceding century, the town leaders had come to recognize the impor-tance of "useful knowledge" and set out to ensure quality schooling for their young ones. In 1791, on an undoubtedly cold day in January, Parson John Tompson set out on horseback for Boston to present a petition requesting that Berwick be allowed to found an academy. Unfortunately, the petition was denied on the parson's first attempt, so a second journey was necessary that winter.

In February the town leaders announced the initiation of a fund for a new school to be called Berwick Academy, and in March the charter was finally approved by Governor John Hancock—the same patriot with whom then Lieutenant Colonel Goodwin had worked at the Provincial Congress in Watertown, and that same noted American who had pardoned Joshua Abbot, the man accused of murdering his neighbor. With the charter officially ap-proved, the founding members began to solicit the funds they needed to proceed. Many of the town's most prominent citizens were behind the efforts to establish the academy, includ-ing the General, the shipping merchant Jonathan Hamilton, who donated £100, and Judge Benjamin Chadbourne, who contributed six acres of land on which the school was built. Not only was our General part of this illustrious group, but he was also the—undoubtedly proud—father of two alumni, James and Dominicus.

Berwick Academy continues to this day as a private day school, now educating both boys and girls from Berwick and beyond. Perched high on the hill, the original school build-ing still stands and is fondly and appropriately referred to as *The 1791 House*. After expand-ing, the academy's beautiful campus came to include the lovely house William Allen Hayes built at the beginning of the nineteenth century. The handsome William Hayes Fogg Memo-rial Library was added later at the end of that same century.[173]

1829: THE GENERAL'S DEATH   On a recent depressingly rainy, foggy morning at the close of December, when it could not possibly have been much darker, I was in the dining room, staring out the window. As I pulled my robe ever tighter against the chill, I turned to the fireplace to close the damper to shut out the cold. My mind wandered back to another year that I had read about in my research—1829, a year when the weather had been sim-ilarly dreary, with an inordinate amount of rain and snow.

In April of that year, spring rains had caused much flooding in South Berwick, the Salmon Falls producing a "deafening roar" with the "abyss below boiling and foaming in endless turmoil."[174] The water from the rainfall had combined with the spring thaw, washing away numerous bridges, including the one Lafayette had crossed just a few years before. (Newspapers referred to this weather phenomenon as a *freshet*.) Some of the houses along Main Street, including that of Dr. Hovey, were flooded with two feet of standing water. To this day, South Berwick struggles with the same issue, as any heavy rain will flood the area where Liberty Street flows into Route 236, the very area where Dr. Hovey resided those many years ago.

One New England gentleman who kept a daily meteorological journal noted that between May 1828 and May 1829 there were seventy-three inches of "water" (meaning a mixture of rain, snow, and hail). Thunder and lightning had filled the skies for forty-five days—this area is not known for thunderstorms—and the skies were cloudy for a hundred and thirty-nine days. The journal also notes that March was colder than December.[175]

In 1829 the General was eighty-six years old. He had lost his beloved wife, Molly, four years earlier. President Andrew Jackson had just begun his first term, continuing the Republican dominance over the now much-weakened Federalist Party. At this point in his life, the General must have been content to let his son Andrew manage the family affairs. By 1829, Andrew was head of Old Fields, his two other brothers, Ichabod and Dominicus, having both died in 1814. The General's third son had proven himself worthy of the inheritance of the Goodwin name and property.

On May 29, 1829, the *Christian Mirror* reported that the "kind," "affectionate," and "charitable General Ichabod Goodwin" had "gone down to the grave deeply lamented."[176] The lengthy obituary states that the General "lived a life of usefulness" and enumerates his service to the country as a secretary of the "Colonial Convention," officer in the revolutionary war [sic], the first major general of Maine, and high sheriff of the county of York. The article, possibly due to the religious affiliation of the journal, goes into much detail on the General's religious sentiments and peaceful "passage to the tomb." Seconding the notion that Ichabod's passing was relatively tranquil, William Willis in his *A History of the Law, the Courts and the Lawyers of Maine* noted that he died "without a struggle and without a pang."[177]

With his ties to the militia, the government, and various commercial activities as well as the two years he had recently served as president of Berwick Academy, we know that the General was an important member of his community. Moreover, the family was quite wealthy by early-nineteenth-century standards and had been living at Old Fields for more than eighty-five years. It can be assumed that his funeral was well attended and the foods offered at the Goodwin home afterward especially fine. I can envision Andrew and his wife Elizabeth's dining room, its bountiful table laden with a delectable baked ham as its centerpiece. A white cloth was likely spread over the dining table, the family silver polished, and the blue-and-white Staffordshire plates stacked on the hutch in the keeping room for the mourners to help themselves.

For this important occasion I imagine they would have had baked white rolls—a treat reserved for special occasions, as white flour was very expensive at the time [178]—to accompany the ham, and perhaps corn bread, a salad, and pickled beets. There may very well have been a roast leg of lamb to supplement the ham and a rich cake and boiled custard to finish. The numerous family and friends who would have come to honor this distinguished citizen would surely have been impressed by such a lavish display.

Baked Ham with Madeira

Serves 15–20

15-pound country ham
  (I use the uncooked, bone-in ham from Edwards in Virginia)
3½ cups Madeira (I use Rainwater Madeira)
½ cup maple syrup
½ cup rum

Soak the ham in cold water for 48 hours (less time if you like a stronger, aged flavor), changing the water every 12 hours or so.

Put the ham in a large pot, and add the Madeira and enough water to cover. Bring to a boil, reduce heat and simmer for 1 hour.

Preheat oven to 350F, or fire up a brick oven to 400F.

Drain the liquid, and reserve for sauce. Put the ham in a baking pan and rub with maple syrup. Cover with lid (or foil if no lid). Place in a Dutch oven and bake for 4 hours, removing cover or foil for last half hour, or until internal temperature is about 155F.

Place the reserved wine in a saucepan, bring to a boil, and reduce to 1½ cups. Add rum and continue to boil for 3 minutes.

Serve ham warm or at room temperature, with sauce on the side.

Walking the Walk: Our Weekend in the Eighteenth Century

Harvey and I woke up on a Monday morning in our typical twenty-first-century manner. We turned on the lights, started the coffee brewing in the Breville coffeemaker, and checked our emails. It was warm, it was easy, but a part of us wanted to go back down the winding front staircase, back into the old keeping room, and back to the simulation of an eighteenth-century lifestyle we had created that past weekend.

It was fall of 2014 and we had been living at Old Fields for ten years by this time. From that first morning I woke up in the General Ichabod Goodwin home, I have often tried to envision what it must have been like to walk in the footsteps of the Goodwins, the effort and time it took every day just to keep the house running, even to cook a simple meal. Now I wanted to re-create, to the best of my ability, my own time-consuming eighteenth-century lifestyle (though one notably less laborious than that lived by those early Goodwins). The plan was to "walk the walk," as they say, using the hearth-cooking skills we had acquired, the eighteenth-century accessories (or their reproductions) we had purchased, and what knowledge we had gleaned of that past world. With the completion of the furnishing of the house—the music book being our last acquisition, in 2010—Harvey and I both felt we had been successful in our attempt to re-create a sense of the world of the Ichabods, but by the spring of 2014 we each felt we wanted to go even further with our attempts. So we started to plan a whole weekend in which we would forgo modern appliances, electricity, any processed food—in other words, to shed as many of the trappings of our twenty-first-century lifestyle as we felt capable of, recognizing that a purist might dismiss our concessions.

For our experiment we chose a weekend in early November, confident that we could count on the weather being cold enough for three days of continual hearth cooking. (I recall reading that if we suddenly found ourselves back in time, in the palace of Queen Elizabeth I, we would probably not survive, the intimation being that our twenty-first-century selves could not survive even the most pampered lifestyle of the sixteenth century.) This time our "going back in time" would be a well-orchestrated adventure, not an unwanted condition imposed by Mother Nature as we had experienced our first spring here, when that heavy, wet snowstorm knocked out the electricity for six days.

We turned the heat down to forty-five degrees (the temperature outside was about the same), swore off electricity, and ate almost exclusively what we cooked ourselves in the fireplace or beehive oven using the keeping room's unheated, enclosed entryway as our refrigerator. We shut off our cell phones and ignored our laptops. Due to the cold, visitors were entertained in either the keeping room or the dining room, where the fires were kept going. We ourselves strayed no farther into the twenty-first century than our modern-day kitchen, where some of our pots and pans and most of our provisions were stored. I must confess that we also made use of the second floor *necessary* (or bathroom, as we now call it).

PREP DAY Friday was to be our preparation day, the day we had set aside for some of the hearth cooking that could be prepared in advance, before we immersed ourselves in our imagined eighteenth-century lifestyle of the Goodwins. The recipes we would make today were ones I believed the first two Goodwin wives might have prepared a day or two before the meal, ones that would keep overnight in the keeping room "refrigerator" centered on the eastern wall of the room.

Undoubtedly, both Elizabeth and Molly would have set aside one day each week for baking, so I knew that making the two yeast-based recipes—Sally Lunn bread and Election Day cake—would be the obvious choices for our pre-experiment preparations. We had already decided that Harvey would do the bread while I made the cake. For all the thought we had put into the organization of this weekend's prep day, we had not thought to allow time in our schedule for two doughs with different rising times. Nor had we thought to coordinate their baking. The cake and the yeast-based bread were both scheduled to go into our one brick oven, despite each requiring a different temperature. Furthermore, yeast doughs are somewhat unpredictable even in a modern room with central heating, so here, in our eighteenth-century keeping room, all we could do was make an educated guess as to the time needed for the dough to rise.

The day before, while reviewing the historic recipes I had chosen to make that weekend,

I noted that one original source called for potato yeast as the sole leavening agent. After looking up how to make that old-time fermentation agent, I thought, *Great, sounds easy, I can do that*. Unfortunately, as I read through the whole process more carefully, it became clear that I would need several days to complete the task, not the one day I had before baking. Promising myself I would make the potato yeast-based Sally Lunn bread someday soon, I settled on store-bought fresh yeast—this less-processed product is a distinctly better option than the powdered dry, or instant, yeasts found in most supermarkets.

On Friday, we woke early to find that everything had been covered by a gentle snowfall the night before. The resulting picture-postcard, snow-covered New England views from our windows helped to soften the unavoidable modern intrusions such as the asphalt road and cable wires. By eight o'clock, what passes for sun on a late-autumn morning in Maine was struggling to clear the treetops. The post-snow, powder-blue sky was spectacular. The first blazing rays of sunlight peered through dusky gray streaks, then luminous white clouds appeared sharply silhouetted against a darkening blue sky that then changed back to layers of light and dark gray. As the day proceeded, the sky began to brighten, lighting up the snow-covered evergreens on the hillside opposite the Salmon Falls River. It was one of those wonderful Maine days with an extraordinarily changeable sky that I so enjoy.

After my brief indulgence of watching Mother Nature's artistry, I gathered the ingredients needed for the two recipes. Harvey started first, as the Sally Lunn bread dough needed numerous risings, presumably requiring more time. I started the yeast cake about an hour after Harvey began. The process of creaming the sugar with the butter, even with an electric mixer, takes a fairly long time; thinking of my wimpy muscles, I wondered how much longer it would take to do it by hand. I was pleasantly surprised that the time needed to complete the process manually was not that different from using an electric mixer. Moreover, it was fascinating to watch the transformation as the sugar and butter became one.

Without our usual dependence on machines, we both noticed a similar phenomenon—through the process of manual labor, we became much more aware of the chemical changes as the ingredients slowly came together. For me, the creaming process and the effect of adding the eggs were initially discouraging. I remember thinking that these are tasks best done by machine. Upon adding the first egg, the mixture looked worryingly sloppy, and I despaired of ever achieving a cohesive mixture. With the second egg, however, everything came together rather quickly. Soon I had a beautiful base for the yeast that was happily bubbling away in its warm water bath, "proving" its viability; hence, *proofed* yeast.

While the yeasts for the two doughs were working their magic, I made a cranberry relish that, according to the website for Lamb's Artillery, was based on the English concept of a red currant sauce. Clearly a fellow historic-food enthusiast, John Lamb notes that the "meals prepared over an open fire from eighteenth-century recipes are simply mouth-watering." I wholeheartedly agree.

After a quick lunch, Harvey started the fire in preparation for our baking. We checked our doughs to see if they had risen sufficiently to go into the preheated beehive oven. Neither was quite ready. Of course, the brick oven *was*. Trying to guess how much longer we should feed the fire so that it would remain hot but not get too hot by the time the doughs were ready was a definite challenge for us novices. When I think about it now, I should have realized that a yeast dough with sugar (sugar impedes the ability of the yeast to expand quickly) would rise much more slowly than my usual, more savory breads; and the added weight of the currants in the Election Day cake dough slowed the process down even more. Fortunately, it all worked out.

The Sally Lunn bread finished its many risings first and was ready to go into the bee-hive oven before the oven had a chance to cool down. Harvey's bread was fully baked an hour before the cake was even ready to go into the oven, giving us sufficient time to reheat the brick oven to the correct temperature.

The remainder of the prep day proceeded relatively problem-free as Harvey and I discussed the activities, recipes, and chores that would take place over the weekend. We wanted to make sure there would be no further competition for the use of the beehive oven or the hearth, its crane, or the trivet. As bedtime approached, we were faced with the first of a number of decisions we would have to make, depending on how "purist" we wanted to be in replicating life in the 1700s.

We both agreed on the need for an early rising, and as five-thirty is a fairly typical start for us, that hour sounded fine. But would we get up without the use of an electric alarm clock? Waking up to that contemporary sound would not exactly set the tone for our travel back in time. So we agreed to each set a mental alarm clock and we hoped at least one of us would be reliable. I then turned the heat down to forty-five degrees, and Harvey banked the fire. We were in bed by nine that evening. For full disclosure, our electric clock, while hidden in a cubby in our bedroom desk, was easily accessible for a quick peek first thing in the morning. I had already decided that we could steal a look at our kitchen clock to record the start and finish times for each dish as there was a need to provide accurate information in the recipes that would be included in this book. And, of course, there needed to be images of the dishes, so we had arranged for Sandy, our photographer friend, to return with her equipment to record the midday meal on Saturday. As we went to bed, Harvey and I hoped the photo shoot the next day would not affect our ability to immerse ourselves in our version of eighteenth-century life.

SATURDAY We both awoke at five-twenty the next morning, appropriately chilled and in need of our morning cup of coffee. First, however, the fire had to be rekindled, the water brought to a rolling boil, the coffee beans ground in the hand grinder, the heated water poured over the grounds, and the egg shell cracked and added to the mixture to settle the grounds. By six-fifteen, almost an hour later, we were ready to drink our first cup of the day. Welcome to the eighteenth century.

By the first light of dawn, Harvey went out to the woodshed to get a large batch of wood that would provide sufficient coals for cooking breakfast and the midday dinner. Meanwhile, I sliced the Sally Lunn bread for toast and some country ham for frying. It was now seven-fifteen and we had the wood, the sliced bread, and the pieces of ham for our first meal. Only one element was missing— the *sufficient coals* part. The fire would need to burn quite a bit longer. Breakfast would have to wait.

Knowing that the preparations for the midday dinner would need to start pretty soon if the meal was to be ready for the photo shoot planned at two o'clock that afternoon, I assembled the ingredients for the afternoon dish—the meats, stale bread, vegetables, and stock— and the necessary utensils. Of course, since the photo shoot was scheduled to take place at the hour traditionally reserved for a midday meal, we would need to eat later than was typical in the eighteenth century.

By eight o'clock the coal situation was not a great deal better, but we needed to move on with the day. We set the toaster in front of the main fire, got as many shovelfuls of the available coals as possible, and placed them under the trivet upon which sat a cast-iron pan ready to fry the ham. We then arranged a smaller bed of coals to rewarm the coffee from earlier in the day. Just like watching a pot of water come to a boil, the bread seemed to take forever to toast in front of our still skimpy bed of coals, or at least fifteen minutes. But it was well worth the wait. I am not exaggerating when I say that I have never had a better slice of buttered toast, or a more flavorful piece of country ham. Even if you have only a small fireplace, or just a wood-burning stove, I highly recommend that you purchase an old toasting iron and try this at home. Every slice was toasted completely through; there was no soft, untoasted interior. Each bite was crunchy but not dry, as the butter soaked through, melting instantly on the sizzling-hot bread. As for the ham, the slow cooking over the coals must have allowed the fat to melt, basting the meat as it did so, resulting in a moist and mellow bit of ham. The coffee rewarmed beautifully and was, to our surprise, not the least bit bitter. Harvey and I quickly concluded that this hard-earned eighteenth-century-style breakfast easily merited the amount of effort involved.

It was now eight-thirty. We had eaten in haste, but the morning preparations took longer than planned. We had to immediately turn our attention to making dinner. I hoped it was not too late to start the syllabub, as this dessert needs to set for at least eight hours. We had arranged for Sandy to arrive at two o'clock, so we would not be sitting down for dinner until four-thirty at the earliest, and it was unlikely we would get to the dessert course before six-thirty, giving me some hope that the syllabub would have sufficient time to set.

That morning I recognized that there was no way I (unlike probably most eighteenth-century housewives) could have gotten breakfast on the table all on my own, with no servant, or in my case, husband, to assist. Not only would I have been overwhelmed, but breakfast would have, at best, become the midday meal.

The menu for the first midday dinner of our eighteenth-century weekend was:

STUFFED LEG OF VEAL WITH CABBAGE AND PARSNIPS

CHESTNUT FRICASSEE

CRANBERRY RELISH

HARD CIDER

SYLLABUB

ELECTION DAY CAKE

The syllabub was first on my agenda. This sweet dates back to the seventeenth century and was quite popular into the 1700s. According to the recipe I found in *Dining with the Washingtons*, if prepared in a modern kitchen the mixture needed to be whipped by machine for ten minutes, so I knew in advance that, without the aid of an electric mixer, I would need some stamina for my initial recipe of the day. As with the cake dough, I enjoyed my intimate connection to the process and was pleased that the syllabub seemed to be adequately

thickened after only a bit more than fifteen minutes of vigorous whisking.

Upon finishing the dessert preparations and placing the dish to set in the
unheated entryway, I turned my attention to the forcemeat that was to be used
to stuff the veal shanks. I must confess
that, despite all our efforts toward an authentic historic experience, I allowed for
the occasional anachronistic element.
So, in the spirit of full disclosure, I admit
that I had ordered veal and pork already
ground for the forcemeat, with the pork
preseasoned as sausage. In my mind,
this was a legitimate use of a modern
convenience, as it allowed me more time
to accomplish what needed to get done;

and, equally important, my purchase supported local suppliers of healthily grown meats.

Grating the pound of bread went relatively quickly, and adding the herbs, eggs, and
butter to the meat also took little time, so by ten o'clock, I was already making incisions into
the two shanks and forcing the stuffing into the slits. The shanks were then ready to be
placed into Harvey's hot oven. I have one more admission to make. Unable to find fresh
chestnuts for the day's chestnut fricassee, and not unhappy about it, I purchased a jar of
peeled chestnuts. If you have ever peeled your own chestnuts, you might understand my
decision to allow myself this modern convenience. My fingers definitely thanked me, as
bits of the hard chestnut skin have a tendency to wind up under one's fingernails, a painful
experience indeed.

At this point in the day, I was an old hand at setting up the trivet over a bed of fresh
coals. I did so again and sautéed an onion in the bacon fat left over from the large batch
of bacon Harvey had just fried up for today's fricassee and tomorrow's johnnycakes. To the
sautéed onion I added the chestnuts, broth, and cream. The dish was now complete and
indeed quite lovely. All this time, Harvey had been tending to the fire in the beehive oven.
To hold the four-hundred-degree starting temperature, the interior bricks needed to

thoroughly absorb enough heat. That way, with luck, the bricks would cool down to no less than three hundred degrees by the time the veal was done, about three hours later. Halfway through the projected cooking time, Harvey removed the door to the beehive oven and inserted his hand to see if the bricks were still providing adequate heat. This is always my husband's job, as I am not willing to leave my hand in the oven until the heat becomes unbearable. Having bravely served as the human thermometer, Harvey found that the temperature was holding steady at around the necessary three hundred degrees to cook the veal. We were on schedule.

By two o'clock that afternoon, the cooking was basically done. We were now ready for our twenty-first-century photo shoot. Upon arriving, Sandy stepped through the keeping room and into the dining room, where she happily declared the lighting perfect. Bright sunlight was streaming into the room, highlighting the reflective surfaces of silver, glass, and crystal on the marble-topped table. Sandy was thrilled, rapidly taking shot after shot of the colorful table—the epergne with its unblemished oranges, the crystal bowl resplendent with a deep red cranberry relish, and the cream and white layers of syllabub clearly visible in the champagne flutes (surprisingly, the syllabub had set by the time Sandy arrived at two-thirty). As we watched, assisting as needed, Harvey and I gradually became aware of how quickly Sandy had to work, as the setting sun changed each successive photo.

Sandy finished the shoot in the dining room and returned to the keeping room to capture a few photos of the fricassee simmering on the hearth and the veal as it came out of the oven. We made final preparations as the shanks rested. After about twenty minutes, Harvey carved while I set the dining room table. I used an antique linen cloth and laid out our best dishes and cutlery, the appropriate white linen napkins, and our diminutive eighteenth-century wineglasses. Sandy was staying for dinner and her husband, Carl, arrived just as she finished shooting. We took our seats around the table, each of us pausing to enjoy the warmth of the fire and the aromas of our hearth-cooked meal.

The veal was lovely to behold, although it would have benefited from another hour or so of cooking time. The parsnips were tasty, if also decidedly undercooked. Everything else was wonderful. The forcemeat was excellent and provided a flavor I had never before experienced. The sausage I purchased already had sage in it, but I had added more from our herb garden, along with marjoram, suffusing the meat-and-bread mixture with a subtle herbal quality. The cabbage that was roasted with the veal was a nice addition. The chestnut fricassee was one of the biggest hits of the evening as it looked like a typical fricassee (think mushrooms in cream sauce), but the chestnuts added a lovely sweet and nutty nuance to the familiar creamy sauce. The eighteenth-century additions to the cranberry relish—spices, orange juice, wine, and brown sugar—gave this refreshing condiment an extra layer of complexity we all appreciated. To conclude, the syllabub made a perfect, lightly sweet, slightly winey finish to this eighteenth-century feast, along with the Election Day cake that offered a nicely dry contrast to the liquid-based dessert course.

The photo shoot had not broken the spell. We were all quickly transported back to the past as soon as we entered the candlelit dining room, welcomed by the sounds of the soft-crackling fire and the enticing aromas of the hearth-cooked dinner, and, of course, lively conversation with our friends (and not one head bent over a cell phone). We had completed our immersion into the eighteenth-century world of our Ichaobds.

At eight-thirty that evening we bid our guests a warm farewell. We were a bit tired, but as we climbed the winding stairs to our bedroom, Harvey and I had a real sense of satisfaction from the first day of our eighteenth-century weekend.

SUNDAY   Thankfully, on Sunday, the second day of our experiment, I had not scheduled the dreaded laundry; so without any additional chores to worry about, the early-morning routine went quite smoothly—get the fire going, the water heating, the coffee ground, and begin the necessary preparations for breakfast, which on this morning was to be a popular New England dish known as johnnycakes.

As with our breakfast on the first day, we found that the basic act of getting the meal to the table took significantly longer than anticipated. To test the recipe, I had made johnny-cakes earlier in the week. But for that practice run, I had done the actual frying on a modern stovetop, and it took about twenty-five minutes per batch. Over the coals in the hearth, this step took closer to forty minutes. Most likely, I needed to refresh the coals under the trivet more frequently than I was used to, to replicate the constant medium-heat setting on the stovetop. Once again, though, the final result was well worth the additional time needed to cook the cakes over hot coals. The texture of the hearth-cooked johnnycakes was significantly better, as the surface was lacy and much crisper. The interior of the cake was drier and the whole was far less greasy.

Part of the improved texture could, of course, have been due to the fact that this was my second time making the recipe; now that I was more familiar with the procedure, my technique would have improved. I made a mental note to try the recipe again, before my memory of these hearth-fried johnnycakes faded, but, like the first time, I would fry the cakes on a modern stovetop for a more accurate comparison. In any event, these cornmeal cakes topped with molasses were extremely appetizing, closely resembling that other cornmeal-based New England specialty, Indian pudding.

The plan for the midday dinner on Sunday was a little less ambitious than that of the previous day:

STEWED RUMP OF BEEF WITH STUFFED SAVOY CABBAGE

PICKLED BEETS*

ELECTION DAY CAKE

*I had planned to serve pickled beets as a refreshing accompaniment to the beef; however, the eighteenth-century recipe I used called for all vinegar and no sugar and was unappealing to our modern palates. So as not to waste them, I later drained the beets, warmed the vinegar, and added some sugar. Both Harvey and I thoroughly enjoyed this revised side dish over the next few days.

As the itinerary for the day included two guests, expected to arrive around midmorning, I decided to cook what I envisioned would have been a typical meal of a busy housewife in the eighteenth century—centered around a piece of boiled meat with vegetables. I wanted an extra touch, so I found a recipe for boiled beef that included braising packets of parboiled cabbage leaves stuffed with forcemeat in the same pot as the meat.

Similar to yesterday's forcemeat preparation, I grated the bread, chopped the herbs, and mixed in the eggs and butter. Then on to the now-familiar task of scooping out some coals under the trivet, on top of which I set a pot of water to boil for the cabbage. (As an aside, both Harvey and I realized that, for our next eighteenth-century experimental weekend, it would be good idea to keep a kettle of hot water on hand for any cooking needs or simply for a cup of tea.) Once the leaves had softened, I drained the cabbage. Looking at the limp leaves still securely stuck to the cabbage head, I wisely handed the vegetable to Harvey, who has the patient, gentle hands of a philatelist. Harvey did a beautiful job, managing to pull off enough leaves to make six beautifully intact packets for the stew.

The fire had been going since first thing that morning, so we had the requisite bed of hot coals by nine-thirty. Harvey hoisted the heavy pot of beef, vegetables, and liquid onto the crane and positioned it directly over the coals. Frankly, without Harvey I could not have used the crane, as the filled pot was far too heavy for me to lift. Once again I found myself awed by the strength of those early New England housewives. As we brought the liquid to a simmer, Harvey and I took turns positioning the pot either away from or closer to the heat source to ensure that the meat and vegetables cooked as slowly as possible. Swinging back and forth to adjust the temperature of a simmering liquid, cranes are wonderfully flexible and no more difficult to manipulate than turning the knob on a stove.

Our neighbor Wendy and her granddaughter Lily were the midmorning guests who had readily offered their services to help prepare the midday meal. Our younger visitor was appropriately dressed as a colonial-era girl. This prompted me to don my Martha Washington cap, and we each proceeded to embrace our role that day. These helping hands were put to work in exchange for a meal and a generous bouquet of herbs leftover from what they themselves had picked that very morning in their herb garden. I think Harvey and I got the better end of that exchange!

Arriving punctually at eleven in the morning (according to Wendy's twenty-first-century watch), the guests were given their chores, and we all began the preparations. The two unpaid hands were excellent helpers indeed, and soon we had beautifully stuffed and wrapped cabbage leaves, which were promptly placed into the simmering stew.

Wendy and Lily had clearly earned their meal. But as they had other chores to attend to that day, they could not join us for the meal they were helping to prepare. So, while that day's meal was cooking, I reheated a medley of leftovers from both that day's breakfast and Saturday's midday dinner, and as a special treat we let Lily make toast using the antique toasting iron. She announced that the toast was a most pleasing reward for her hard work.

Not one to neglect her duties, our young "servant" girl washed down the table and swept the floor after finishing her meal. A fine job it was, too. Evidently, Lily was quite well trained. We were sad to see them go.

By late afternoon, it was just the two of us. We sat down to our midday dinner in the fading daylight of the keeping room, now illuminated by a single pair of candles and the dying embers of the fire. In this peaceful atmosphere, we took our first bites of the stew and cabbage, the preparations for which seemed to have been started so long ago. We both had the exact same impression—the dish tasted positively medieval, in the best sort of way. Even after all the other amazing flavors of the weekend—and of the many hearth-cooked dishes prior to that weekend—we were still astonished at the experience of tasting these novel flavors. Fortunately, the meal felt complete without the additional vegetable course, and the porter we drank was an adequate palate cleanser for the meat, vegetables, and relatively rich stuffing. Feeling relaxed after dinner, we read by the faint light of the candles until, pleasantly exhausted, we again climbed the winding front stairs and went to bed.

And so, to end as we began, there was, indeed, a part of us that wanted to go back—back to our eighteenth-century reenactment. Our experiment was immensely rewarding, so much so that we soon found ourselves eagerly contemplating another weekend of walking in the footsteps of Molly and the General.

Recipes That Evoke the Flavors of the Eighteenth Century

SALLY LUNN BREAD
Adapted from Nathalie Dupree and Cynthia Graubart's
Mastering the Art of Southern Cooking
Yields 1 loaf

As wheat was much more readily available south of New England, I suspect that the recipe for Sally Lunn Bread never traveled as far north as Maine, or even Massachusetts; however, it is definitely a historic bread that was popular in Georgian England and enjoyed by early colonists, albeit probably only those living in southern climes.

⅔ ounce fresh yeast
2 teaspoons sugar, plus an additional 4 teaspoons
¼ cup warm water, about 110F
2 cups whole milk
3 tablespoons butter, melted
1 tablespoon salt
3 large eggs, beaten
3 cups bread flour
2 cups pastry flour, or more, depending on the moisture content of the flour

Dissolve the yeast and 2 teaspoons sugar in the warm water in a large mixing bowl. Let sit for 10 minutes.

Scald the milk and add the butter, salt, and 4 teaspoons sugar. Cool to less than 115F. Stir mixture into the dissolved yeast. Add the eggs and bread flour plus 1 cup pastry flour and stir until the dough holds together. If the dough remains very wet, which mine did, add pastry flour ¼ cup at a time until shaggy but not dry. Sometimes I have needed to add 2½ cups total of pastry flour. I have learned that the heirloom flour I use has a high moisture content, hence the need for additional flour. Fortunately, the moist dough does not require kneading.

Place the dough in an oiled bowl and cover lightly with a damp dishtowel.

Let the dough double in bulk, then punch down, double once more, and punch down again.

Oil a bundt or tube pan. Scoop the dough into the oiled pan and let double one more time.

Preheat oven to 400F.

Place the pan in the oven and turn down to 350F. If using a beehive oven, place pan in the oven and do not replace the oven's door during the first 15 minutes of cooking. This will allow some of the heat to dissipate. Bake for 50 to 60 minutes until brown and crusty. Cool on a wire rack for 10 minutes and then remove from the pan.

As you can tell from the recipe, this dough is quite different from a typical bread dough as it tends to almost resemble a batter bread. Do not be discouraged, as the result is excellent.

We sliced the bread into sippets—strips about ¾ inch wide by 3 inches long—toasted them by the fire, and then dipped them in the rump roast juices. I cannot imagine why sippets seem to be a lost tradition. The only time I find them on a menu is in Colonial Williamsburg.

ELECTION DAY CAKE
Adapted from Sandra L. Oliver's Saltwater Foodways *and Brett Moore's website*
Yields 2 loaves, approximately 8½ x 4½ x 2½ inches

Many of the recipes for Election Day cake I found begin with the words "Take thirty quarts flour." Given its name, I believe that such a quantity of flour was called for so there was enough cake to serve all a town's voters. Eventually, after checking at least a half dozen sources, I was able to find measurements more appropriate for a home cook.

Oliver has nicely reduced quantities, like 4½ cups of flour. I decided on a slightly adjusted version of Oliver's cake; and on Brett Moore's website, I found an appealing recipe for the cake that instructs the baker to soak dried fruit in a sugar syrup laced with whiskey. I ended up soaking my fruit (currants were my preference) in a sugar syrup with rum, as I thought rum more appropriate for a New England recipe.

DRIED FRUIT MIXTURE
½ cup sugar
½ cup water
1 cup currants
½ cup rum

DOUGH
½ ounce fresh yeast
1 cup warm milk, about 90 to 100F
¾ cup sugar
4½ to 5 cups pastry flour
⅓ cup butter
2 eggs
1 teaspoon ground cinnamon
1 teaspoon ground nutmeg

ICING
1 cup confectioner's sugar
6 tablespoons reserved syrup from the drained fruit

Preheat oven to 350F.

DRIED FRUIT MIXTURE

Combine the sugar with the water in a small saucepan and bring to simmer. Place the currants in a small bowl, cover with the rum, and then add the warm sugar syrup. Set aside.

DOUGH

Crumble the fresh yeast in the warm milk with 1 tablespoon of the sugar and 2 tablespoons of the flour. Let the yeast proof as you proceed with the recipe. Cream the butter and the remaining sugar until fluffy and the sugar is completely dissolved. Beat the eggs one at a time and add to the butter-and-sugar mixture.

Sift the flour with the spices and stir into the eggs, butter, and sugar mixture. Stir the drained rum-and-syrup-soaked currants into the dough.

Turn the dough onto a floured board and knead for about 5 minutes, adding additional flour if necessary. My dough needed another ½ cup of flour.

Butter two small loaf pans. Place one half of the dough in each pan and cover with damp dishtowel. Put the pans in a warm spot and let the dough rise until doubled in bulk. I usually raise yeast dough in a cool room, but a heavy, buttery yeast dough such as this one seemed to need a warmer environment to help with the rising, especially with the additions of the sugar and soaked fruit, so I kept it in the main space of the keeping room. Even with the warmer temperature, the dough needed four hours to double.

Bake in preheated oven for 40 to 45 minutes.

Turn out onto a wire rack to cool.

ICING

Combine the confectioner's sugar with the reserved syrup from drained fruit. Glaze the cooled loaves with icing and serve.

STUFFED LEG OF VEAL
Adapted from Amelia Simmons's American Cookery
Serves 12

Not wanting to cook an entire leg of veal, an approximately 135-pound joint, as I was told by my local butcher, I used two shanks instead. After the usual research, I chose to follow the recipe by Amelia Simmons in *American Cookery* as the instructions were quite clear and the ingredients sounded just right (with a few minor adjustments, of course).[179]

Two 5-pound veal shanks, salted
1 pound stale bread, preferably brioche or challah, grated
¾ pound ground veal
½ pound pork sausage (breakfast-sausage style)
3 tablespoons parsley, finely chopped
4 tablespoons fresh sage, finely chopped
1 tablespoon dried marjoram, crumbled
6 tablespoons butter, softened, plus an additional 2 tablespoons
3 eggs, lightly beaten
4 tablespoons cream
Salt, to taste
1 quart veal broth, preferably homemade
3 parsnips, parboiled or sliced into ½-inch chunks
1 green cabbage, cored and sliced
2 tablespoons flour, for dusting
8 tablespoons melted butter, if necessary

Preheat beehive oven for about an hour and a half, then let it cool until it has reached approximately 400F (if you are using a modern stove, simply preheat oven to 400F).

Set aside the veal shanks.

Combine all the forcemeat ingredients—grated bread crumbs, veal, pork, herbs, eggs, butter cream and salt—in a large bowl.

Make an incision about 2 inches long and 1 inch deep in each of the veal shanks, and fill the incisions with the forcemeat mixture. I had a lot of stuffing left over, so I patted the extra over the surface of each shank, about ½ inch thick. Since the tops of the shanks were now covered with the force-meat, I omitted the step of dusting them with flour.

Pour the veal broth into the bottom of a large roasting pan, place the 2 shanks in the pan side by side, and add the parsnips and cabbage.

Put the pan uncovered into the oven and let temperature slowly lower to around 325F (or turn thermostat down to 325F on a modern stove). If the forcemeat gets too brown, baste with the melted butter.

Bake the veal and vegetables for 4½ hours, refiring the oven if the tempera-ture drops much below 300F.

Remove the pan from the oven and let the veal rest in its broth for at least 20 minutes.

While the meat is resting, break up the 2 tablespoons butter into small pieces and roll in flour. Place the pan juices into a saucepan, bring to a boil, and slowly add the floured butter, bit by bit, letting one piece melt before adding the next, stirring constantly. Once butter is thoroughly incorporated, pour into a sauce- or gravy boat.

Slice the veal and serve with the vegetables and gravy.

CHESTNUT FRICASSEE
Serves 6

Although I have yet to find an eighteenth-century recipe that includes chestnuts, we know that the American chestnut tree was found in New England and was used in early building construction. I did find a recipe for mushroom fricassee and extrapolated from that to arrive at the procedure here.

2 tablespoons bacon fat
½ onion, diced
1 pound shelled chestnuts (I used presteamed chestnuts and spared my fingers)
¼ cup Madeira wine
½ cup beef broth, preferably homemade
½ cup heavy cream
Salt and pepper to taste

Heat the bacon fat in a medium cast-iron pan. Sauté onion in the fat until lightly browned. Add the chestnuts, and stir in the pan until glazed, about 2 minutes. Add the Madeira, bring to a boil, then reduce heat and simmer until reduced by half. Add broth, bring to a boil, and simmer again until reduced by about one-third. Add heavy cream, stir, and warm through.

Season with salt and pepper, and serve.

CRANBERRY RELISH
Serves 4

1½ cups fresh cranberries
1 cup sugar, mix of brown and white
Zest, and juice, of one orange
¼ cup dry sherry
Cinnamon and ginger to taste

Take a few shovelfuls of coals from your wood fire and bring to the front of the hearth. Center the trivet over the coals.

Combine the ingredients in a small saucepan and place on the trivet. Bring to a simmer, stirring occasionally for about 5 minutes or until the cranberries are cooked down and soft.

Remove the pan from the trivet and set aside to cool.

SYLLABUB
Adapted mainly from Stephen A. McLeod's Dining with the Washingtons,
in which the recipe is said to be based on the eighteenth-century recipes of
E. Smith and Elizabeth Raffald [180]
Serves 6–8

There are dozens of recipes for this extremely popular dessert. According to *Dining with the Washingtons*, the sweet is actually a beverage, although the author suggests serving it with a "long-handled spoon."[181] My syllabub could be consumed only with a spoon—perhaps because I used a thick, local heavy cream from Jersey cows—until the very bottom, where some of the liquid component had separated out and was drinkable.

2½ cups heavy cream
¾ cup sugar
1 lemon, zested and juiced, preferably a Meyer lemon, as it is less acidic
1 cup sweet white wine—I used an inexpensive Sauterne
¼ cup dry sherry
¼ cup dessert sherry

Combine the cream, sugar, and lemon zest in a large bowl; then combine the lemon juice, wine, and both sherries in a separate small bowl.

Stirring constantly, pour this liquid combination into the cream-and-sugar mixture, then whip vigorously with a wire whisk for about 15 minutes (or about 10 minutes if using an electric mixer; just be careful not to over mix, as the cream could turn into butter), until somewhat thick and opaque.

Refrigerate for about 4 hours, then ladle into individual serving glasses.

Refrigerate for an additional 4 hours, or overnight, by which time the cream will have thickened considerably and risen to the top, and a small amount of the winy liquid will have settled to the bottom.

JOHNNYCAKES
Adapted from A Young Woman's Memory of How Her Aunt Made Johnnycakes, *as related in Sandra L. Oliver's* Saltwater Foodways [182]
Yields 10-12 cakes

As I had made this recipe previously, I knew that the pancakes would be heavy. In trying to find a solution I came across Anna Coit's family recipe, passed down from her aunt Jetti, born in 1869. Anna recalls her aunt's instructions that the mixture should be quite loose, warning that the batter can get stiff. To solve the stiffness, her aunt suggests letting the batter rest and then adding a sufficient quantity of milk to the now-thickened mixture, using enough until the batter is loose again. Brilliant.

2 cups johnnycake meal
1½ teaspoons salt
2 cups vigorously boiling water
¼ cup heavy cream or milk, plus additional milk as needed
Bacon fat
Molasses or maple syrup to taste

Mix the johnnycake meal with salt.

Take the boiling water and add it into the meal, stir, and let stand 15 minutes. Be certain that the water is at a vigorous boil before pouring; if the meal is not thoroughly cooked there is a chance of a bitter aftertaste.

Remove from heat. Stir in the milk or cream until smooth and let batter rest for about 30 minutes.

So far, this essentially follows the traditional recipe. Then, as per Aunt Jetti's instructions, I added about ¼ cup of heavy cream after the batter had rested. I switched to milk for the final ½ cup needed to loosen the batter, not wishing to add extra fat and calories.

Heat a medium cast-iron pan over a hot bed of coals or use the "high" setting on a regular stove. Melt the bacon fat and portion out the cakes, using a ladle—about ⅓ cup of batter per cake. Drop in as many cakes as you can without crowding the pan, remembering that you want to be able to maneuver your spatula as you flip the cakes.

Let the first side stiffen and become golden brown, then flip the johnnycake to the other side, flattening it lightly. Let that side stiffen and brown, then flip from time to time until the cakes are quite brown. The whole process may take as long as a half hour or more, depending on the heat from your bed of coals or your stove.

Serve with molasses or maple syrup. I used molasses, as it is also appropriate for an early New England recipe.

STEWED RUMP OF BEEF WITH STUFFED SAVOY CABBAGE
Adapted from Ms. Cole's Lady's Complete Guide;
or Cookery in All Its Branches [183]
Serves 10–12

I have come across many seventeenth- and eighteenth-century renditions of this evidently common dish. I had tried another version of this dish, as described in chapter 9, yet wishing to stay more authentic for this weekend, I decided to use the more typical rump roast rather than the chuck I had substituted for the General's meal while on furlough.

STEWED BEEF
8 slices bacon, approximately
3 medium parsnips, sliced thinly
6 large carrots, sliced in ¾ inch chunks
2 onions, cut into ½ inch slices
6 pounds bottom round of beef
2 quarts beef broth, preferably homemade
6 sprigs thyme
8 sprigs parsley

STUFFED CABBAGE

½ pound stale brioche, grated
¼ pound sausage
½ pound ground veal
4 tablespoons sage, chopped
2 tablespoons parsley, chopped
½ onion, diced
1 egg
¼ cup beef broth
1 savoy cabbage, blanched
8–10 pieces of twine

Lay the bacon across the bottom of the Dutch oven. Place the vegetables over the bacon, then place the beef over the vegetables. Pour in the beef broth and add the parsley and thyme.

Bring to a boil, then reduce heat and simmer, lid on, for 1½ hours.

For the stuffing, mix the brioche, sausage, veal, herbs, onion, egg, and broth.

Carefully peel off 8 blanched cabbage leaves and move them onto a cutting board.

Place 3 tablespoons of stuffing in the center of each cabbage leaf. Wrap the leaf around the stuffing to make a packet. Tie horizontally and vertically with twine.

Lift the lid on the Dutch oven, place the cabbage packets into the simmering broth, replace the lid, and cook for another 1½ hours.

When the meat is cooked, let it cool in the broth.

When ready to serve, remove the meat and bring the broth to a boil. Let the liquid boil until it is sufficiently concentrated to your taste. Gently rewarm the meat in the broth. Remove and place on carving board to slice.

Serve the meat with the vegetables and stuffed cabbage leaves, with the broth on the side.

A SPECIAL RECIPE FROM OLD FIELDS TO THE NEXT GENERATION A few weeks prior to that weekend in November 2014, sixty York County middle school children were invited to the Spencer-Goodwin-Bennett Tavern to learn more about the archaeological dig and how life hundreds of years ago was centered around a keeping room. Since the weather forecast was too warm to have a simmering pot of soup ready to ladle into their "colonial" paper cups as we had done the year before, I decided to bake cookies in the brick oven a few days ahead of time, when the temperature promised to be no more than in the mid-fifties. The future electorate of York County, Maine, seemed to enjoy these cookies.

GINGERBREAD COOKIES
Adapted from Colonial Williamsburg's blog History Is Served
Makes 3 dozen

1¼ cups molasses
½ cup cream
6 cups all-purpose flour,
    plus extra flour as needed for rolling out dough
8 ounces sugar
2 tablespoons ginger
1½ teaspoons nutmeg
Pinch of salt
8 ounces softened butter

Preheat modern oven to 375F or brick oven to 400F. If baking in a brick oven, place a few bricks on the oven floor so baking sheet does not rest directly on surface.

Warm the molasses and cream. Stir to blend. Do not let the mixture get hot.

Place the dry ingredients in a large mixing bowl and stir. Work in the softened butter until the mixture resembles bread crumbs of the type made on the coarse holes of a grater, not the perfect dots of those made by machine. Add the molasses-and-cream mixture to the dry mix, and stir until a stiff dough forms.

Roll out on a lightly floured board until ¼ inch thick. Cut with cookie cutter or a small biscuit cutter.

Bake on a greased baking sheet for 8 to 10 minutes.

The cookies will still be a bit soft but will harden as they cool.

EPILOGUE

A New Year's Toast to Old Fields

Looking back, I am forever grateful for that steamy July day in 2003 when I found myself browsing in a bookstore. If I had not stumbled across that design book on American farmhouses, we might never have been drawn to the Goodwin home, whose keeping room perfectly resembled my *epiphany* picture; in fact, Harvey and I might never even have moved to Maine.

I think of everything Harvey and I have learned about the Goodwins and the times in which they lived, and I am deeply satisfied with all that we have accomplished here, re-creating a space that evokes the house's origins. It will be extremely difficult to leave the eighteenth-century abode we have had the privilege to live in for over ten years. We loathe the thought of leaving, even as we are now planning for our move to Boston. Yes, Harvey and I are heading south, or at least as far south as the nearest big city. At our age, we feel it is time to downsize. I had also promised myself that someday I would live in a city where I could walk everywhere, just as I did as a child in Baltimore. From our new apartment, we will be able to get to the farmers' market, to the Boston Public Library and gardens, to shops and restaurants, to the opera, ballet, and symphony, without having to drive.

As I sit down to record my thoughts this morning, I realize that almost two years ago today Harvey and I were organizing our experimental eighteenth-century weekend. I wish I could say that in the intervening months I made my own potato yeast, made the johnny-cakes one more time on the modern cookstove for comparison, or at least organized another weekend immersed in the eighteenth century. Alas, none of these events took place. Instead, after our annual Maryland vacation at the close of 2014, we were immediately up against the catalog deadline for a February public auction in New York City. Soon after, the wife of a devoted, and unfortunately quite ill, client requested that we auction the final sections of his extensive collection. Recognizing how the holding would benefit from the venue of a stamp show, we scheduled the auction for May and found ourselves on another deadline. Then, barely recovered from that auction, we took on another obligation when yet another collector with whom we were close realized it was time to sell his collection of United States stamps, and wished to do this before the end of 2015. So, there we were, on deadline once more, for our third major auction last year. And no, in case you were wondering, I would not label this a semi-retired lifestyle.

Due to the fairly constant stream of auction deadlines, I regret to say that Harvey and I have simply not had time to pursue to the fullest our love of an eighteenth-century lifestyle. In fact, for much of the time that we have lived here, it has been necessary to let business take precedence over such pursuits. I wish we had had more time to make those additional fires for more festive meals in the dining room, or those rustic hearth-cooked dinners in the keeping room. I am also sorry I never had a chance to study piano so that, as my ambitious imagination hoped, I would have been able to play an early Mozart sonata on our Broadwood square piano. Of course, purchasing a few more pieces of antique American-made furniture would have been nice as well.

Aside from our need to start downsizing at our age there is one more, rather significant and overriding factor behind our difficult decision to leave South Berwick and our eighteenth-century home. As we are both nearing our eighth decade, we cannot ignore the importance of living close to a great hospital, and, regrettably, South Berwick is not close enough to Boston's Massachusetts General to give me any sense of security. This urgency was brought home to me in my mid-thirties, when in separate instances my parents each needed serious medical care—while my mother, living near the University of Maryland, received excellent cancer treatment, my father was in an isolated rural town when he had his stroke at age fifty-nine and did not get the immediate medical attention that might have prevented some of the damage to his brain.

Thus, Harvey and I have made the decision to move to Boston, the prominent New England city that played such an important role in the founding of our nation. It feels like a happy choice. We will enjoy walking to the Old South Meeting House, where the Boston Tea Party was first plotted. Moreover, I was pleased to discover that the condominium we have chosen comes with its own historic name and its own past, albeit one not quite as old as that of our General Ichabod Goodwin home.

For now, as we anticipate our move, my most important wish is that our home, the home of our Ichabods and of so much American history, will find a new owner who preserves and furthers what we have accomplished. Preservation is quite often one of the overriding ambitions of those who purchase historic houses, so our hope is that whoever buys our house will be interested in the many documents and artifacts relating to the Goodwins that we have assembled. And, as long as I am making my wish list, I like to think that the new owner will want to continue our research, documentary as well as archaeological, adding to the knowledge of this prominent Berwick family and their house. Perhaps they might even find that diary Harvey had hoped to locate.

Meanwhile, with Boston in our future, I have begun research on the man after whom our new home is named—Albert A. Pope. The man whom we have already begun to affectionately call our Colonel established the first American bicycle manufacturing company, running the business from the building that now bears his name.[184] What I found even more fascinating was that the Colonel was a significant investor in progressive journalism during its critical era in the late-nineteenth and early-twentieth centuries.

In fact, I soon discovered that Pope saved *McClure's*, the very influential and progressive magazine, from folding in 1895 (it eventually ceased publication in 1929).[185] That year, when founder Sam McClure was on the verge of closing its doors, he went in search of Pope for financial assistance. Eventually McClure found Pope at his summer home in Cohasset, Massachusetts, where the Colonel immediately offered a loan in the amount of $5,000.[186] I can imagine the scene at the Colonel's waterfront home, the two men doubtless enjoying the fresh sea breeze as McClure pressed his case for the importance of keeping his journal active in the American conversation.

But for now, we have just rung in one last festive New Year's at Old Fields, toasting with a popular eighteenth-century beverage called *flip*—named perhaps after the large beaker-shaped glass into which the drink would be poured and then passed around from one patron to the next at the local tavern. One of the shards discovered in our dig was, in fact, a fragment of just such a glass. It seems that those in the eighteenth century would have enjoyed something akin to the eggnog we drink today. Historic recipes indicate that the drink could be made from rum mixed with sherry, Madeira, or cognac; with an added measure of beer or ale; a little cream or milk; egg or egg white; and some sweetener. To finish, the flip was often heated by inserting a hot poker into the glass vessel, a lovely touch that Harvey and I repeated on this bleak winter afternoon.

As we celebrate our twelfth New Year's as stewards of the Goodwin homestead, I am thinking about the most recent discovery made at the dig last summer, a royalist button with the British king's emblem of a lion, probably from a waistcoat. Harvey and I still marvel at how each artifact connects us to history; I will especially miss the thrill of anticipation at the start of each summer's field school as students and volunteers begin to sift through the soil of a new pit, and I remain ever hopeful that the next discovery will provide answers to the remaining mysteries surrounding the history of Old Fields.

Thanks to a long-awaited visit by Tom Johnson, the prominent New England architectural historian, and a colleague of his this past fall we were able to fill in a few more of the missing puzzle pieces. After a two-hour inspection from attic to basement, Tom shared his thoughts over a glass of Madeira and a pudding. He theorized that the front-door pediment could very likely be original to the earlier house that burned in 1794. Soon after his visit, Tom wrote in an email that he and his colleague were:

> [F]airly certain that the present house is a single 1794 build with salvaged Georgian elements from the previous house on the site, and that the front door, which probably originally faced south, was moved to reorient it toward Hamilton House using the earlier door surround.

Moreover, being familiar with the architecture of the Hamilton House across the street, Tom suggested that the same architect was responsible for both the Hamilton House and the Goodwin home that was rebuilt after the fire (to whatever extent). He based his theory on the unique profile of the raised paneling above the fireplace in our best parlour which, he pointed out, is identical to that of the Hamilton House. Given the individuality of the paneling and the fact that Berwick was a small town, it does seem likely that both houses were done by the same builder. I am quite fond of the idea that our home was actually built by the same person responsible for the elegant house across the street.

Because of the configuration of the beehive oven inside the hearth and the chamfered paneling of the eastern wall, Tom and his colleague further believe that the entire keeping room, not just the hearth, dates back to a pre-1760 construction. By the time of Tom's visit, Neill had already begun to suspect as much. And while he, Harvey, and I have had many conversations about the possibilities over the past few years, Neill, the consummate professional, rightly avoids definitive statements without the archaeological evidence to back them up. I find it fascinating how the various fields—in this case, archaeology and architectural history—work together to provide a fuller picture.

When Tom examined the foundation under the 1870 addition, Harvey and I mentioned the Goodwin family anecdote stating that the nineteenth-century addition was placed over the foundation of the William Spencer Garrison. Tom said that this family story passed down through the years could be true, pointing out that the stone walls of the cellar predate the eighteenth-century walls of our Georgian home.

Before leaving Maine, I will type up a summary of all that I have learned regarding life here at Old Fields and the house. It will ceremoniously be inserted into that spiral-bound notebook so graciously left us by Kent MacNown. But for now, seated at our bedroom desk, I have set the computer aside, abandoning its mechanized typing, and I am starting my own lengthy letter, handwritten, to the next stewards of Old Fields.

The antique desk in our bedroom in South Berwick, where I wrote much of this book and where I often imagined Sophia Hayes Goodwin writing her lengthy letters to her husband, while he was stationed in Washington, D.C. Alas, the Boston bedroom will not accommodate our desk, so a small writing table in the main room will have to suffice.

Then later this afternoon, to celebrate the first day of the year, Harvey will build a fire in the keeping room and roast a leg of venison, unfortunately a farmed animal, unlike the one we had previously bartered for with a local farmer for a cookbook on nose-to-tail eating.[187]

For this New Year's Day feast I have planned a long-overdue reprise of the chestnut fricassee. For the vegetable we will rely on the easily stored cabbage and leftover Election Day cake—which I confess went into the freezer after that eighteenth-century weekend. A local porter will accompany the venison. Madeira, of course, will be the appropriate beverage to serve with the cake. If we are lucky, as we set the table in the dining room, nature will provide us with yet another of her lovely sunsets. This past fall, we were treated to many, reminding us of how lucky we are to have those west-facing windows with their view of the rolling countryside beyond.

After dinner, we will withdraw to our modern Great Room in the 1985 addition. This room has our modern media, the high-definition television and a DVD player. Harvey, the opera lover, needs his New Year's tradition—a viewing of *Die Fledermaus*. By nine o'clock, our New Year's Day will have come to an early end. We will climb the winding stairs, light a single candle in a gleaming brass candlestick, and enjoy a quiet conversation in Molly and Ichabod's master's bedchamber.

I invite my readers, and future generations of readers, to turn off their computers and cell phones, consider lighting their own candle at the end of an evening, and experience for themselves the beauty and quiet of a world without electricity—the world of my Ichabods.

ACKNOWLEDGMENTS

I would like to acknowledge the generous contributions of the many individuals who embraced this project. Everyone I contacted, everyone with whom I spoke, of whom I asked questions, from whom I requested information and clarification, all of those who gave so freely, I thank you. There are too many to thank by name; that said, the following organizations and men and women are among those I wish to individually recognize here.

It makes sense to begin with the society I first approached when I decided to start my research on Old Fields—the Old Berwick Historical Society (OBHS). The members of this society are quick to share their deep knowledge of the history of their beloved town, and the vast archives they have assembled since their founding in 1962. Their many maps, books, and original papers added to my understanding of the town I came to call home.

Historic New England is another of our invaluable regional societies. Their websites for each of the properties offer much detail and insight into the various owners of the historic houses. At the Colonel Samuel Pierce House in Dorchester, Massachusetts, I was able to read the colonel's daily entries in his journal with its colorful descriptions of a time period that overlapped with the Captain's and the General's, helping me understand their day-to-day lives. Moreover, each tour of the many properties I have taken offered insights into how eighteenth century homes would have appeared and how its owners may have lived.

Other archives that proved indispensable were the Dartmouth College library in Hanover, New Hampshire; the Maine Historical Society; the records at the York County Courthouse in Alfred, Maine; and, the Massachusetts Archives.

Kent MacNown, former owner of the General Goodwin home served as one of my initial inspirations when he came to our door and offered his collection of notes on some of the history of both the area of Kittery/Berwick and anecdotes and letters of the Goodwin family.

Even more important to my research was the invaluable assistance of Dr. Neill De Paoli. He began excavating on our property in the fall of 2010. Supported by the OBHS, his excavations have provided us the evidence we had hoped for, and he has given so freely of his time to discuss his findings as well as his theories on those findings. In addition to the physically demanding dig, Neill made time in his already busy life for travel to various institutions in order to research the documentary evidence and then writing reports based on those documents to create informative timelines on the Spencers and the first two Ichabod Goodwins.

I want to also acknowledge the work of Neill's team: Laura Wolfer, Jim McDevitt and Steve Woodman. United by their love of history, these individuals labored alongside Neill throughout the long, hot days of summer and the frigid, blustery ones of late Fall.

Closer to home, I want to acknowledge the invaluable support of my family. Without that support I would have never had the confidence to proceed. Upon finishing the first ten pages or so, with some trepidation, I sent a draft to our daughter, one of my best friends, but also one of the toughest, most objective critics I know. When I got back the response "Wow," I thought, "Maybe I really can do this."

Additional thanks must go to Sandy Agrafiotis, a talented photographer and a woman who I have grown to appreciate and admire over the many hours she spent here setting up all of her equipment and then waiting for just the right lighting to achieve her goal. Her beautiful photographs are an invaluable addition to my book, and Harvey and I fervently hope our hearth-cooked dinners felt like sufficient recompense for the incalculable amount of effort she expended so willingly.

Throughout the year-long-plus process of writing, from August, 2013 to September, 2014, no one offered more time and energy than my husband Harvey. From searching the internet for physical documents associated with the town of Berwick and its inhabitants, to helping to interpret those original papers as well as ambiguous newspaper articles, to ensuring that I never gave into despondency, thinking this project could ever become a book anyone would want to read, Harvey has been with me, reading draft after draft, until we thought it was ready for more professional eyes.

Thus it was in September of 2014, I approached Bauer and Dean and soon met with publisher Beth Daugherty. At the outset of that first encounter I knew I had found someone with whom I would love to work. I showed her the manuscript in its very raw, first state and crossed my fingers. By the end of our meeting, Beth had signed on as editor for what would prove to be a year-plus-long project. Without the insane number of hours she devoted to this book, the finished product would have been nowhere near the accuracy, polish, or flow. I wish every author could experience this kind of devotion.

To those who volunteered their services to read, and re-read the book, catching typos and providing constructive suggestions that made my narrative notably better, I thank you all for your priceless assistance: Janet Daugherty, Jennifer Gyr, Michael Kathrens, Maureen Lischke, Pam Martin, Wendy Pirsig, Jeanie Thackrey, Dan Matthew Wood, and especially Wendy Kenney who thoroughly and adeptly marked up two versions of the manuscript.

To Chandra Wohleber and Elizabeth Wagner, I must express my gratitude and great admiration of their professional talents that helped guide the final manuscript to its current state. Their attention to detail, their knowledge of grammar and their skill with words are incomparable.

To Betty Eng, whose imagination and creativity took my text and images and turned the book into an aesthetic work of art, I am most appreciative. I want to also thank Kathy Hart who was indispensible by helping Betty with the front and back matter.

I am also especially grateful to Tad Baker, Patricia Laska, Dennis Robinson, and Betsy Widmer, who each took the time to read the final manuscript and agreed to write a "blurb" for the back jacket. I am touched by their wonderful words. I was also deeply moved that Dennis and Tad, both well-established writers, embraced me as a "fellow" author and provided astute guidance in understanding what is to come, especially as it relates to the world of social media.

And then there are the Goodwins themselves. From the first day after I moved into their home, I started to imagine them walking the wide-planked floors of what was now our own keeping room, preparing their meals and engaging with their neighbors. When contemplating the countless fires that were started in our hearth, the numerous children born in our bedroom and the many deaths endured, I can only say "thank you." May their ancestral home remain a part of New England's heritage for at least another 250 years.

SOURCES

INGREDIENTS During the decades of the 1950s, '60s, and '70s, as Elizabeth David was writing her cookbooks of traditional French, Italian, and English recipes, she despaired over her inability to really know what many of the historic foods actually tasted like. In her chapter on traditional Christmas dishes, in the lovely compilation *Elizabeth David's Christmas,* she complains that even if we were to follow every detail of historic recipes, "our ancestors would have considerable difficulty in recognizing them. Chemical feeding stuffs and new systems of breeding and fattening animals for market…the pasteurizing of milk and cream, the production of eggs from battery hens…have caused our food to deteriorate…[and have] changed the nature of almost every single ingredient which comes into our kitchens."[188]

Today, through the work of locally based dairies that carry raw milk and cream, the raising of historic breeds of meat and poultry, and the proliferation of farmers' markets with their heirloom varieties of fruits and vegetables, I believe we are much closer to knowing the flavors of earlier times. The following sources specialize in just these products.

SEACOAST GROWERS ASSOCIATION
seacoastgrowers.org
Greenmarkets are proliferating everywhere. The Seacoast Growers Association serves the coast of southern Maine and the Portsmouth area of New Hampshire. Their markets feature grass-fed meats and poultry, milk, cheese, and eggs, as well as a wide variety of fruits and vegetables. As there are different regulations for different localities, you may want to make sure the products sold at your area markets are grown locally. In the Seacoast markets, each vendor may sell only products he or she raised or grew.

ANSON MILLS
ansonmills.com
1922 C Gervais Street
Columbia, SC 29201
(803) 467-4122
info@ansonmills.com
Wheat flour, cornmeal, oats, rice, buckwheat flour, popping corn

EATALY NYC (Also in Chicago and Boston)
eataly.com/nyc
200 Fifth Avenue
New York, NY 10010
(212) 229-2560
guestrelations@eataly.com
Grass-fed meat as well as a wide array of Italian oils,
vinegars, cheese, and pasta; seafood; produce; house-baked breads

EDWARDS VIRGINIA SMOKEHOUSE
www.edwardsvaham.com
Unfortunately, in January 2016 the smokehouse was consumed by fire.
To receive updates on their planned reopening, subscribe to their online newsletter.

KENYON'S GRIST MILL
kenyonsgristmill.com
21 Glen Rock Road
P.O. Box 221
West Kingston, RI 02892
(800) 753-6966 or (401) 783-4054
Johnnycake meal

MAINE MEAT
memeat.com
7 Wallingford Square, #104
Kittery, ME 03904
(207) 703-0219
inquire@memeat.com
Local, pasture-raised beef, lamb, pork, chicken, plus special orders

PATRIDGE FARM
583 County Road
North Haverhill, NH 03774
(603) 989-5589 or (603) 918-1451
Pasture-raised lamb, pork, chicken, turkey, geese

PENZEY SPICES
penzeys.com
Check website for store locator.
(800) 741-7787
customerservice@penzeys.com
Spices and herbs

THE NEW YORK BAKERS
nybakers.com
2934 National Avenue, Suite E
San Diego, CA 92113
(619) 508-7720
Baking supplies, a great source for fresh yeast

TURKEY SHORE DISTILLERIES
turkeyshoredistilleries.com
23 Hayward Street, Unit 8
Ipswich, MA 01938
(978) 356-0048
Old Ipswich rum

INTERIOR DESIGN I was surprised how challenging it was to find sources that would help me interpret the eighteenth century as authentically as possible. For example, a number of paint companies try to duplicate colors of colonial America but many of them do not achieve the right look, at least to my eye. I ended up using paints from the London-based Farrow & Ball. They are known for formulating colors inspired by the great eighteenth- and nineteenth-century homes of England. Producing products perfectly suited to historic interiors, the following companies have proven good sources for anyone looking to incorporate the beauty of eighteenth-century décor in his or her own home.

FARROW & BALL
See website for store locator: us.farrow-ball.com
Liddens Estate
Wimborne, Dorset BH21 7NL
United Kingdom
(888) 511-7121
NAsales@Farrow-Ball.com
Eighteenth-, nineteenth-, and twentieth-century paint colors and finishes

J. R. BURROWS & COMPANY
burrows.com
393 Union Street
Rockland, MA 02370
(800) 347-1795 or (781) 982-1812
merchant@burrows.com
Distributor of Stourvale Mill Collection of documentary carpets

MOLE HOLLOW CANDLES
molehollowcandles.com
208 Charlton Road/Route 20
P.O. Box 223
Sturbridge MA, 01566
(800) 445-6653
info@molehollowcandles.com
Beeswax candles

ROBERT ORTIZ STUDIOS
ortizstudios.com
207C South Cross Street
Chestertown, MD 21620
(410) 810-1400
ortizstudios@verizon.net
Artisan furniture inspired by George Nakashima and Shaker design

THE GAINSBOROUGH SILK WEAVING COMPANY LIMITED
gainsborough.co.uk
Alexandra Road
Sudbury CO10 2XH
United Kingdom
+44 1787 372081
sales@gainsborough.com.uk
Wool and silk textiles woven on eighteenth-century-style looms; to the trade only

ANTIQUES I would need an additional fifteen pages to list all of the shops, fairs, and auctions we visited while creating the look we sought for each room of the Goodwin house. Whenever we traveled for business, which was often, Harvey and I always tried to take a few hours to explore the local antique stores. Hence, we have objects and furnishings from Connecticut, New York, Maryland, and the District of Columbia. Farther afield, we found little treasures in Canada, London, and Zurich. You never know where a special piece might show up, so, my recommendation? Take a nice Sunday drive, check out the Internet, and have fun shopping. Even Harvey, an anti-consumer, enjoyed the hunt. And remember: always negotiate; these are not department stores.

FISKE AND FREEMAN
fiskeandfreeman.com
35–37 South Main Street
Ipswich, MA 01938
(802) 236-4391
Mostly seventeenth- and eighteenth-century English oak furniture

GEORGE SPIECKER
fineamericana.com
P.O. Box 40
North Hampton, NH 03862
(603) 964-4738
gspiecker@comcast.com
Eighteenth- and early nineteenth-century American furniture and New England art

HARPSICHORD CLEARING HOUSE
harpsichord.com
9 Chestnut Street
Rehoboth, MA 02769
(800) 252-4304 or (508) 252-4304
Sales and restoration of new, used, and antique keyboard instruments

JAMES D. JULIA INC.
jamesdjulia.com
203 Skowhegan Road
Fairfield, ME 04937
(800) 566-9298 or (207) 453-7125
info@jamesdjulia.com
Auction sales of furniture, paintings, ceramics, firearms, and documents

R. JORGENSEN
rjorgensen.com
502 Post Road, U.S. Route 1
Wells, ME 04090
(207) 646-9444
Mostly eighteenth- and nineteenth-century American and European furniture,
and American country furniture

SKINNER
skinnerinc.com
63 Park Plaza
Boston, MA 02116
(617) 350-5400
Auction sales of decorative arts, European furnishings, and Americana

THE ANTIQUARIUM
theantiquariumportsmouth.com
25 Ceres Street
Portsmouth, NH 03801
(603) 427-1690
Early American antiques and artifacts

THE FARM ANTIQUES
thefarmantiques.com
294 Mildram Road
Wells, ME 04090
(207) 985-2656
info@thefarmantiques.com
Mostly eighteenth- and nineteenth-century English furniture, and English and Oriental accessories

HOUSE MUSEUMS For me, there is nothing more inspiring than entering an eighteenth-century historic home. There were a dozen or so house museums that we visited while we were decorating our home. The ones below came closest to my vision for the Goodwin House. The most inspiring, I must say, turned out to be the farthest away: The Dennis Severs' House, in Spitalfields (an interesting word deriving from *hospital*), London. Dennis Severs was a quirky Californian who bought this house in Central London and set it up as a sort of "living" museum. The museum represents a house as it would have been inhabited from 1724 to the dawn of the twentieth century, specifically by the fictitious Jarvis family—immigrant French Huguenot silk weavers—who climb the social ladder as their wealth increases through the demise of their last ne'er-do-well offspring. As the visitor tours the house, he or she gets the impression that a member of the Jarvis family has just stepped out of whichever room, leaving nightclothes on the bed, half-drunk wine glasses and a knocked-over candlestick on the dining table, and dishes on the old kitchen table. Severs, who died in 1999, had even set up a soundtrack of a horse's hooves clip-clopping over cobblestones, and had devised some way of creating aromas of foods prepared by a long-absent cook. Our visits to the Dennis Severs' House were enchanting, showing us another interpretation of a different long-ago time, in this case late seventeenth-, eighteenth-, and nineteenth-century London.

The following house museums provide tours of the house and gardens. Make sure to check their opening hours as many are seasonal.

DENNIS SEVERS' HOUSE
dennissevershouse.co.uk
18 Folgate Street
Spitalfields, London E1 6BX
United Kingdom
+44 (0) 20 7247 4013
info@dennissevershouse.co.uk

HISTORIC NEW ENGLAND
historicnewengland.org
Check website for information on the individual house museums
141 Cambridge Street
Boston, MA 02114
(617) 227-3956

Historic New England is dedicated to preserving historic properties of Connecticut, Maine, Massachusetts, New Hampshire, and Rhode Island, providing house tours and educational courses throughout New England. I always enjoy visiting the towns where these properties are located, as many of them have wonderful examples of seventeenth- and eighteenth-century architecture. In particular, be sure to visit Hamilton House, Jackson House, Sarah Orne Jewett House, Otis House, Pierce House, and Sayward-Wheeler House. Allow time to explore the areas near the house museums.

HUNTER HOUSE
newportmansions.org/explore/hunter-house
54 Washington Street
Newport, RI 02840
(401) 847-7516
info@newportmansions.org

JEREMIAH LEE MANSION
marbleheadmuseum.org/propertieslee-mansion/
161 Washington Street
Marblehead, MA 01945
(781) 631-1786
info@marbleheadmuseum.org

MOFFATT-LADD HOUSE
moffattladd.org
154 Market Street
Portsmouth, NH 03801
(603) 436-8221
moffattladd@gmail.com

VAN CORTLANDT HOUSE MUSEUM
historichousetrust.org/house/van-cortlandt-house-museum
Van Cortlandt Park
Broadway at West 246th Street
Bronx, NY 10471
(718) 543-3344

WARNER HOUSE
warnerhouse.org
150 Daniel Street
P.O. Box 895
Portsmouth, NH 03802
(603) 436-5909

WEBB-DEANE-STEVENS MUSEUM
webb-deane-stevens.org
211 Main Street
Wethersfield, CT 06109
(860) 529-0612

ARCHIVES Scans and copies of historic documents are nice; however, there is nothing like working with old papers, papers that were in the hands of individuals, famous and not so famous, who lived hundreds of years before us. Local sources—libraries, historical societies, universities, and town halls—are treasures everyone should cherish and use. Every town, every city, every county that has kept its tax records, deeds, newspapers, and letters provides invaluable information that help us understand and re-create the past.

DARTMOUTH COLLEGE LIBRARY
library.dartmouth.edu
6025 College St.
Hanover, NH 03755
(603) 646-1110

MAINE HISTORICAL SOCIETY
mainehistory.org
489 Congress Street
Portland, ME 04101
(207) 774-1822
info@mainehistory.org

MASSACHUSETTS HISTORICAL SOCIETY
masshist.org
1154 Boylston Street
Boston, MA 02215
(617) 536-1608

OLD BERWICK HISTORICAL SOCIETY (OBHS)
AND COUNTING HOUSE MUSEUM
oldberwick.org
Main and Liberty Streets
P.O. Box 296
South Berwick, ME 03908
(207) 384-0000
info@oldberwick.org

PORTSMOUTH ATHENAEUM
portsmouthathanaeum.org
9 Market Square
Portsmouth, NH 03801
(603) 431-2538
info@portsmouthathanaeum.org

YORK COUNTY COURTHOUSE
45 Kennebunk Road
Alfred, ME 04002
(207) 234-1576

The courthouse holds original records of the sale and purchase of property, and wills and probate inventories for York County, Maine. The earliest records date to the late 1600s. These are located in the Registry of Deeds and Registry of Probate on the first and second floors of the courthouse, respectively. A second source at the courthouse is the *York Deeds*. This eighteen-volume set, published from 1884 to 1910, contains transcriptions of the original deeds for York County dating from 1642 to 1737. The *York Deeds* also include a number of probate inventories—itemized lists of what the deceased owned at the time of his or her death—of York County residents. The third source at the courthouse is the *Province and Court Records of Maine*. This six-volume set, published from 1928 to 1975, contains transcriptions of all court cases handled by the several judicial bodies that operated in Maine from 1636 to 1727. Both the *York Deeds* and *Province and Court Records of Maine* are available at the Maine State Library in Augusta, as well as at a number of local libraries and historical societies scattered about Maine, or as locals like to say, the "Pine Tree State."

NOTES

1. Todd, *The Thing Itself*, 3.
2. The "facts" of history are not always written in granite. They change according to new research and discoveries. For example, if you look at the website for the government of Dover, New Hampshire, www.dover.nh.gov, you will read that "Dover was founded in 1623." However, Dennis Robinson in his article entitled "Portsmouth and Dover Still Feuding Over 1623 NH Founding Date," on his website on the history and culture of the New Hampshire seacoast, http://www.seacoastnh.com/History/History-Matters/portsmouth-and-dover-still-feuding-over-1623-nh-founding-date/, cites the work of Elwyn Page and John S. Jenness, in which they "concluded that the Hilton brothers probably established what would become the town of Dover in 1628."
3. The terms *first period* and *second period* refer to early architectural styles in colonial America (roughly, seventeenth-century colonial and eighteenth-century Georgian, respectively). I have the impression that the terms are not commonly used outside of New England, where one can still find numerous examples of each architectural period; or perhaps the terms are used only colloquially (or regionally) as I have not seen them used in mainstream architectural studies.
4. Rosch, *American Farmhouses*, 70–71. The keeping room was similar to today's open-plan kitchen/family room, and in the colonial era was the room where meals were prepared and consumed; and chores such as laundering, spinning, husking, and bathing would take place.
5. Terry Heller, The Sarah Orne Jewett Text Project, Coe College, www.public.coe.edu/~theller/soj/ttl/ttl-frm.htm, chapter XXVIII. This site by Terry Heller is devoted to the works of Sarah Orne Jewett and offers extensive information and background on the people and places in her novels and short stories. The novel quoted here is *The Tory Lover*, published in 1901 by Houghton Mifflin.
6. Twin parlours are commonly found in Georgian domestic architecture, underscoring the period's characteristic symmetry. The "best" parlour was reserved for important guests and special occasions, while the informal parlour was similar to the family room or library of today.
7. Deed found in the York County Registry of Deeds by Dr. Neill De Paoli.
8. Technically, a *cover* is the outer portion of an item that has gone through the mail. It may or may not have stamps (stamps were an 1840 invention; covers mailed prior to 1840 are usually referred to as *stampless covers*). The cover typically will be a sheet of paper folded and sealed (often with wax) or an envelope that contains the letter or other contents.
9. Historic New England, originally SPNEA, or Society for the Preservation of New England Antiquities, was founded in 1910 and has over two dozen properties from Maine to Rhode Island. Their goal is to "keep history alive" in the region through the collection and preservation of objects, buildings, and land, as stated on their website, www.historicnewengland.org. The Colonial Dames of America, founded in 1891, is located in forty-three states and the District of Columbia. They work to preserve our "shared American history." More information can be found on their website, www.nscda.org.
10. The gill (pronounced like Jill, as in Jack and Jill) is a liquid measure of four ounces, originally used for spirits.
11. The first document found mentioning Daniel Goodwin in America is a land grant from the town of Kittery dated 1652; however, according to a genealogy.com forum on the surname "Goodwin," he emigrated from Suffolk County, England, in the early 1600s.

The Broadwood square piano, found at Harpsichord Clearing House in Rehoboth, sits in the corner of our best parlour. The General or the Governor's music book is displayed on top.

12. Nylander, *Our Own Snug Fireside*, 76–79. In this colorfully entitled section, "Frosty Mornings and Stinging Fingers," you will find excerpts from diaries describing just how cold it could get in New England interiors.

13. The hearth serves as our stove and oven for many of the meals we prepare from the start of each fall through late spring, while the majority of our summer dinners continue to be cooked over coals, albeit outside in the Egg, a ceramic cooker based on early man's oval clay cooking vessels. We think of this outdoor cooker as our version of the summer kitchen, a separate building where hearth cooking took place during the warmer months. Its smaller hearth, designed for cooking purposes only, meant smaller fires and less heat generated during meal preparation. Dining could then take place in the main house, kept cooler without having had to light a fire for cooking.

14. A crane is an iron bar used in cooking over an open fire. Our crane is attached by two round brackets to the left wall inside our hearth. The brackets have openings, allowing the arm of the crane to pivot. The handle of a pot or kettle is hung from the bar and the cook can control the temperature by swinging the pot closer to or farther away from the coals. The cook might also use a trammel, an arrangement of links and hooks for lowering or raising the pot, to bring the contents to a boil or maintain a simmer.

15. Popular from around 1796 to about 1850, the Rumford fireplace, designed by Count Rumford (1753–1814), was a superior form of fireplace, one that was taller and shallower and able to reflect heat more efficiently. A typical design would have the following dimensions: front width 24", rear width 13.5", depth 12", opening height 24."

16. Elisabeth Donaghy Garrett, *At Home*, 78–94.

17. McLeod, *Dining with the Washingtons*, 157. Throughout the book, the author frequently mentions that this beverage was Washington's favorite. The citation on page 157 is an anecdote of a hotel owner in Virginia informing Washington that there was a good supply of canvas-back ducks, to which Washington responded, "Give us some of them … and a bottle of good Madeira, and we shall not complain." Earlier in this same book, on page 98, we learn that at the end of his life, Washington had an inventory of eight pipes (one pipe is equal to 126 gallons) of "old Wine"—a term used at the time for Madeira. Madeira was a common import to the colonies as it appears frequently in shipping logs and merchant ledgers (these documents can be found in the archives of local historical societies such as the Old Berwick Historical Society, or OBHS, here in South Berwick.)

18. Elisabeth Donaghy Garrett, *At Home*, 39–54.

19. The music book was part of a small lot from the Decatur-Armsden Collection of Kittery Point, Maine. This trove of historical ephemera was owned by a number of important people who had lived in the area, including Colonel Tobias Lear, General George Washington's aide de camp and one of General Goodwin's best friends.

20. Listed in the younger Ichabod Goodwin's inventory of 1829 found in the Registry of Deeds at the York County Courthouse in Alfred, Maine were "2½ dozen edged plates." The set owned by the General and Molly might have been the popular Staffordshire pottery.

21. In the hopes of preventing war with Britain, which was interfering with American trade, President Jefferson imposed an embargo prohibiting all American ships from sailing to England. He believed that the king and Parliament would realize Britain could not live without American goods and would cease hostilities.

22. "John Jay's Treaty, 1794–5," U.S. Department of State, Office of the Historian, www.history.state.gov/milestones/1784-1800/jay. John Jay was assigned to negotiate with the British with the goal of preventing war, a situation the new country was anxious to avoid. Jay was successful, and though the public was not happy with the treaty, it accomplished its objective of maintaining peace, at least until the start of fresh hostilities with Britain during the War of 1812.

23. "Furness Family, Men of the Sea," Nina Maurer, Old Berwick Historical Society, www.oldberwick.org/index.php?option=com_content&view=article&id=538&Itemid=293. The Barbary pirates operated in the Mediterranean Sea. It was here that the *Olive Branch* was captured.

24. *New-Hampshire Gazette*, March 15, 1794, p. 3, col. 3. As quoted by Terry Heller, The Sarah Orne Jewett Text Project, Coe College, www.public.coe.edu/~theller/soj/ttl/sup/hofer-jh.html.

25. Jobe and Kaye, *New England Furniture: The Colonial Era*, 299. The caption reads: "Provenance: The table came from the 1797 General Ichabod Goodwin House in South Berwick, Me., and is believed to have been in that house for several generations."

26. James C. Massey and Shirley Maxwell, "A View from the Attic," *Old House Journal*, 34 (2006): 62.

27. These reproduction carpets are based on documentary evidence of both pattern and colorways found in the archives of Grosvenor Wilton Company, Ltd., under the title Stourvale Mill Collection.

28. Howard, *Houses of the Founding Fathers*, 280.

29. MacNown, ed., *Old Fields, The General Goodwin House*, unpaginated. William A. H. Goodwin notes in his letter to his daughter that a door was removed from the south side of the house "and a bay window substituted by my mother."

30. Mather, *Magnalia Christi Americana*, 399.

31. Terry Heller, The Sarah Orne Jewett Project, Coe College, www.public.coe.edu/~theller/soj/ttl/extend.html. In his extended notes on Jewett's *Tory Lover*, the author discusses the return (or "redemption") of the captives from the raid on Berwick. Mehitable Goodwin was among those who were brought home.

32. Often the restoration of old New England homes reveals interior walls stuffed with old shoes. This type of stuffing was used not as insulation but in the superstitious belief that an old shoe would keep away bad luck.

33. Stackpole, *The First Permanent Settlement in Maine*, 18–19.

34. MacNown, ed., *Old Fields, The General Goodwin House*, unpaginated.

35. "South Berwick Garrison Houses," Pete Payette, www.northamericanforts.com/East/me4.html#sberwick also mentions that the garrison was located at or near the General Ichabod Goodwin Home.

36. Dr. Neill De Paoli, Old Fields archaeology report, 2014.

37. "Humphrey Chadbourne (1615–1667), Pioneer of Old Berwick," Old Berwick Historical Society, www.oldberwick.org/index.php?option=com_content&view=article&id=472&Itemid=278. Between 1995 and 2007, the seventeenth-century Chadbourne estate (not far from Old Fields) was the site of an archaeological dig headed by Emerson Baker. Professor Baker notes that the site is amazingly well preserved, resulting in an important collection of relics from the earliest settlement period of the region. The collection is housed at the Counting House Museum of the Old Berwick Historical Society.

38. Dr. Neill De Paoli, Old Fields archaeology report, 2013.

39. "Deep-Water Anchorages Near the Head of Tide, Salmon Falls River, 1600s and 1700s," Old Berwick Historical Society, www.oldberwick.org/index.php?option=com_content&view=article&id=362:deep-water-anchorages-near-the-head-of-tide-salmon-falls-river-1600s&catid=49&Itemid=70. The article discusses the deep-hole anchorages of the Salmon Falls River.

40. Dr. Neill De Paoli, timeline of William Spencer, the elder, 2014. Indentured servitude was common in colonial America. The servant was not paid for his service but was free to leave after a specified period of time, often seven years. The unpaid labor was frequently in exchange for passage from England to this country.

41. Salinger, *Taverns and Drinking in Early America*, 56. The following blog also offers a discussion of literacy in colonial America: www.colonialquills.blogspot.com/2011/06/literacy-in-colonial-america.html.

42. "Historical Background on Traveling in the Early Nineteenth Century," Teach US History, www.teachushistory.org/detocqueville-visit-united-states/articles/historical-background-traveling-early-19th-century. This statement is based on the length of a trip from Boston to New York at the end of the eighteenth century.

43. "William Chadbourne (b. 1582), Pioneer Millwright of 1634," Old Berwick Historical Society, www.oldberwick.org/index.php?option=com_content&view=article&id=234&Itemid=252. The mill was founded by three of the earliest settlers of Berwick, who arrived in 1634.

44. Eighmey, *Abraham Lincoln in the Kitchen*, 187–88.

45. Baker, *A Storm of Witchcraft*, 104.

46. Hardy, *Settlement & Abandonment on Tatnic Hill*, 36.

47. The website www.measuringworth.com, offering various bases for the calculations used in determining monetary equivalency, points out the difficulty in calculating an exact ratio between older currencies and today's. One must take into account such issues as how few people had anything resembling wealth at all, the relative scarcity of goods, and the importance of various kinds of possessions in earlier times. For the purposes of this book, I used the retail price index rather than the higher multipliers of the GDP deflator, average earnings, per capita GDP, or the highest of all—share of GDP. Hence, when trying to figure out the value of the Chadbourne estate—which was £1700 according to the Old Berwick Historical Society's website—using the retail price index, we might calculate the estate at £228,000, or $353,392 in today's currencies. Another way to consider the value might be to use average earnings as the qualifier, bringing the amount to as high as £3,300,000, or $5,114,884.50. To put that vast sum into context of the times, one of the Goodwin documents from the mid-eighteenth century states that only men of means could serve on a grand jury, with the definition of "means" being a household worth the modest amount of £50. This helps to understand the substantial wealth Humphrey Chadbourne had accumulated.

48. "Humphrey Chadbourne (1615–1667), Pioneer of Old Berwick," Old Berwick Historical Society, www.oldberwick.org/index.php?option=com_content&view=article&id=472&Itemid=278. The article on the OBHS website goes into great detail on the prominence of the seventeenth-century family of Humphrey Chadbourne and his wife, Lucy Shapleigh Chadbourne.

49. Stackpole, *The First Permanent Settlement in Maine*, 16.

50. Dr. Neill De Paoli, timeline of William Spencer, the elder, 2014.

51. Dr. Neill De Paoli, timeline of Humphrey Spencer, 2014.

52. Earl, *Customs and Fashions in Old New England*, chapter XV.

53. The taverns of Colonial Williamsburg have adapted historic recipes, perhaps revising them to be less labor intensive and more appealing to the wide range of visitors they serve; however, there are also several working kitchens in which re-enactors demonstrate hearth cooking using original methods and authentic equipment.

54. Salinger, *Taverns and Drinking in Early America*, 164.

55. The difficulty of comparing the value of currency from different time periods has been discussed in note 47. The website www.measuringworth.com suggests 10 shillings might be equivalent to a little more than $100 in today's dollars. Dr. Neill De Paoli's research uncovered records of two additional debts within a few years, one of eight pounds fifteen shillings and another of five pounds fifteen shillings. The fact that Humphrey and Mary Spencer's son, William, could not afford to pay the ten-shilling tax is rather revealing of his financial situation.

56. Lardons are cubes of pork fat that have been cut from the slab.

57. A roux is a cooked paste made by stirring flour into melted butter or fat, used to thicken a sauce.

58. Leaf lard is rendered from the fat found around the kidneys and loin of the pig. It is considered the highest grade of pork fat and, with little noticeable pork flavor, is preferable for baking pastry crust.

59. Pie weights are small metal weights placed on top of the unbaked pastry crust to prevent it from bubbling. Dried beans may also be used.

60. "Growth. The Colonies: 1690–1715," National Humanities Center, nationalhumanitiescenter.org/pds/becomingamer/growth/text1/text1read.htm. The population grew from 260,000 in 1700 to just over 2 million by 1770. (In 1740, the number was over 900,000.)

61. *Transcript of Diary of Colonel Samuel Pierce*, 23. Courtesy of Historic New England. Samuel Pierce (1738-1815) lived during the time of our first two Ichabods. While reading the fascinating entries of this New Englander, I noted that he wrote he would be entering "the marriage state." I loved the turn of phrase and could picture the Captain and Elizabeth using those words on their own wedding day. The Colonel also mentions that he was married the day after he "plasterd" the house; rather a pedestrian thought to append to the new phase of his life.

62. Determined by using a calculator at www.measuring worth.com.

63. "At the Very Core of Apple Cookery," Burton Wolf, The Washington Post, www.washingtonpost.com/archive/lifestyle/1979/08/26/at-the-very-core-of-apple-cookery/d55e83b8-a738-494b-8e3e-6c44d04ec104/. The article discusses this most American of fruits, the apple, and the invention of the utilitarian machine that would relieve the cook of the time-consuming tasks of peeling and coring.

64. Oliver, *Saltwater Foodways*, 26. Sandra Oliver is a native of Maine and a noted food historian. For a decade I have relied on her cookbook for historical information on eighteenth- and nineteenth-century New England foodways and recipes. Here, the noted author and food historian refers to the bread by its alternate name, thirded bread.

65. www.foodtimeline.org.

66. The Gerrish diary was transcribed by historian Nina Maurer and can be found in the Maine Historical Society archives.

67. "Pierce House History," Historic New England, www.historicnewengland.org/historic-properties/homes/pierce-house/pierce-house-history. The article on the history of the house points out the considerable wealth needed to purchase and maintain a pair of oxen. With this in mind, I imagine bartering for the use of these animals was a common occurrence.

68. Nylander, *Our Own Snug Fireside*, 130–39.

69. Through the archives of GenealogyBank, www.genealogybank.com, with its thousands of complete newspapers, editions starting as early as 1690, I was able to find much contemporary information on life in eighteenth-century New England, and specifically, on events here in South Berwick involving families such as the Goodwins.

70. *Boston Post-Boy*, October 28, 1745, Issue 570, 2, via www.genealogybank.com.

71. *Maine at Louisburg in 1745*, Henry S. Burrage, www.archive.org/stream/maineatlouisburg00burruoft/maineatlouisburg00burruoft_djvu.txt. There were two historic sieges at Louisburg in Cape Breton, Nova Scotia, one in 1745 and the second in 1758. Historian Henry S. Burrage highlights what was, in his estimation, the outsized role of Maine at the Siege of Louisburg in 1745.

72. *Boston Post-Boy*, October 24, 1743, 4, via www.genealogybank.com.

73. *Boston Post-Boy*, October 29, 1744, 4, via www.genealogybank.com.

74. Stavely and Fitzgerald, *America's Founding Food*, 14–15. It seems the Adams family did, for whatever reason, consume the pudding before the main meal. Presumably, this habit was the basis of a political statement for Federalists, who went along with the Adams's tradition, as opposed to Jefferson and his followers, who chose to eat the pudding at the conclusion of the meal.

75. Marty Davidson, *Grandma Grace's Southern Recipes: Very, Very Old Recipes Adapted for a New Generation* (Tennessee: Rutledge Hill Press, 2005), 174.

76. "Hasty Pudding: Indian Pudding Recipe and History," Linda Stradley, What's Cooking, America?, www.whatscookingamerica.net/History/HastyPudding_IndianPudding.htm. The author provides a recipe as well as the background of Indian pudding, tracing its ancestry to the British hasty pudding.

77. Simmons, *American Cookery*, 22.

78. "Maple Syrup Heritage," Triple Creek Maple, www.triplecreekmaple.com/maple_heritage.html. The article on this heritage food points out that the Native Americans had learned how to tap the maple tree and boil down its sap into syrup prior to the arrival of the Pilgrims.

79. Regina Cole, "A Georgian Home in Maine," *Early Homes*, Fall–Winter 2012.

80. Craig Muldrew, *Food, Energy and the Creation of Industriousness*, (Cambridge: Cambridge University Press, 2011), 142. A laborer in eighteenth-century England might consume close to 4,500 calories per day, while his child would have consumed just under 2,000 calories. To put that in perspective, an average man today is said to need only 2,200 to 2,800 calories per day, according to government-issued dietary guidelines.

81. Andrew F. Smith, ed., *Oxford Encyclopedia of Food and Drink in America* (New York: Oxford University Press, 2004), 1:459. Olive oil in the New World. The author states, "The only oil regularly available to colonial Americans was olive oil. (Fats that remain liquid at room temperature are generally referred to as oils.)"

82. Generally, I found historic recipes to include a wider array of these herbs and spices than we find listed today. For example, borage, an uncommon herb in today's world, had a variety of uses in the eighteenth century. It was suggested in cases of coughs and fevers; it was added to salads and soups; its flowers were candied and made into jams. Its flavor is somewhat reminiscent of cucumber.

83. Goodwin family papers from the Dartmouth College Library archives.

84. "Letter from Abigail Smith to John Adams, 12 September 1763," Massachusetts Historical Society, www.masshist.org/digitaladams/archive/doc?id=L17630912aa&hi=1&query=eaquil&tag=text&archive=all&rec=1&start=0&numRecs=. Eighteenth-century spelling was quite flexible as witnessed in the letters between Abigail and John Adams.

85. Using the calculator at www.measuringworth.com, I determine that the rewards for his slaves ranged from $562 to $1,410 in today's dollars.

86. *Boston Post-Boy*, July 2, 1750, 2, via www.genealogybank.com.

87. *Boston Post-Boy*, February 1, 1748, 2, via www.genealogybank.com.

88. *Boston Post-Boy*, July 30, 1750, 2, via www.genealogybank.com.

89. *Lewiston Journal*, November 27, 1982, 4A.

90. "French and Indian War: Battle of Carillon," Kennedy Hickman, About.com, www.militaryhistory.about.com/od/frenchindianwar/p/battle-of-carillon.htm. Unlike the successful siege of the fort in 1745, this time the French were prepared to repulse an attack by the British.

91. *Boston Evening-Post*, July 24, 1758, 2, via www.genealogybank.com.

92. Dr. Neill De Paoli, timeline of Captain Ichabod Goodwin, 2014.

93. Wondrich, *Punch*, 241–42. In his book on historic recipes for punch, the famed mixologist discusses one that he found "sandwiched between the leaves" in the memoirs of the Schuylkill Fishing Club, an organization founded in the early eighteenth century and devoted to angling. Intrigued, Harvey and I researched the many variations of this famous drink and devised our version using a much higher alcohol to water ratio, a ratio more suited to our taste.

94. The Provincial Congress (v2:1375), American Archives, Northern Illinois University Libraries, www.amarch.lib.niu.edu. The document in the American Archives lists the attending delegates from the colony of Massachusetts who were chosen to convene at the Second Provincial Congress of Watertown in 1775.

95. Secretary of the Commonwealth, *Massachusetts Soldiers and Sailors of the Revolutionary War: A Compilation from the Archives*. This compendium of deployments can also be found online at the Massachusetts state archives, https://archive.org/stream/massachusettssol00mass#page/n1/mode/2up.

96. No More Commissions (v2:1478), American Archives, Northern Illinois University Libraries, www.amarch.lib.niu.edu.

97. Ichabod's speech at the Provincial Congress of Watertown can be found on the website of the Old Berwick Historical Society, www.oldberwick.org, as well as on the website of an affiliate of ancestry.com, www.rootswebancestry.com, where they cite the work of W. C. Spencer's *A List of REVOLUTIONARY SOLDIERS OF BERWICK*. Compiled from the Records of the Town in 1898. This same work also quotes the first speech given by Ichabod Goodwin, Jr., at another Provincial Congress held the following year in 1776, which states in part:

> *The melancholy state of this Province, of which this town is a part, calls upon us, the inhabitants, to declare our sentiments and show how they agree with those of our brethren in this and the neighboring colonies of North America, relating to the improprieties of the Parliament of Great Britain in taxing North America. But the distance we are from the metropolis of this Province, and the little acquaintance we have with the nature of the dispute, renders it needless for us to attempt to say much upon the subject; yet as the cause is general we are in duty bound to declare our sentiments upon this important dispute, and so far as we understand it, we join with our brothers in this and the neighboring colonies in opposing the operation of those late acts of the British Parliament.*

98. *New England Chronicle*, November 24, 1775, 1, via www.genealogybank.com.

99. "Revolutionary Soldiers of Berwick," Old Berwick Historical Society, www.oldberwick.org/index.php?option=com_content&view=article&id=132&Itemid=146.

100. Colonel Scammon was related to Captain Ichabod's wife, Elizabeth Scammon Goodwin, but I have yet to determine the specific connection.

101. Siskin, Ed and Jean, *Collection of Colonial and Early United States Mails*, Matthew Bennett International, Sale 290, October 7, 2005.

102. Ibid., Lot 127, page 80. As the auction catalog for the Siskin Collection was being written, the Siskins had not been able to locate the contents of one of the covers—this letter describing the battle at Trenton, New Jersey. We included the cover and its missing letter in the catalog hoping that it would eventually show up, but when it did not, the lot was withdrawn from the sale. Siskin found the letter three months after the sale, so we were able to offer the cover and letter, as a private sale, to a collector of historical documents. It is still one of our favorite documents that we have handled.

103. www.legalgenealogist.com. The website offers a detailed description of the negotiations between British General Burgoyne, George Washington, and the Continental Congress that led to the "prisoners of convention" for whom Lt. Colonel Goodwin had responsibility.

104. Judy G. Russell, "America's First POW Camps," *The Legal Genealogist* (blog), February 21, 2012, www.legalgenealogist.com/blog/2012/02/21/americas-first-pow-camps/. The author discusses the dismay of both George Washington and the Congress over the consequences of letting Burgoyne's troops return to England. Once overseas, these troops could replace British troops fighting elsewhere, who in turn could come to fight on American soil for the British king.

105. http://archive.org, The Military Journal of Colonel Ichabod Goodwin, *The Collections and Proceedings of the Maine Historical Society*, 1894, Second Series, 5:33–71.

106. *London Evening Post*, May 21, 1778, 1, via www.genealogybank.com. The newspaper article consists of a letter sent to Lord of English Treasury, signed by Benjamin Franklin, Silas Deane, and Arthur Lee.

107. www.mainememory.net. The Military Journal of Colonel Ichabod Goodwin, 65. In the introduction to the journal, written by William A. H. Goodwin, we also learn some details of the shooting of a Lieutenant Brown, a British prisoner who, Goodwin tells us was in a chaise with "two women of the town," obviously a British officer enjoying the lenient lifestyle granted by General Washington's terms for the acceptable treatment of prisoners. During that ride, an altercation ensued with one of Colonel (our General) Goodwin's sentries, and the lieutenant was shot. The newspaper *The Independent Chronicle*, in its issue of July 23, 1778, states that a letter was sent to Major General Heath, inquiring whether Brown should be given a Christian burial.

108. "Massacre and Retribution: The 1779–80 Sullivan Expedition," Ron Soodalter, HistoryNet.com, www.historynet.com/massacre-retribution-the-1779-80-sullivan-expedition.htm. The article's detailed description of the brutality of the massacres attempts to put Washington's response in context.

109. General Sullivan's brother and law partner was James Sullivan, who was elected governor of Massachusetts in 1807.

110. Siskin, Ed and Jean, *Collection of Colonial and Early United States Mails*, Matthew Bennett International, Sale 290, October 7, 2005, Lot 202, page 131. Letter dated May 24, 1779, and written by General Sullivan's aide-de-camp.

111. Secretary of the Commonwealth, *Massachusetts Soldiers and Sailors of the Revolutionary War: A Compilation from the Archives* (Boston: Wright and Potter Printing Co., State Printers, 1896) 6:97.

112. Cecere, *To Hazard Our Own Security*, 268–270.

113. "Peleg Wadsworth to Ichabod Goodwin, Sept. 28, 1780," Maine Memory Network, www.mainememory.net/artifact/10274. Order by Peleg Wadsworth, dated September 28, 1780.

114. Secretary of the Commonwealth, *Massachusetts Soldiers and Sailors of the Revolutionary War: A Compilation from the Archives* (Boston: Wright and Potter Printing Co., State Printers, 1896) 6:97.

115. www.mountvernon.org/digital-encyclopedia/article/ice-cream/. The website for Mt. Vernon mentions that a "Cream Machine for Ice" was purchased for Mt. Vernon in 1784 and that during George Washington's presidency "ice cream moulds" were purchased in 1792 and 1795.

116. "Seven Famous Fourths: How Independence Day Has Transformed," Laura Geggel, July 3, 2015, Live Science, www.livescience.com/51427-july-4-celebrations.html. From the first years of the United States, the Fourth of July was celebrated in commemoration of the signing of the Declaration of Independence.

117. *New-Hampshire Gazette*, July 10, 1784, 3, via www.genealogybank.com.

118. *Massachusetts Spy*, July 22, 1784, 2, via www.genealogybank.com.

119. *Daily Eastern Argus*, July 4, 1868, 3, via www.genealogybank.com.

120. *Portsmouth Journal of Literature and Politics*, May 4, 1872, 1, via www.genealogybank.com.

121. Oliver, *Saltwater Foodways*, 359.

122. *New-Hampshire Gazette*, November 25, 1784, 4, via www.genealogybank.com.

123. "New England Weather: 1786 Snow Storms," Colonial Sense, www.colonialsense.com/Society-Lifestyle/Signs_of_the_Times/New_England_Weather/1786_Snow_Storms.php.

124. *Massachusetts Gazette*, February 22, 1788, 3, via www.genealogybank.com.

125. John Mottley, *Joe Miller's Jests; Or, the Wits Vade-Mecum* (New York: Dover, 1963), 220. The book is a compilation of jokes put together by eighteenth-century writer John Mottley. Joe Miller was an actor who had not written but had gathered the humorous anecdotes.

126. A mechanical device that turns a spit automatically by means of a clock mechanism and weighted ropes, thus replacing the human or animal power previously needed.

127. *New-Hampshire Spy*, February 6, 1790, 119, via www.genealogybank.com.

128. The inventor of the hulling machine was Benjamin Chadbourne (1718-1799), a prosperous judge who lived about one mile away from Old Fields, at the junction of Liberty and Vine Streets. He was also the great grandson of Humphrey Chadbourne.

129. *Cumberland Gazette*, December 13, 1790, 2, via www.genealogybank.com.

130. "Society for Effecting the Abolition of the Slave Trade," Saylor Academy, www.saylor.org/site/wp-content/uploads/2011/05/Society-for-Effecting-the-Abolition-of-the-Slave.pdf. The group was largely founded by Quakers, with a strong female membership.

131. *New-Hampshire Spy*, February 6, 1790, 119, via www.genealogybank.com.

132. "Statistics of Slaves," United States Census Bureau, www2.census.gov/prod2/decennial documents/00165897ch14.pdf

133. *American Apollo*, October 5, 1792, 322, via www.genealogybank.com

134. *New Hampshire Gazetteer*, July 18, 1792, 3, via www.genealogybank.com.

135. *Oracle of the Day*, July 30, 1793, 4, via www.genealogybank.com.

136. *Eastern Herald*, May 14, 1792, 2, via www.genealogybank.com.

137. Ibid.

138. MacNown, ed., *Old Fields, The General Goodwin House*, excerpt from letter by William A. H. Goodwin, unpaginated.

139. Jobe and Kaye, *New England Furniture*, 298–99.

140. MacNown, ed., *Old Fields, The General Goodwin House*, excerpt from letter by William A. H. Goodwin, unpaginated.

141. Denys Myers in Thompson, ed., *Maine Forms of American Architecture*, 61.

142. Ibid.

143. *Newhampshire and Vermont Journal*, June 6, 1794, 3, via www.genealogybank.com.

144. Little, *American Decorative Wall Painting 1700–1850*, 101.

145. Ibid., 102.

146. *Oracle of the Day*, March 8, 1797, 2–3, via www.genealogybank.com.

147. Ibid. Dr. Hovey toasted with the words: "May negotiations in Europe triumph over the horrors of war and form the basis of an honourable and permanent peace." Jonathan Hamilton spoke the following: "The survivors of our unfortunate brethren [he refers to the kidnapping by pirates of his ship and William Furness] who have been in slavery at Algiers—having returned to their native country in poverty and distress—may they have speedy and suitable relief from their fellow citizens."

148. Ibid.

149. *New-Hampshire Gazette*, January 16, 1810, 3, via www.genealogybank.com.

150. "Citizen, Merchant, Community Leader: A New Interpretation of Jonathan Hamilton," Margaret Kugelman Hofer, Old Berwick Historical Society, www.oldberwick.org/index.php?option=com_content&view=artic le&id=361:Jonathan-hamilton-citizen-merchant-community. The article offers a detailed biography of this prominent citizen from his birth into a poor family to his rise as a successful merchant and community leader to the downfall of the Hamilton family.

151. "Hamilton House History," Historic New England, www.historicnewengland.org/historic-properties/homes/hamilton-house/history. The article traces the history of the Hamilton property through the ownerships of the Hamiltons, the Goodwins (one branch of the Goodwin family owned the Hamilton estate in the 1800s just prior to Tysons), the Tysons, and now Historic New England.

152. Willis, *A History of the Law, the Courts, and the Lawyers of Maine*, 685–89.

153. *Boston Gazette*, March 26, 1812, 2, via www.genealogybank.com. The article includes the cartoon showing "a new species of Monster" with the new boundaries formed under Governor Gerry's leadership. These borders were shaped to enhance the ability of the Republican Party to maintain their majority through the practice now known as *gerrymandering*.

154. Willis, *A History of the Law, the Courts, and the Lawyers of Maine*, 688.

155. Ibid. I would imagine by "the necessary duties of the occasion" the author is suggesting that the change-over was conducted in a most civil manner, perhaps with a glass of Madeira.

156. *Yankee*, March 18, 1814, 3, via www.genealogybank.com.

157. *Boston Patriot*, March 26, 1814, 4, via www.genealogybank.com.

158. *American State Papers: Documentary, Legislative and Executive* (Washington, DC: Gales Seaton, 1860), 3:892.

159. *New-Hampshire Gazette*, October 4, 1814, 3, via www.genealogybank.com.

160. *Dartmouth Gazette*, October 12, 1814, 2, via www.genealogybank.com.

161. *Darmouth Gazette*, November 2, 1814, 4, via www.genealogybank.com.

162. "Timeline Middle Ages and Early Modern Period," Environmental History Resources, www.eh-resources. org/timeline-middle-ages/. This site on environmental history discusses the severity of the winters between 1300 and 1870, with the height of the impact occurring between 1600 and 1800.

163. Hardy, *Settlement & Abandonment on Tatnic Hill*, 135–36.

164. *Portsmouth Oracle*, July 6, 1816, 1, via www.genealogybank.com.

165. Hardy, *Settlement & Abandonment on Tatnic Hill*, 137–38.

166. MacNown, ed., *Old Fields, The General Goodwin House*, unpaginated. The depiction of Sophia Hayes Goodwin as an enthusiastic conversationalist is based on her rather lengthy letters, often over 4 pages long and occasionally written horizontally as well as vertically on the same page. The letters, written to her husband, Ichabod, who worked in Washington, DC, during the Civil War, were replete with the minutiae of her daily life.

167. "Image of the American Patriot, Part V. Rekindling the Spirit of Liberty: Lafayette's Visit to the United States, 1824–1825," William Jones, The Schiller Institute, www.schillerinstitute.org/educ/hist/lafayette.html. The Schiller Institute, founded by Helga Zepp La Rouche, works to enhance human rights throughout the world, hoping to rekindle the thoughts and feelings behind the American Revolutionary War.

168. *Columbian Centinel*, October 6, 1824, 2, via www.genealogybank.com.

169. Terry Heller, "Two Accounts of General Lafayette's June 24, 1825 Visit to South Berwick, Maine," The Sarah Orne Jewett Project, Coe College, www.public.coe.edu/~theller/soj/u-rel/lafayette.html. In this section of his site, Mr. Heller offers two articles on Lafayette's visit to Berwick. One is from the newspaper *Eastern Argus*, and the second is the reminiscence of Sophia Goodwin.

170. MacNown, ed., *Old Fields, The General Goodwin House*, unpaginated.

171. Terry Heller, "Two Accounts of General Lafayette's June 24, 1825 Visit to South Berwick, Maine," The Sarah Orne Jewett Project, Coe College, www.public.coe.edu/~theller/soj/u-rel/lafayette.html.

172. Ibid.

173. "People," Old Berwick Historical Society, www.oldberwick.org/index.php. The historical society website includes an extensive list of prominent citizens of the seventeenth, eighteenth, nineteenth, and twentieth centuries.

174. *Portsmouth Journal of Literature and Politics*, April 11, 1829, 2, via www.genealogybank.com.

175. *Portsmouth Journal of Literature and Politics*, June 20, 1829, 3, via www.genealogybank.com.

176. *Christian Mirror*, June 25, 1829, 3, author's collection.

177. Willis, *A History of the Law, the Courts, and the Lawyers of Maine*, 689.

178. White flour was more expensive than browner whole wheat flour because of its more extensive processing. It had long been associated with privilege and wealth because of the cost and was reserved by many households for feast-day recipes.

179. Simmons, *American Cookery*, 11–12.

180. McLeod, *Dining with the Washingtons*, 209.

181. Ibid.

182. Oliver, *Saltwater Foodways*, 160–61.

183. Mary Cole, *Lady's Complete Guide*, 63.

184. "Colonel Albert Pope and His American Dream Machine," Pedersen Bicycles, www.corvallistoday.com/Europe/pederonall.htm.

185. Doris Kearns Goodwin, *The Bully Pulpit: Theodore Roosevelt, William Howard Taft and the Golden Age of Journalism* (New York: Simon & Schuster, 2013). In this expansive book, the role of Sam McClure's magazine is laid out in detailed descriptions of the work of journalists such as Ida Tarbell, Lincoln Steffens, and Ray Stannard Baker. One of the most renowned series of articles was Ida Tarbell's thoroughly researched pieces exposing the unethical business practices of the Standard Oil Company.

186. Stephen B. Goddard, *Colonel Albert A. Pope and His American Dream Machine: The Life and Times of a Bicycle Tycoon Turned Automotive Pioneer* (Jefferson, NC: McFarland, 2000), 11.

187. Fergus Henderson, *The Whole Beast: Nose to Tail Eating* (New York: Ecco, 2004).

188. Norman, *Elizabeth David's Christmas*, 89–90.

I have long enjoyed the elegance of creamware serving pieces such as the soup tureen at top and the chestnut basket below, both displayed in our dining-room cabinet. One can easily appreciate the aesthetic sensibility of those 18th-century craftsmen who designed these beautiful pieces for fine dining.

BIBLIOGRAPHY

COOKBOOKS AND CULINARY HISTORIES

Blumenthal, Heston. *Historic Heston*. New York: Bloomsbury, 2013.

Bullock, Helen. *The Williamsburg Art of Cookery*. Richmond, VA: Dietz Press, 2006.

Carter, Charles. *The Complete Practical Cook*. London: St. Paul's Church-yard, 1730. Reprint, London: Prospect Books, 1984.

Cole, Mary. *Lady's Complete Guide; Or, Cookery in All Its Branches*. London: G. Kearsley, 1788.

Crump, Nancy Carter. *Hearthside Cooking: An Introduction to Virginia Plantation Cuisine, Including Bills of Fare, Tools and Techniques, and Original Recipes with Adaptations for Modern Fireplaces and Kitchens*. McLean, VA: EPM Publications, 1986.

DeWitt, Dave. *The Founding Foodies: How Washington, Jefferson, and Franklin Revolutionized American Cuisine*. Naperville, IL: Sourcebooks, 2010.

Dupree, Nathalie, and Cynthia Graubart. *Mastering the Art of Southern Cooking*. Layton, UT: Gibbs Smith, 2012.

Eighmey, Rae Katherine. *Abraham Lincoln in the Kitchen: A Culinary View of Lincoln's Life and Times*. Washington, DC: Smithsonian Books, 2013.

Elverson, Virginia T., and Mary Ann McLanahan. *Revolutionary Cooking: Over 200 Recipes Inspired by Colonial Meals*. Reprint, New York: Skyhorse Publishing, 2014.

Farley, John. *The London Art of Cookery and Housekeeper's Complete Assistant*. London: Scatcherd, 1789. Reprint, Carlisle, MA; Applewood Books, 2008.

Fowler, Damon Lee, ed. *Dining at Monticello: In Good Taste and Abundance*. Charlottesville: Thomas Jefferson Foundation, 2005.

May, Robert. *The Accomplisht Cook, or, the Art and Mastery of Cooking*. London: Obadiah Blagrave, 1685. Reprint, Devon, England: Prospect Books, 1994.

McLeod, Stephen A. *Dining with the Washingtons: Historic Recipes, Entertaining, and Hospitality from Mount Vernon*. Chapel Hill: University of North Carolina Press, 2011.

Norman, Jill. *Elizabeth David's Christmas*. London: Penguin, 2003.

Oliver, Sandra L. *Saltwater Foodways: New Englanders and Their Food, at Sea and Ashore, in the Nineteenth Century*. Mystic, CT: Mystic Seaport Museum, 1995.

Phipps, Francis. *Colonial Kitchens, Their Furnishings, and Their Gardens*. New York: Hawthorn Books, 1972.

Recipes: American Cooking: New England, Foods of the World. New York: Time-Life Books, 1970.

Simmons, Amelia. *American Cookery*. Hartford: Hudson & Goodwin, 1796. Reprint, New York: Dover Publications, 1984.

Sloat, Caroline, ed. *Old Sturbridge Village Cookbook: Authentic Early American Recipes for the Modern Kitchen*. Chester, CT: Globe Pequot Press, 1984.

Stavely, Keith, and Kathleen Fitzgerald. *America's Founding Food: The Story of New England Cooking*. Chapel Hill: University of North Carolina Press, 2004.

———. *Northern Hospitality: Cooking by the Book in New England*. Amherst: University of Massachusetts Press, 2011.

Tennant, Jane. *Our Founding Foods: Classics from the First Century of American Celebrity Cookbooks*. Minocqua, WI: Willow Creek Press, 2008.

Washington, Martha. *Martha Washington's Booke of Cookery; and Booke of Sweetmeats*. Transcribed by Karen Hess. New York: Columbia University Press, 1995.

Wondrich, David. *Punch: The Delights (and Dangers) of the Flowing Bowl*. New York: Perigee, 2010.

BOOKS INCLUDING EARLY AMERICAN HISTORY, ARCHITECTURE, AND LIFESTYLE

Baker, Emerson W. *A Storm of Witchcraft: The Salem Trials and the American Experience*. Oxford: Oxford University Press, 2014.

Bradford, William. *Of Plymouth Plantation, 1620–1647*. Revised edition, New York: Knopf, 2006.

Bryson, Bill. *At Home: A Short History of Private Life*. New York: Doubleday, 2010.

Cecere, Michael. *To Hazard Our Own Security: Maine's Role in the American Revolution*. Westminster, MD: Heritage Books, 2010.

Chamberlain, Samuel, and Narcissa G. Chamberlain. *New England Rooms 1639–1863*. Stamford, CT: Architectural Book Publishing,1993.

Deetz, James. *In Small Things Forgotten: The Archaeology of Early American Life*. Updated and revised edition, New York: Anchor Books, 1996.

Earle, Alice Morse. *Customs and Fashions in Old New England*. New York: Charles Scribner's Sons, 1893.

Garrett, Elisabeth Donaghy. *At Home: The American Family, 1750–1870*. New York: Abrams, 1990.

Garrett, Wendell D. *American Colonial: Puritan Simplicity to Georgian Grace*. New York: Monacelli Press, 1995.

Goodman, Dena, and Kathryn Norberg, ed. *Furnishing the Eighteenth Century: What Furniture Can Tell Us About the European and American Past*. New York: Routledge, 2007.

Hardy, Joseph W. *Settlement and Abandonment on Tatnic Hill: An Eclectic History of Wells, Maine, 1600–1900*. Portsmouth, NH: Back Channel Press, 2008.

Howard, Hugh. *Houses of the Founding Fathers: The Men Who Made America and the Way They Lived*. New York: Artisan, 2007.

Jayne, Thomas. *The Finest Rooms in America: 50 Influential Interiors from the Eighteenth Century to the Present*. New York: Monacelli Press, 2010.

Jenrette, Richard Hampton. *Adventures with Old Houses*. Charleston, SC: Wyrick, 2000.

Jewett, Sarah Orne. *The Tory Lover*. Boston: Houghton, Mifflin and Company, 1901.

Jobe, Brock, and Myrna Kaye. *New England Furniture: The Colonial Era*. Boston: Houghton Mifflin, 1984.

Larkin, Jack. *The Reshaping of Everyday Life, 1790–1840*. New York: Harper & Row, 1988.

———. *Where We Lived: Discovering the Places We Once Called Home: The American Home from 1775 to 1840*. Newtown, CT: Taunton Press, 2006.

Little, Nina Fletcher. *American Decorative Wall Painting, 1700–1850*. New York: E. P. Dutton, 1972.

MacNown, S. Kent, ed. *Oldfields, The General Goodwin House: An Assemblage of Oldfields' History, Pictures, Happenings & Memorabilia*. Dover, NH: self-published, ca 2000.

Mather, Cotton. *Magnalia Christi Americana*. London: Thomas Parkhurst, 1702. Reprint, Books on Demand, 2015.

McCullough, David. *John Adams*. New York: Simon & Schuster, 2001.

———. *1776*. New York: Simon & Schuster, 2005.

Meacham, Jon. *Thomas Jefferson: The Art of Power*. New York: Random House, 2012.

Messer, Sarah. *Red House: Being a Mostly Accurate Account of New England's Oldest Continuously Lived-In House*. New York: Viking, 2004.

Miller, Judith. *The Style Sourcebook*. New York: Stewart, Tabori & Chang, 1998.

Nylander, Jane. *Our Own Snug Fireside: Images of the New England Home, 1760–1860*. New York: Knopf, 1993.

Nylander, Jane C., with Diane L. Viera. *Windows on the Past: Four Centuries of New England Homes*. Boston: Bulfinch Press, 2000.

Parissien, Steven. *The Georgian Group Book of the Georgian House*. London: Aurum Press, 1999.

Roberts, Kenneth. *Boon Island*. New York: Doubleday, 2012.

Rosch, Leah. *American Farmhouses: Country Style and Design*. New York: Simon & Schuster, 2002.

Salinger, Sharon V. *Taverns and Drinking in Early America*. Baltimore: Johns Hopkins University Press, 2002.

Schuler, Stanley. *Old New England Homes*. Exton, PA: Schiffer Publishing, 1984.

Secretary of the Commonwealth. *Massachusetts Soldiers and Sailors of the Revolutionary War: A Compilation from the Archives*. Boston: Wright & Potter Printing Company, State Printers, 1809.

Severs, Dennis. *18 Folgate Street: The Life of a House in Spitalfields*. London: Chatto & Windus, 2002.

Stackpole, Everett. *The First Permanent Settlement in Maine*. Dover-Foxcroft, ME: 1926. Reprint, South Berwick, ME: Old Berwick Historical Society, 1968.

Stephenson, Michael. *Patriot Battles: How the War of Independence Was Fought*. New York: HarperCollins, 2007.

Sweeney, John A. H. *Treasure House of Early American Rooms*. New York: Viking, 1963.

Thompson, Deborah, ed. *Maine Forms of Architecture*. Camden, ME: published under the auspices of the Colby Museum of Art by DownEast Magazine, 1976.

Todd, Richard. *The Thing Itself: On the Search for Authenticity*. New York: Riverhead Books, 2008.

Ulrich, Laurel Thatcher. *A Mid-wife's Tale: The Life of Martha Ballard, Based on Her Diary, 1785–1812*. New York: Knopf, 1990.

Wharton, Edith, and Ogden Codman, Jr. *The Decoration of Houses*. Reprint, New York: W. W. Norton & Company, 1978.

Willis, William. *A History of the Law, the Courts, and the Lawyers of Maine, from Its First Colonization to the Early Part of the Present Century*. Portland, ME: Bailey & Noyes, 1863. Reprint, Clark, NJ: Lawbook Exchange, 2006.

Wood, Gordon, S. *Empire of Liberty: A History of the Early Republic, 1789–1815*. New York: Oxford University Press, 2009.

CHILDREN'S BOOKS

Forbes, Esther. *Johnny Tremain*. Boston: Houghton Mifflin, 1943. Winner of the Newbury Medal, 1944.

Lowrey, Janette Sebring. *Six Silver Spoons*. New York: HarperCollins, 1971.

Stevenson, Augusta. *Molly Pitcher, Girl Patriot*. Indianapolis: Bobbs-Merrill, 1952. Ms. Stevenson wrote a number of other books as part of the Childhood of Famous Americans series. These include titles such as *Ben Franklin, Printer's Boy*, and *Clara Barton, Girl Nurse*.

Thane, Elswyth. Thane wrote the Williamsburg series of books, based on American history from the Revolutionary War to World War II. Originally published between 1943 and 1957, these titles have been reprinted many times since: *Dawn's Early Light* (1943), *Yankee Stranger* (1944), *Ever After* (1945), *The Light Heart* (1947), *Kissing Kin* (1948), *This Was Tomorrow* (1951), and *Homing* (1957).

MAGAZINE AND NEWSPAPER ARTICLES

Cole, Regina. "A House Accommodating Change: A Georgian in Maine." *Early Homes* (Fall–Winter 2012): 30–37. (Article features the Bennetts and the General Ichabod Goodwin House.)

Curtis, Wayne. "Life on the Northern Frontier." *American Archaeology* (Winter 2015–2016): 38–43. (Article features Neill De Paoli and the excavation he heads on the property.)

Donahue, Marie. "Keeping Alive the Spirit of the Past." *Lewiston Journal* magazine section, November 27, 1982. (Article features the General Ichabod Goodwin House.)

Jewett, Sarah Orne. "The Old Town of Berwick." *New England Magazine* (July 1894).

Svenson, David. "Lucky Strike." *Portland Monthly* (September 2012). (Article features the excavation on the property and the discovery of the Spanish real.)

"USM Student Uncovers Centuries-Old Spanish Coin." *The Weekly Sentinel*, July 13, 2012.

WEBSITES

colonialsense.com

genealogybank.com

lambsartillery.org

mainememory.net

measuringworth.com

oldberwick.org

public.coe.edu\~theller\soj\sj-index.htm (The Sarah Orne Jewett Text Project)

recipes.history.org (History is Served blog by Colonial Williamsburg Historic Foodways)

savoringthepast.net

INDEX

References are to page numbers: Recipes are differentiated by ALL capital letters, and illustrations are indicated by (ill.) after page number.

*The view from our keeping room
into the dining room. For our last
New Year's Day here at Old Fields,
Harvey has lit the fire. The delft
tiles in the dining-room fireplace
surround were one of the first details
about the General Ichabod Goodwin
House to capture my imagination.*

Imagining Ichabod

Illustration credits: Unless noted below, all photographs by Sandy Agrafiotis

Author's private collection: Pages viii, 5, 15, 38, 82, 130, 170
Harvey Bennett: Pages 120, 143
Neill De Paoli: Pages v., site plan on 58–59, 67, 69, 70, 73, 74
Courtesy of Kent MacNown: Pages 165, 166, 167
Courtesy of Maine State Archives: Page 157
Matthew Bennett International: Page 132
Reproduced by permission from Old Berwick Historical Society: Image on pages 76–77
Courtesy of Rauner Special Collections Library at Dartmouth College: Page 120

Editor: Beth Daugherty
Cover and book design: Betty Eng
Front and back matter design: Kathy Hart
Copyediting and proofreading: Chandra Wohleber and Elizabeth Wagner
Printing and binding: Pimlico Book International

Typeset in Palatino and Daisy Lau
Printed on 100gsm Chinese Ji Long Creamy Woodfree

First edition, 2016

Printed and bound in China

ISBN-10: 0-9838632-4-5 (cloth)
ISBN-13: 978-0-9838632-4-3 (cloth)

Library of Congress Control Number: 2016933942

Published by Bauer and Dean Publishers, Inc.
P.O. Box 98
Times Square Station
New York, NY 10108
www.baueranddean.com

Distribution by National Book Network (NBN)
Orders also through ACC Art Books
6 West 18th Street, Suite 4B
New York, NY 10011
Tel (212) 645-1111 or (800) 252-5231
sales@antiquecc.com